CREATIVITY IN THE VEDIC ASTROLOGY CHART

Music, Dance and Film

Michael A. Sugarman

CREATIVITY IN THE VEDIC ASTROLOGY CHART

Michael A. Sugarman

Copyright © 2024 by Michael A. Sugarman

Published by 1st World Publishing
P.O. Box 2211, Fairfield, Iowa 52556
tel: 641-209-5000 • fax: 866-440-5234
web: www.1stworldpublishing.com

First Edition

ISBN: 978-1-4218-3558-7

LCCN: Library of Congress Cataloging-in-Publication Data

All rights reserved. No part of this book may be reproduced or utilized in any form or by any means, electronic or mechanical, including photocopying or recording, or by any information storage and retrieval system, without permission in writing from the author.

This material has been written and published for educational purposes to enhance one's well-being. In regard to health issues, the information is not intended as a substitute for appropriate care and advice from health professionals, nor does it equate to the assumption of medical or any other form of liability on the part of the publisher or author. The publisher and author shall have neither liability nor responsibility to any person or entity with respect to loss, damages, or injury claimed to be caused directly or indirectly by any information in this book.

Table of Contents

Acknowledgments 7
Chapter 1 - Houses, Planets, Nakshatras & Drekkanas 13
Chapter 2 - Music 23
Chapter 3 - Dance 151
Chapter 4 - Theater, Film & Photography 243
Bibliography 354

Acknowledgments

I have been blessed by a series of wise, generous teachers, including Juliana Swanson, Penny Farrow, Dr. K. S. Charak, Vinay Aditya, Gayatri Devi Raman, Chakrapani Ullal, Marc Boney, and the books and recordings of Mr. K. N. Rao.

Much of my learning has occurred, and continues, at Arsha Vidya Gurukulam in Saylorsburg, Pennsylvania. Continuous thanks to all those (too many to name) who help to make Arsha Vidya a wonderful source of spiritual knowledge, inspiration, and kind hospitality.

I value the friendships I have made through my studies and practice of astrology, including those with Kumar, Luciana, Neelima, Simon, Roy, Michiel, and Murali. In Fairfield, I am grateful for the love and steady support from oldest friends David & Carol, Karen & Ark, Meret, and Karen Smith, who patiently read through a very rough first draft, and offered helpful suggestions. The love and inspiration of Mindy Jones will never be forgotten.

Thanks to Susan Lalji for her usual excellent and thorough editing job. It has been a most enjoyable and rewarding process to associate with Rodney Charles and 1st World Publications in the presentation of this contribution.

*"The meaning of life is to find your gift.
The purpose of life is to give it away."*

– Pablo Picasso

*"Imagination is more important than knowledge.
Knowledge is limited. Imagination encircles the world"*

– Albert Einstein

To my two favorite artists, Adelia and Cora Jane.

Chapter 1
Houses, Planets, Nakshatras & Drekkanas

For all its considerable utility in revealing information about family, career, marriage, health, finances, etc., the Vedic astrology chart can also be employed to illustrate one's gifts. I believe that many of us, perhaps even most of us, come into this world possessed of creative talents and abilities – some means of individual expression which also serves to reflect and glorify the spiritual beauty of nature. As a practicing Vedic astrologer, but also as a lover of music and the fine arts I have often made it a point to recognize the presence of artistic potential when it appears in a chart. The client may choose not to pursue that potential in his/her life, or wait any number of years to begin to do so, but I will highlight it all the same, out of the belief that art and artistic expression enrich the life of the client as well as the lives of those around him/her.

With this in mind, we will investigate a set of charts whose owners by any standard would be considered artists. Although there are any number of categories of artistic expression, we will focus on three: music, dance, and the visual arts of theater, film, and photography.

Houses

Certain houses of the chart (and their lords) will naturally play a more important role when creative potential is under consideration. The ascendant and its ruler will demonstrate basic tendencies, talents, abilities, and temperament. The 2nd house of mouth and voice will be activated in charts of singers and orators. The 2nd is also the house of the face, i.e., the appearance, and can be instrumental in the charts of film actors whose appearance is part of their craft and overall appeal. As the house of one's own efforts, courage, self-expression, skillfulness, and communication in general, the 3rd house often figures prominently in the charts of artists. In the *Jyotish* physical scheme, the 3rd house is that of the hands and manual dexterity so any form of artistic expression which involves use of the hands, i.e., playing a musical instrument, painting, or drawing, etc., will be reflected through the 3rd. It is also the house which represents the ears and the sense of hearing, so it connects to music and musical expression and appreciation, music as its own language, via musical notes instead of words. One of our case studies, Brian Wilson, is quoted as saying "I believe that music is God's voice." The 5th is the house of creative intelligence, inspiration, and imagination, in addition to its primary signification as the house of children. Much as children are seen to possess the innocence and spontaneous joy of creativity, the 5th house and lord can confer that same creative spark in a given chart. When artistic authority is seen in a chart, as in the case of musical producers, choreographers and film directors, the 5th house will play a prominent role, as traditionally, the 5th house and sign of Leo, with the Sun as its natural ruler, represent royalty, the throne, and authority.

As the 10th from the 10th, the 7th house can signify the career, but as reflection house from the ascendant, tends to represent a more independent, self-driven career. The 9th house, as reflection to the 3rd, and as 5th from the 5th, can also play a role in the creative process, especially if/when it highlights the *dharma* of creative purpose or potential in a chart. For creative artists fortunate enough to forge a career from their artistry, the 10th house of highest visibility, worldly achievement and essential and primary activities will reveal that artistry to one extent or another. The 11th house turns out to be another crucial house related to the theme of creativity and creative potential. As the house of gains, awards and successes, the fulfillment of goals and dreams, of multiples, large groups and the masses, a strong 11th house and/or lord can bring mass exposure and widespread popularity to the artist and his/her creative endeavors. More specifically, the 11th house, as the house of the calves, shins, and ankles, is the primary house of dance, as we will see in the section related to dance and our analysis of the charts of dancers. Finally, the 12th house also becomes a house related to creative expression, specifically the media of theater, film, photography, and video. Why might this be? The 12th is the house of sleep and dreams, dreams being our most intimate and compelling form of visual illusion. It can be said that theatrical performance, film, and the photographic arts are another rendition of visual illusion, and in many ways dream-like. We will see the 12th house consistently represented in our consideration of the charts of theatrical and film actors, directors, photographers, and the like.

Planets

In the consideration of planetary influences in a chart, and the ways in which planets encourage and activate creative potential, the planet Venus will consistently take on a prominent role. In astrology, Venus represents the qualities of beauty, harmony, balance, romance, and aesthetic refinement, and is therefore assigned rulership of the fine arts. Planets residing in signs owned by Venus, or otherwise influenced by Venus, will display some of the same capabilities as Venus. According to their respective natures and tendencies other planets can support a chart's basic creative nature; Sun by means of identity and the soul's perceived purpose, Moon through artistic sensitivity and an emotional identification with a particular means of artistic expression, Mars by means of energy, focused effort, courage, and determination, Mercury through mental and manual dexterity, communication, cleverness and wit, Jupiter by means of grace, faith, connection, expansion, and fortunate opportunity, and Saturn through its ability to provide structure, longevity, and patient endurance during any creative process. The influence of the lunar nodes, *Rahu* and *Ketu*, can significantly enhance the qualities of invention, subtlety, intuition/cognition and the singularity of the artist's particular vision.

Nakshatras

There is wide variety in the nature of the 27 *nakshatras*, as some tend to enhance creative expression more than others. As we move through each section and the example charts therein, we will notice that certain *nakshatras* recur with some frequency. These will include:

Ashwini (0 degrees to 13 degrees 20 minutes Aries) – As one of three *nakshatras* in the *laghu* (light, swift, nimble) category, *Ashwini* can support physical manifestation of the creative impulse, certainly including dance. The first ten degrees of *Ashwini* occur in a weapon *drekkana*, emphasizing instrumental skill. (See the *Drekkana* section below.)

Bharani (13 degrees 20 minutes Aries to 26 degrees 40 minutes Aries) – Secondary to *Bharani's* womb symbolism, planets located in *Bharani* may favor a creative process which resembles pregnancy and childbirth, i.e., a prolonged period of growth and gestation of a creative project before it ultimately comes to fruition.

Krittika (26 degrees 40 minutes Aries to 10 degrees Taurus) – *Krittika* can bring aesthetic refinement and the desire and ability to see a creative endeavor through to its completion. *Krittika's* deity is *Agni*, the god of fire. Planets placed in *Krittika* can demonstrate qualities of genius and may be driven by passion and great enthusiasm, as well as by strong determination to overcome obstacles. *Krittika's* razor symbolism renders it especially skilled in cutting away excess, such as in editing, in the service of artistic economy of expression. *Krittika* is an energetic and physically fine-tuned *nakshatra*, particularly when manifested by planets tied to the ascendant or its lord. The last ten degrees of *Krittika* fall in the sign of Taurus where an occupying planet will be disposited by Venus.

Rohini (10 degrees Taurus to 23 degrees 20 minutes Taurus) – In Vedic mythology, *Rohini* was one of the Moon's wives, and his favorite. *Rohini* was possessed of culture, beauty, and refined artistry, particularly in the realms of music and dance. *Rohini nakshatra* will be frequently and prominently featured in charts of artists, musicians, dancers, actors, writers, etc. Planets in *Rohini* tend to flourish and can benefit from *Rohini's* tendency to yield a seemingly inexhaustible source of creative inspiration, secondary to *Rohini's* deity, Lord *Brahma* the creator. Although not the only *nakshatra* capable of conferring creativity and originality in a horoscope, *Rohini* distinguishes itself with its subtlety, elegance, beauty, and abundance, particularly when occupied by the Moon or Venus.

Mrigashira (23 degrees 20 minutes Taurus to 6 degrees 40 minutes Gemini) – *Mrigashira's* first 6 degrees 40 minutes occurs in Venus-ruled Taurus, and can confer artistic beauty and sensitivity.

Punarvasu (20 degrees Gemini to 3 degrees 20 minutes Cancer) – *Punarvasu's* deity is *Aditi*, the mother of the Gods, and possessed with boundless creativity and imagination. Planets occurring in this *nakshatra*, whose meaning is "good again," or "light again," benefit from *Punarvasu's* tendency to provide renewal and fresh inspiration in an ongoing manner.

Purva Phalguni (13 degrees 20 minutes Leo to 26 degrees 40 minutes Leo) – *Purva Phalguni* is one of the most purely creative *nakshatras* and is consistently seen in the charts of artists of all kinds. *Purva Phalguni* is said to symbolize fertility and the marriage bed, the creation of children, and activities which promote relaxation and enjoyment, all of which meanings imply spontaneity, creative talent and the gifts associated with creative inspiration.

Hasta (10 degrees Virgo to 23 degrees 20 minutes Virgo) – The meaning of the Sanskrit term "*Hasta*" is "hand," so activation of this *nakshatra* can confer manual dexterity. *Hasta* also places high value on words and sounds, so skill in writing, including lyrical composition, can sometimes be indicated when this *nakshatra* is emphasized in a chart. The Sanskrit root of the word "*Hasta*" is "*Has*" which means laughter, so planets or the ascendant degree in *Hasta nakshatra* may indicate a sense of humor and/or career in the field of comedy. Like *Ashwini*, *Hasta* is categorized as a *laghu nakshatra*, whose first 10 degrees fall in a weapon *drekkana*.

Chitra (23 degrees 20 minutes Virgo to 6 degrees 40 minutes Libra) – *Chitra's* deity is *Vishwakarma* the celestial architect, and *Chitra's* symbol is a luminous jewel, so themes of beauty, harmony, aesthetic balance, and proportion are all activated in this *nakshatra*. Planets in *Chitra* may have a propensity for visual expression through colorful, appealing, and well-designed imagery. The last 6 degrees 40 minutes of *Chitra* occur in the Venus-owned sign of Libra.

Swati (6 degrees 40 minutes Libra to 20 degrees Libra) – *Swati* falls entirely in the sign of Libra so any planet there is disposited by Venus. *Swati's* deity *Vayu* is lord of the winds, and is the deity associated with breath and *prana*. In Hindu mythology, *Vayu* is recognized as king of the *Gandharvas*, celestial beings whose males are graced with beautiful singing voices and whose females are elegant dancers.

Shravana (10 degrees Capricorn to 23 degrees 20 minutes Capricorn) – *Shravana's* symbol is the human ear and therefore implies skill at listening in the context of musical appreciation and sensitivity, i.e., an "ear" for music. As will be seen in some of our example charts, *Shravana* can confer a distinctive sense of internal melody. *Shravana's* deity *Vishnu* is the protagonist in the story of the three footsteps, so dance and choreography can also be activated in this *nakshatra*.

Dhanishtha (23 degrees 20 minutes Capricorn to 6 degrees 40 minutes Aquarius) – Because *Dhanishtha's* symbol is the drum, musical ability and a keen sense of rhythm are often manifested through planets which are placed in this *nakshatra*. The occupation of space, particularly by light and sound, is a predominant theme of *Dhanishtha*.

Shatabhisha (6 degrees 40 minutes Aquarius to 20 degrees Aquarius) – *Shatabhisha's* deity is *Varuna*, who is said to rule the firmament, i.e., the all-encompassing sky, and to possess the quality of omniscience. Planets in *Shatabhisha* may take on a visionary quality, secondary to the characterization of *Varuna* as all-seeing. Because of the power of acute observation associated with this *nakshatra*, we will see the activation of *Shatabhisha* in the charts of photographers, theatrical/film actors, and directors, etc.

Purva Bhadrapada (20 degrees Aquarius to 3 degrees 20 minutes Pisces) – Not unlike the previous *nakshatra*, planets who reside in *Purva Bhadrapada nakshatra* are also often granted skill in visual aesthetics, i.e., film, photography, and videography.

Revati (16 degrees 40 minutes Pisces to 30 degrees Pisces) – Like *Dhanishtha*, *Revati's* symbol is the drum and therefore may confer rhythmic and/or musical ability on planets placed there. Regarded as a wise, sensitive, and intuitive *nakshatra*, *Revati* can serve to enhance the imaginative powers of *grahas* occurring there.

Drekkanas

Drekkanas are 10-degree increments, 3 in each sign, 36 in total. Each *drekkana* has its own set of symbols and brief narrative description. There are several categories of *drekkanas*, and some of the *drekkanas* which will figure prominently in charts of artists and musicians are those termed *"ayudh"* or weapon. Weapon *drekkanas* will confer a degree of manual skill and dexterity to the native, particularly when there is additional emphasis on the 3rd house and/or its planetary ruler. (Readers should bear in mind that although the term "weapon" is employed to characterize this set of *drekkanas*, and is the most literal translation of the Sanskrit word "*ayudh*," the concept extends to any sort of tool or instrument. Activation of weapon *drekkanas* can frequently be seen in the charts of athletes, for example, who may wield a tennis racket or golf club for a living, or surgeons, acupuncturists, skilled woodworkers or jewelers, or anyone who enjoys simple hobbies like gardening or knitting.) Keeping in mind that each *drekkana* covers a span of 10 degrees, the weapon *drekkanas* are: the 1st and 3rd of Aries, the 2nd and 3rd of Gemini, the 2nd and 3rd of Leo, the 2nd of Virgo, the 1st and 3rd of Sagittarius and the 3rd of Capricorn. Although not strictly a weapon *drekkana*, the 1st *drekkana* of Gemini, whose description is of "a woman with hands raised, skilled in needle work" may also be seen in charts of those who possess skill in precise use of the hands. Additionally, there are 4 *drekkanas* which fall under the category of "*pakshi*" or bird. These include the 2nd *drekkana* of Gemini, the first of Leo, the 2nd of Libra, and the first of Aquarius. Planets in *pakshi drekkanas* may take on qualities of swiftness, lightness, and movement, all of which nicely lend themselves to the art of dance, particularly ballet. (Annotation and description of the 36 *drekkanas* are to be found in Varahamihira's *Brihat Jataka*. The second volume of James Kelleher's two-volume set *Path of Light* contains expanded commentary and interpretation of each of the *drekkanas*.)

The Jaimini System

Although the approach taken in this work will implement the perspective of *Parashara Jyotish*, the *Jaimini* system will also be employed, especially including the use of *Jaimini Chara dasha*, to demonstrate timing of periods of creative inspiration and career achievement. Just as it is expected (and recommended) that the reader will have some familiarity with planetary yogas in the *Parashara* system, the same recommendation is made regarding *Jaimini* yogas. When *Jaimini* standard *karakas* (indicators) are mentioned in the discussion, abbreviations will be employed – *Atma Karaka* (AK), *Amatya Karaka* (AmK), *Bhratri Karaka* (BK), *Matri Karaka* (MK), *Putra Karaka* (PK), *Gnati Karaka* (GK), *Dara Karaka* (DK). The seven *karakas* employed in the *Jaimini* scheme correspond symbolically, in descending order by degrees, to the first seven houses of the horoscope. In any given chart, as planet of highest degree, the AK will represent the ascendant and therefore the chart's owner, as well as the individual soul's life purpose. The AmK symbolizes resources and means (2nd house) as well as career and essential activities. As 3rd highest, the BK represents siblings, co-workers, and neighbors, as well as skills, including skills in the service of artistic expression. The MK of a chart will represent motherhood along with other 4th house themes – home, property, secure assets, and permanence. The *Jaimini* PK is associated with the 5th house of intelligence, children, creativity, wisdom, and inspiration. The planet 6th highest in degree, the GK, is connected to 6th house themes, such as illness, enemies, obstruction, hard work/continuous focused effort, etc., and of the seven *Jaimini karakas* is the most adverse. As the planet of 7th highest degree, the DK will represent the spouse or partner.

In the *Jaimini* scheme, the AK, AmK, PK, DK, and natal 5th house lord are possessed of *Raj* yoga-forming capability. Both PK and natal 5th lord will represent themes of intelligence and creative inspiration in the *Jaimini* system; a chart's creative potential is therefore heightened when the 5th lord and PK enjoy mutual activation, or when they happen to be the same planet. Although the BK is not specifically thought of as yoga creating, it does represent 3rd house significations and as such will often figure prominently in the charts of creative artists. The mutual and/or combined influence of Venus and the Moon is auspicious and potentially *Raj* yoga-forming, depending on the strength of each *graha*; the combined influence of Jupiter and Mercury is also beneficial. As in *Parashara Jyotish*, a house is fortified and rendered more capable when it contains or is aspected by its lord. The Moon in *Jaimini sambandha* with four or more *grahas* also constitutes a *Raj* yoga. Secondary and alternative ascendants play an important role in the *Jaimini* system; the most significant is known as the *Karakamsha* (*navamsha* sign occupied by the *Atma Karaka*) *lagna*, which will be abbreviated as KL.

In *Jaimini*, the *sthira* (fixed) houses, and occupying planets, aspect *chara* (movable or cardinal) houses, and planets in those houses, except for the adjacent house. For example, Taurus and any planet(s) in Taurus will aspect the signs of Cancer, Libra, and Capricorn in a chart (and any planets in those signs), but *not* the sign of Aries. The converse is also the case: Movable signs and planets in movable signs will aspect the fixed signs, except for the one adjacent, e.g., Libra and any planet(s) in Libra will aspect the signs of Taurus, Leo, and Aquarius, but *not* the sign of Scorpio. The *dwishwabhava* (mutable or dual) signs and residing planets all aspect each other, with no exceptions. (Readers who are not as conversant with the *Jaimini* system are directed to the works and commentaries of such writers as K.N. Rao, P.S. Sastri, Dr. B.V. Raman, and Marc Boney.)

Let us now embark on an exploration of artistic charts, beginning with music.

Chapter 2

Music

Our first chart will be that of prolific composer and pianist George Gershwin (September 26, 1898, Brooklyn in Kings County, NY, 11:09 a.m., Rodden rated A). Well known for his innovative orchestral piece *Rhapsody in Blue*, Gershwin wrote numerous songs for films and Broadway musicals, including such standards as "Embraceable You," "Fascinating Rhythm," "The Man I Love," "I've Got a Crush on You," "But Not for Me," and "Someone to Watch Over Me." In his relatively brief career, George Gershwin composed more than 500 songs. The often-revived American opera *Porgy and Bess,* composed by Gershwin in 1935, is considered his masterpiece. Gershwin was known to sit at the piano, playing and composing for hours at a time, and is quoted as having stated, "When I'm in my normal mood, music drips from my fingers." In 1985, George Gershwin and his lyricist brother Ira were awarded the Congressional Gold Medal. In commemoration of his 100th birthday in 1998, a special Pulitzer Prize was given to George Gershwin, for his "distinguished and enduring contributions to American music."

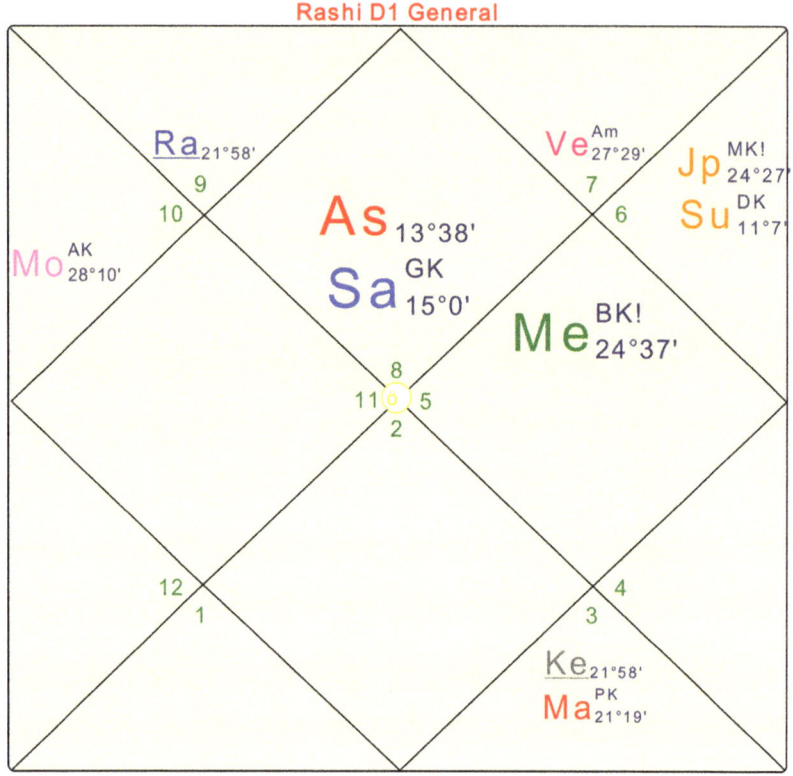

Creativity in the Vedic Astrology Chart

Rashi D1 General

		Ma PK 21°19' Ke 21°58'	
Mo AK 28°10'	ö **George Gershwin** Mon. 9/26/1898 11:09:00 Brooklyn, Kings, NY		Me BK! 24°37'
Ra 21°58'	Sa GK 15°0' As 13°38'	Ve Am 27°29'	Jp MK! 24°27' Su DK 11°7'

George Gershwin's chart has Scorpio rising with 3rd lord Saturn in the ascendant. Our first clear indication of the possibility of creativity, and specifically musical creativity, is the Moon's location in the 3rd house in the musical *nakshatra* of *Dhanishtha*. As lord of the 9th house of highest *dharma* or purpose, the Moon, waxing and benefic, benefits from multiple influences, including those from 3rd lord Saturn and ascendant ruler Mars, but especially significant is Jupiter's 5th glance to the Moon from the 11th house. As ruler of the 5th house of the mind and creative inspiration, Jupiter also aspects back to its own 5th house, which happens to be the 3rd house from the Moon. Jupiter in *Chitra nakshatra* will reflect qualities of beauty and aesthetic balance, while the Sun in *Hasta nakshatra* favors use of the hands (Gershwin was an accomplished pianist) along with writing and compositional skill. Notice also that 10th lord Sun and Jupiter are flanked by natural benefics, and that an *Adhi*-like yoga is formed opposite the 5th house by Venus, Jupiter, and Mercury as Jupiter aspects the 5th and Venus and Mercury aspect the houses on either side of the 5th. 10th lord Sun's flanking constitutes *Ubhayachari* yoga, made more potent by the Sun's association with Jupiter. The 10th house has 8th and 11th lord Mercury in the naturally creative *nakshatra* of *Purva Phalguni*, as Mercury is activated there by 3rd lord Saturn. The owners of the 10th house of career (Sun) and the 11th house of mass entertainment (Mercury) are involved in *Parivartana* yoga. The yoga-forming conjunction of 5th lord Jupiter and 10th lord Sun is energized by Mars' 4th aspect from the 8th house and note that Mars rules the 11th house from the Moon. Although it is found in the 12th house from the ascendant, Venus in its own sign of Libra plays a strong role as lord of the 5th house from the Moon and located in the 10th. What to make of George Gershwin's *lagna* lord Mars in the 8th house of the chart and tightly conjunct *Ketu*? This pairing occurs in the *nakshatra* of *Punarvasu*, offering Mr. Gershwin subtlety and innovation (*Ketu*) along with steady renewal (*Punarvasu*) of his musical themes and concepts. Finally, notice the abundance of *grahas* (6) in *ayudh* (weapon) *drekkanas* in George Gershwin's chart: *Rahu*, Moon, Mars, *Ketu*, Mercury, and the Sun.

Taken from the *Jaimini* system perspective, 5th lord Jupiter and the Sun occupy the chart's KL in the sign of Virgo, with AK Moon in the 5th house in Capricorn and PK Mars directionally strong in the 10th. The Sun and Mars both carry underlying strength; the Sun is exalted in the D-9, and *swakshetra* and *dig bala* in the 10th house of the D-10. Mars, repeating the role of ascendant ruler of both D-9 and D-10 charts, is *swakshetra* in the 6th house of Gershwin's D-9, and is exalted in the 3rd house of artistic skills in the D-10. Both charts benefit from the *Jaimini* aspect back to the ascendant by their strong ascendant ruler. The capability of George Gershwin's D-10 is elevated by activation of the chart's ascendant by all three natural benefics, including Venus as the chart's AmK. The Jupiter – Moon configuration in the D-1, with Jupiter in the KL and Moon in the 5th, is a *Jaimini Raj* yoga (annotated in BPHS Chapter 33, verses 41 – 45 & verses 85 -- 86) said to confer authorship and a writer "well-versed in all branches of learning." The potency of this yoga is amplified by Jupiter's status as 5th lord and Moon's as AK. The chart's creative potential is enhanced by the *Jaimini* mutual aspect between 5th lord Jupiter, Sun, and PK Mars.

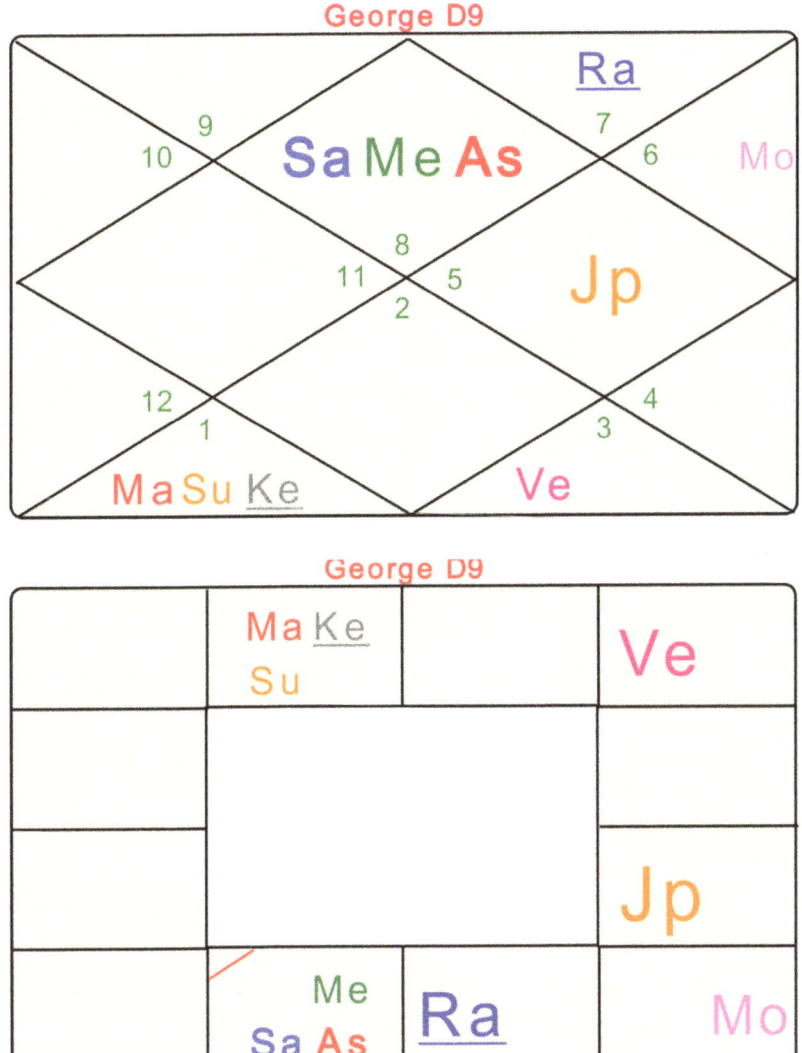

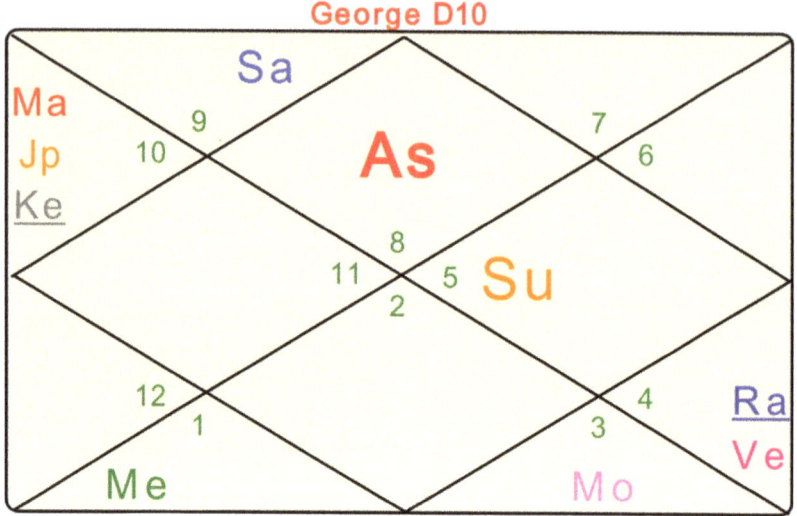

George D10

Creativity in the Vedic Astrology Chart

GG: Vimshottari

Start Date			Age	Dashas	
8/	3/	1898	-0.1	Ma	Sa
9/	12/	1899	1.0	Ma	Me
9/	9/	1900	2.0	Ma	Ke
2/	5/	1901	2.4	Ma	Ve
4/	7/	1902	3.5	Ma	Su
8/	13/	1902	3.9	Ma	Mo
3/	14/	1903	4.5	Ra	Ra
11/	24/	1905	7.2	Ra	Jp
4/	19/	1908	9.6	Ra	Sa
2/	24/	1911	12.4	Ra	Me
9/	12/	1913	15.0	Ra	Ke
10/	1/	1914	16.0	Ra	Ve
9/	30/	1917	19.0	Ra	Su
8/	25/	1918	19.9	Ra	Mo
2/	24/	1920	21.4	Ra	Ma
3/	14/	1921	22.5	Jp	Jp
5/	2/	1923	24.6	Jp	Sa
11/	12/	1925	27.1	Jp	Me
2/	18/	1928	29.4	Jp	Ke
1/	24/	1929	30.3	Jp	Ve
9/	25/	1931	33.0	Jp	Su
7/	13/	1932	33.8	Jp	Mo
11/	12/	1933	35.1	Jp	Ma
10/	19/	1934	36.1	Jp	Ra
3/	14/	1937	38.5	Sa	Sa
3/	16/	1940	41.5	Sa	Me

GG: Chara

Start Date			Age	Dashas	
8/	28/	1919	20.9	Leo	Libr
7/	28/	1920	21.8	Leo	Sco
6/	28/	1921	22.8	Leo	Sag
5/	28/	1922	23.7	Leo	Cap
4/	28/	1923	24.6	Leo	Aqu
3/	28/	1924	25.5	Leo	Pis
2/	26/	1925	26.4	Leo	Ari
1/	27/	1926	27.3	Leo	Tau
12/	27/	1926	28.2	Leo	Gem
11/	27/	1927	29.2	Leo	Can
10/	27/	1928	30.1	Leo	Leo
9/	27/	1929	31.0	Can	Gem
3/	29/	1930	31.5	Can	Tau
9/	27/	1930	32.0	Can	Ari
3/	29/	1931	32.5	Can	Pis
9/	27/	1931	33.0	Can	Aqu
3/	28/	1932	33.5	Can	Cap
9/	27/	1932	34.0	Can	Sag
3/	28/	1933	34.5	Can	Sco
9/	27/	1933	35.0	Can	Libr
3/	29/	1934	35.5	Can	Virg
9/	27/	1934	36.0	Can	Leo
3/	29/	1935	36.5	Can	Can
9/	27/	1935	37.0	Gem	Tau
11/	27/	1935	37.2	Gem	Ari
1/	27/	1936	37.3	Gem	Pis

The timing of George Gershwin's rise in career, which brought him significant acclaim and wealth, is simple – he ran the 16-year *Vimshottari* period of Jupiter from age twenty-two to thirty-eight, and sadly, passed away shortly after the Jupiter period ended, in Saturn -- Saturn. Again, Jupiter's placement in the 11th house with 10th lord Sun, surrounded by natural benefics and in reception of an aspect from ascendant lord Mars, all constitute sufficient justification for George Gershwin's success during his Jupiter period. Notice that 5th lord Jupiter is found in the 10th house of his *vargottama* D-9, and is aspected by 3rd house ruler Saturn. In Gershwin's D-10, (also *vargottama*), 5th lord Jupiter is debilitated in the 3rd house, but participates in a 2 – 3 *Parivartana* yoga with Saturn and is joined in the 3rd by exalted ascendant ruler Mars.

At the age of twenty, George Gershwin began his 11-year Leo *Jaimini Chara dasha*, to be followed by a 6-year Cancer period. The sign of Leo is the 10th house of the chart and holds BK Mercury. Both Leo and the 10th house from Leo, the sign of Taurus, are aspected by the Moon and Venus, rendered more potent by the Moon's status as AK and that of Venus as AmK. The sign of Taurus also benefits from the activation by its *swakshetra* ruling planet. From Cancer, the Moon and Venus occupy angular houses and aspect the 2nd and 11th houses. In Gershwin's D-9, Leo is occupied by natal and local 5th lord Jupiter and aspected by its exalted sign ruler DK Sun and *swakshetra* PK Mars, while in the D-10 Leo holds *swakshetra* Sun. The Sun in the 10th house of the D-10 is influenced by natal/local 5th lord Jupiter, BK Mercury, and exalted PK Mars (also *Ketu*), while the 10th from Leo is activated by aspects from that same Jupiter, Mars, and *Ketu* grouping as well as those from *Rahu* and AmK Venus. George Gershwin's *Jaimini* Cancer period saw him enjoy his period of greatest professional success including the composition and premiere of *Porgy and Bess*. In his D-9, the 10th house from Cancer holds exalted DK Sun and *swakshetra* PK Mars (and *Ketu*) as Sun and Mars obtain further strength due to their *dig bala* status. Notice as well that the three *grahas* in the 10th from Cancer are aspected by Saturn, BK Mercury, and natal/local 5th lord Jupiter. In his D-10 Cancer holds AmK Venus with BK Mercury in the 10th house aspected by DK Sun. Aries sign ruler Mars is exalted in the 7th from Cancer.

The next chart for our consideration will be that of the "Queen of Soul," Aretha Franklin (March 25, 1942, Memphis, TN, 10:30 p.m., AA). As a vocalist, songwriter and pianist, Ms. Franklin had a series of number one hit songs, including "I Never Loved a Man," "Respect," "(You Make Me Feel Like) A Natural Woman," and "I Say a Little Prayer." She recorded 112 songs which listed on the U.S. *Billboard* magazine charts, and 20 songs which reached # 1 on the Rhythm & Blues charts. Aretha Franklin was the winner of 18 Grammy awards, including that for Best Female Rhythm and Blues singer for eight consecutive years, from 1968 to 1975, the first eight years in which that award was given. Possessed of a majestic singing voice, Aretha Franklin began her career at an early age, singing gospel music before her transition to rhythm and blues in her teens. Regarded as the pre-eminent rhythm and blues singer of her time, Ms. Franklin is estimated to have sold more than 75 million records. In 1987 Aretha Franklin became the first female artist to be elected to the Rock and Roll Hall of Fame and in 1999 she was awarded the National Medal of the Arts. Aretha Franklin was named number one on *Rolling Stone* magazine's 2023 ranking of the "200 Greatest Singers of All Time." (*Rolling Stone*, January 1st, 2023).

Creativity in the Vedic Astrology Chart

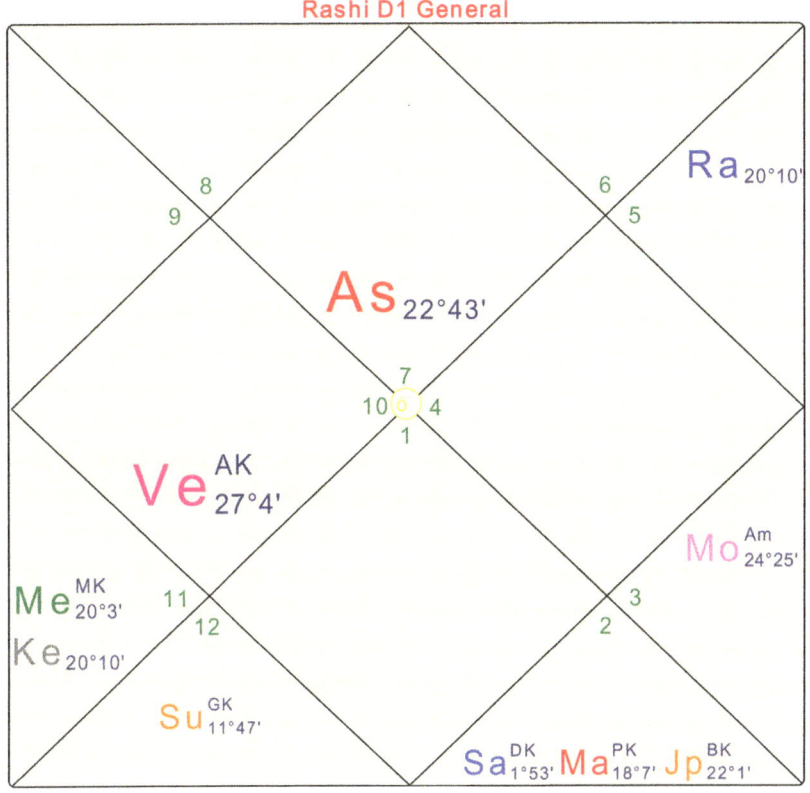

Rashi D1 General

		Sa DK 1°53' Ma PK 18°7' Jp BK 22°1'	Mo Am 24°25'
Su GK 11°47'			
Ke 20°10' Me MK 20°3'	ö **Aretha Franklin** Wed. 3/25/1942 22:30:00 Memphis, TN		
Ve AK 27°4'			Ra 20°10'
		As 22°43'	

Ms. Franklin's Libra rising chart features ascendant ruler Venus in the 4th house where it gains directional strength, occupies the *nakshatra* of *Dhanishtha*, and aspects the 10th house of career. Because of the Moon's placement in Gemini in the 9th, Venus becomes ruler of the 5th house from the Moon. Notice the significant *sambandha* between *lagna* lord Venus and 3rd lord Jupiter, as Jupiter in a sign of Venus aspects Venus with its 9th glance. From the 8th house, Ms. Franklin's 2nd house of voice is aspected by three *grahas*, including 2nd lord Mars and 3rd lord Jupiter, both of whom are in *Rohini nakshatra*. Yoga *karaka* and lord of 5th house of creativity Saturn sits in *Krittika nakshatra* and participates in a 4 – 8 *Parivartana* yoga with Venus. In addition to Venus' influence on the 10th, Saturn as 5th lord also aspects the house of career. The majesty and power of Ms. Franklin's voice is seen through

2nd lord Mars' close association with Jupiter in *Rohini*, as well as the collective aspect to the 2nd house, especially that of Jupiter. Why Jupiter? Jupiter is the *karaka* or indicator of oratory, i.e., expansive, inspiring speech. In a chart such as Ms. Franklin's, where Jupiter rules the 3rd house of music and artistic expression and is placed in a sign of Venus (particularly *Rohini*), Jupiter is more likely to emphasize the singing voice as opposed to that of speech. Recall that Aretha Franklin's career began in the realm of gospel music and it was in churches and religious gatherings where her voice began to attract notice for its soaring, highly inspirational quality. That quality carried over to her career in rhythm and blues, i.e., "soul" music, and resulted in Ms. Franklin's most deserved title as "Queen of Soul."

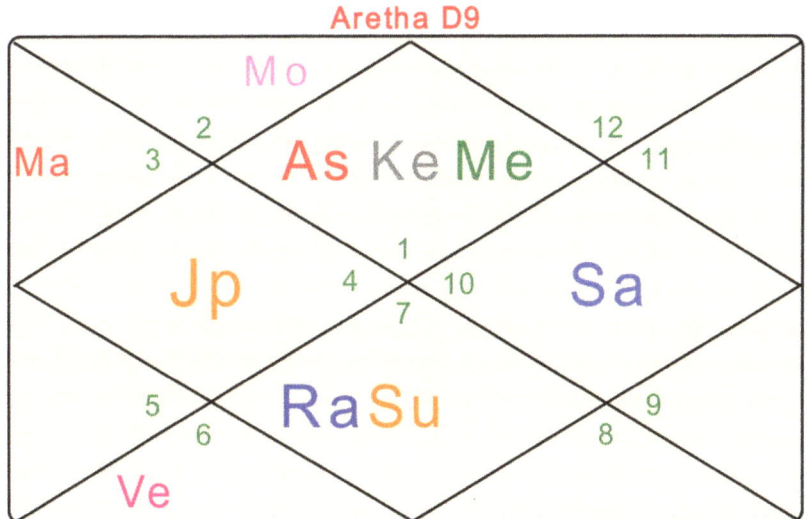

Aretha D9

	Me As / Ke	Mo	Ma
			Jp
Sa			
		Su Ra	Ve

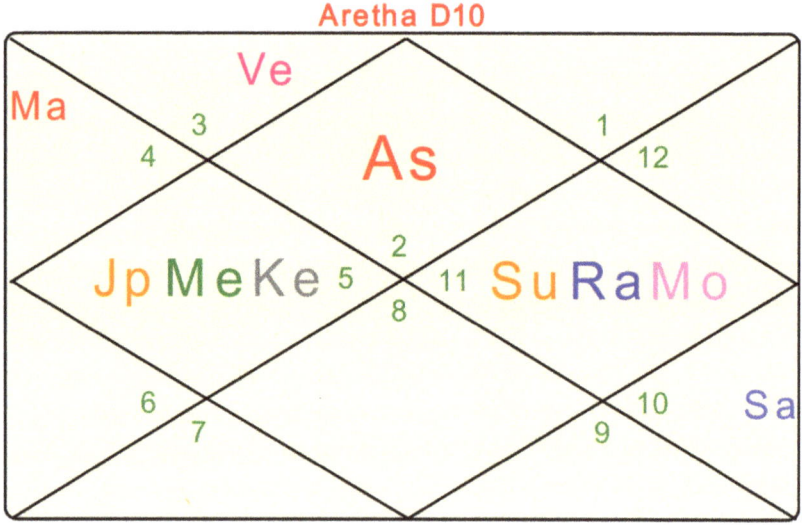

Aretha D10

Aretha D10

		As	Ve
Ra Su Mo			Ma
Sa			Jp Ke Me

AF: Vimshottari

Start Date	Age	Dashas	
4/ 1/ 1948	6.0	Jp	Mo
8/ 1/ 1949	7.4	Jp	Ma
7/ 7/ 1950	8.3	Jp	Ra
11/ 30/ 1952	**10.7**	**Sa**	**Sa**
12/ 4/ 1955	13.7	Sa	Me
8/ 13/ 1958	16.4	Sa	Ke
9/ 22/ 1959	17.5	Sa	Ve
11/ 22/ 1962	20.7	Sa	Su
11/ 4/ 1963	21.6	Sa	Mo
6/ 4/ 1965	23.2	Sa	Ma
7/ 14/ 1966	24.3	Sa	Ra
5/ 20/ 1969	27.2	Sa	Jp
12/ 1/ 1971	**29.7**	**Me**	**Me**
4/ 29/ 1974	32.1	Me	Ke
4/ 26/ 1975	33.1	Me	Ve
2/ 24/ 1978	35.9	Me	Su
12/ 31/ 1978	36.8	Me	Mo
6/ 1/ 1980	38.2	Me	Ma
5/ 29/ 1981	39.2	Me	Ra
12/ 16/ 1983	41.7	Me	Jp
3/ 23/ 1986	44.0	Me	Sa
11/ 30/ 1988	**46.7**	**Ke**	**Ke**
4/ 28/ 1989	47.1	Ke	Ve
6/ 29/ 1990	48.3	Ke	Su
11/ 3/ 1990	48.6	Ke	Mo
6/ 5/ 1991	49.2	Ke	Ma

AF: Chara

Start Date			Age	Dashas	
3/	25/	1956	14.0	Cap	Sag
11/	23/	1956	14.7	Cap	Sco
7/	25/	1957	15.3	Cap	Libr
3/	25/	1958	16.0	Cap	Virg
11/	24/	1958	16.7	Cap	Leo
7/	26/	1959	17.3	Cap	Can
3/	25/	1960	18.0	Cap	Gem
11/	24/	1960	18.7	Cap	Tau
7/	25/	1961	19.3	Cap	Ari
3/	26/	1962	20.0	Cap	Pis
11/	24/	1962	20.7	Cap	Aqu
7/	26/	1963	21.3	Cap	Cap
3/	25/	1964	22.0	Aqu	Pis
12/	24/	1964	22.8	Aqu	Ari
9/	24/	1965	23.5	Aqu	Tau
6/	25/	1966	24.2	Aqu	Gem
3/	26/	1967	25.0	Aqu	Can
12/	25/	1967	25.8	Aqu	Leo
9/	24/	1968	26.5	Aqu	Virg
6/	25/	1969	27.2	Aqu	Libr
3/	26/	1970	28.0	Aqu	Sco
12/	25/	1970	28.8	Aqu	Sag
9/	25/	1971	29.5	Aqu	Cap
6/	24/	1972	30.2	Aqu	Aqu
3/	25/	1973	31.0	Pis	Ari
1/	24/	1974	31.8	Pis	Tau

The astrological influences driving Ms. Franklin's early and continued success in her Saturn major period should be apparent: (As noted) Saturn as yoga *karaka* and 5th lord aspects the 10th house of career in her birth chart. Saturn forms *Shasha* yoga in the 10th house in her Aries rising D-9 as well as a 9 – 10 *Raj* yoga with exalted 9th lord Jupiter. Saturn again owns the 10th house of her D-10 and locates in the auspicious 9th house in its own sign of Capricorn. Aretha Franklin was signed to her first record contract in 1960, with Columbia Records, during the Venus sub-period of her Saturn major period. Ascendant lord Venus participates in *Parivartana* yoga with major period ruler Saturn and is aspected by 3rd and 6th lord Jupiter. In the D-9, Venus owns the 2nd house of vocal expression and is aspected in the 6th by D-9 ascendant lord Mars. As the ascendant ruler of Ms. Franklin's D-10, Venus inhabits the 2nd house.

Aretha Franklin began her 8-year Capricorn *Jaimini Chara dasha* at the age of fourteen, in 1956. From Capricorn the Venus -- Saturn *Parivartana* yoga becomes an auspicious exchange uniting the 1st house and the 5th. There is also *Jaimini* mutual aspect between AK Venus and Taurus occupants 5th lord/DK Saturn, PK Mars, and BK Jupiter. Jupiter's *Jaimini* aspect to Venus in the 5th house from the chart's Virgo KL creates the *Raj* yoga cited in BPHS 39:11. The 10th house from Capricorn is activated by aspects from the three *grahas* in Taurus, as well as by that of Mercury from Aquarius. In her D-9, *Shasha* yoga Saturn is aspected by exalted AmK Moon who also activates the 10th house and resident Sun. In Aretha Franklin's D-10, Capricorn's strength is maintained due to the occupation of its ruling planet as well as by aspects from Jupiter, Mercury, and *Ketu*. The 10th house from Capricorn is influenced by six *grahas*; in addition to the repetition of those from Jupiter and Mercury, the sign of Libra is activated by the Sun and AmK Moon along with *Rahu* and *Ketu*. Ms. Franklin's continued success in her subsequent Aquarius period is evident as exalted BK Jupiter, Mercury, Sun, and *Rahu/Ketu* influence the sign of Aquarius in her D-9, while the 10th house from Aquarius is aspected by Jupiter, Mercury, *Ketu*, and *swakshetra* Saturn. Aquarius is the sign on the 10th house of Aretha Franklin's D-10 and contains AmK Moon, the Sun and *swakshetra Rahu* while receiving an aspect from PK Mars. The 10th house from Aquarius benefits from the aspect by its owner PK Mars, as well as that from natal 5th lord/DK Saturn.

Next, we will analyze the charts of two musicians who happened to be born one day apart. First we will take up the chart of Glen Campbell (April 22, 1936, Delight, AK, 8:14 p.m., B). As a studio musician in the 1960s Glen Campbell played on the recordings of such musical notables as the Beach Boys, Frank Sinatra, Nat King Cole, Elvis Presley, Bing Crosby, the Everly Brothers, Merle Haggard, Doris Day, and countless others. Glen Campbell's *New York Times* obituary states that in the year 1963 alone, the playing and/or singing of Glen Campbell could be found on 586 different recordings (Michael Pollak, *New York Times*, August 9, 2017). Glen Campbell went on to stardom as a recording artist, singer, and performer, also as host of his own television show and actor in a number of Hollywood films. Throughout, Glen Campbell maintained his pre-eminence and thoroughly deserved reputation as one of the most accomplished guitar players in the history of recorded music. In 2012 Glen Campbell was honored with a Grammy Lifetime Achievement Award, and in 2016 he was given the Academy of Country Music's Career Achievement Award.

Michael A. Sugarman

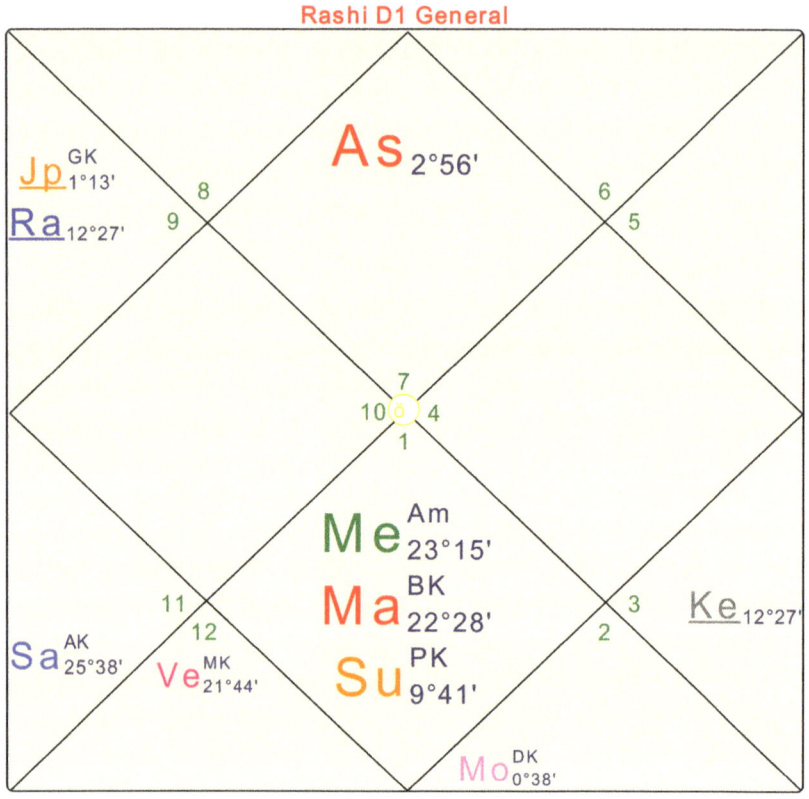

Creativity in the Vedic Astrology Chart

```
                    Rashi D1 General
┌─────────────┬──────────────┬──────────────┬──────────────┐
│             │ Su PK 9°41'  │              │              │
│             │ Ma BK 22°28' │ Mo DK 0°38'  │ Ke 12°27'    │
│ Ve MK 21°44'│ Me Am 23°15' │              │              │
├─────────────┼──────────────┴──────────────┼──────────────┤
│ Sa AK 25°38'│                             │              │
│             │            ö                │              │
├─────────────┤      Glen Campbell          ├──────────────┤
│             │  Wed. 4/22/1936 20:14:00    │              │
│             │        Delight, AK          │              │
├─────────────┼──────────────┬──────────────┼──────────────┤
│ Ra 12°27'   │              │              │              │
│ Jp GK 1°13' │              │ As 2°56'     │              │
└─────────────┴──────────────┴──────────────┴──────────────┘
```

Again we have a Venus ruled chart, Libra ascendant, with Venus exalted in Pisces in the 6th house in the *nakshatra* of *Revati* and stronger by virtue of its *swakshetra* dispositor Jupiter. *Revati*'s symbol is the drum, and with sufficient supporting influence in the chart, can contribute to musical and artistic ability. Glen Campbell's primary skill, honed from a very young age, was as a guitar player, and here we have an abundance of indication of talented use of the hands: As lord and occupant of the 3rd house of skills and manual dexterity and placed at 1 degree 13 minutes of Sagittarius, Jupiter falls in a weapon *drekkana*. In the 7th house of the chart, we find Sun, Mars, and Mercury in the sign of Aries. Sun and Mars are strong, as 11th (popular entertainment) lord Sun is exalted and within 19 minutes of, and approaching, its exact degree of exaltation, while *swakshetra* Mars forms

Ruchaka yoga. Additional strength is conferred to Mercury and Sun who are disposited by Mars. Mercury is 9th lord of the Libra chart and although it assumes a degree of maleficence it is the winner of a planetary war with Mars and contributes to Glen Campbell's guitar mastery and creative ability as lord of the 5th house from the Moon. All 3 planets in the 7th house are aspected by yoga *karaka* and 5th house ruler Saturn, strong in its own sign of Aquarius. In addition to Saturn's aspect from the 5th, the Sun, Mars, and Mercury are aspected by 3rd house ruler and weapon *drekkana* planet Jupiter, and we begin to see the more complete picture of what made Glen Campbell such an extraordinary musician. The planets in the 7th house will naturally aspect the ascendant and notice that all three *grahas* occupy weapon *drekkanas* themselves, Sun in the first *drekkana* of Aries, and Mercury and Mars in creative *Bharani nakshatra* in the 3rd. With the addition of *Ketu* in the 2nd *drekkana* of Gemini, we have a total of five *grahas* in weapon *drekkanas* in Glen Campbell's chart. Aspects by Mars, Moon, and Saturn to Glen Campbell's 2nd house, along with Saturn's and especially Jupiter's aspects to 2nd lord Mars provided Mr. Campbell with a lyrical and pleasant singing voice. Finally, 10th lord Moon is exalted in the 8th house in Taurus, becomes lord of 3rd house from itself, and benefits from dispositor Venus' exaltation.

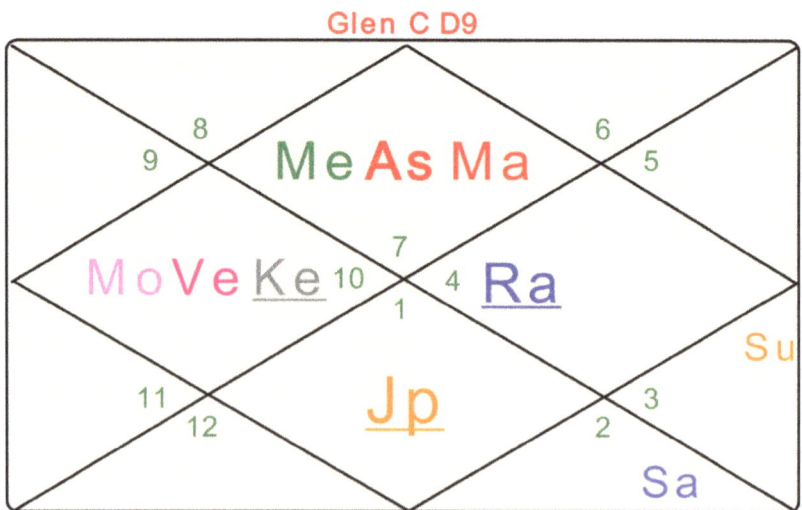

Creativity in the Vedic Astrology Chart

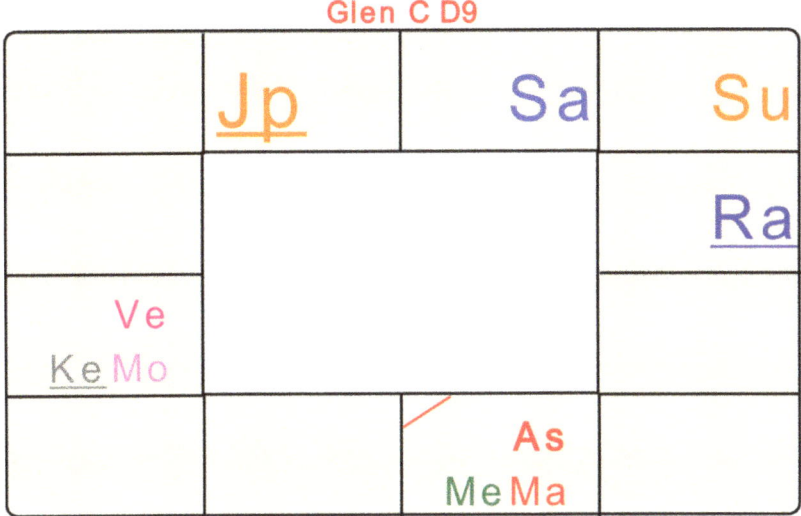

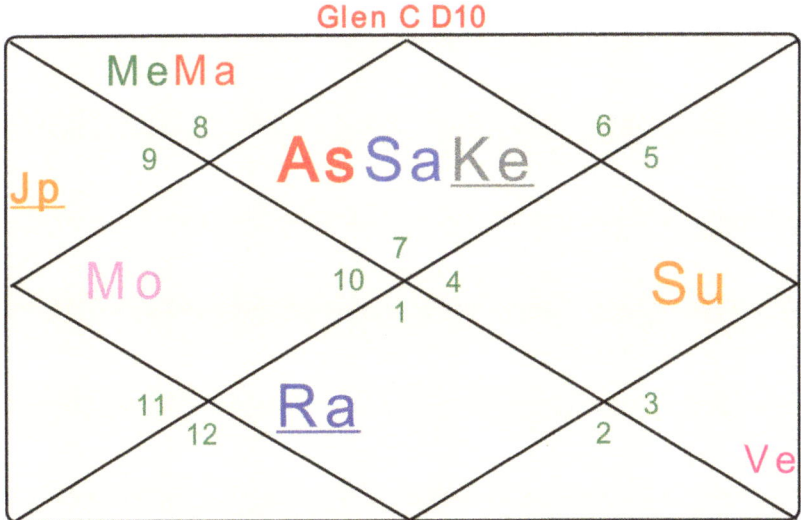

Glen C D10

	Ra		Ve
			Su
	Mo		
Jp	Me Ma	Sa / As Ke	

Glen: Chara

Start Date	Age	Dashas
4/ 22/ 1936	-0.0	Libr
4/ 23/ 1941	5.0	Sco
4/ 23/ 1946	10.0	Sag
4/ 23/ 1958	22.0	Cap
4/ 23/ 1969	33.0	Aqu
4/ 23/ 1971	35.0	Pis
4/ 23/ 1974	38.0	Ari
4/ 23/ 1986	50.0	Tau
4/ 23/ 1996	60.0	Gem
4/ 23/ 2006	70.0	Can
4/ 23/ 2008	72.0	Leo
4/ 23/ 2012	76.0	Virg

Glen : Vimshottari

Start Date			Age	Dashas	
5/	9/	1948	12.0	Mo	Ve
1/	7/	1950	13.7	Mo	Su
7/	9/	1950	14.2	Ma	Ma
12/	5/	1950	14.6	Ma	Ra
12/	24/	1951	15.7	Ma	Jp
11/	28/	1952	16.6	Ma	Sa
1/	7/	1954	17.7	Ma	Me
1/	5/	1955	18.7	Ma	Ke
6/	3/	1955	19.1	Ma	Ve
8/	2/	1956	20.3	Ma	Su
12/	8/	1956	20.6	Ma	Mo
7/	9/	1957	21.2	Ra	Ra
3/	21/	1960	23.9	Ra	Jp
8/	15/	1962	26.3	Ra	Sa
6/	20/	1965	29.2	Ra	Me
1/	8/	1968	31.7	Ra	Ke
1/	25/	1969	32.8	Ra	Ve
1/	26/	1972	35.8	Ra	Su
12/	20/	1972	36.7	Ra	Mo
6/	21/	1974	38.2	Ra	Ma
7/	9/	1975	39.2	Jp	Jp
8/	27/	1977	41.3	Jp	Sa
3/	9/	1980	43.9	Jp	Me
6/	15/	1982	46.1	Jp	Ke
5/	22/	1983	47.1	Jp	Ve
1/	20/	1986	49.7	Jp	Su

Glen Campbell's career escalated and brought him to national prominence during his *Vimshottari Rahu* major period, from ages 21 to 39. *Rahu* in the 3rd falls in the 10th house from ascendant lord Venus, where it is sign disposited by *swakshetra* Jupiter and *nakshatra* disposited by *Ketu*, both in weapon *drekkanas*. Located in the 10th house of Mr. Campbell's *vargottama* D-9, *Rahu* is aspected by its dispositor Moon and ascendant ruler Venus, both of which gain directional strength in the 4th house of the D-9. *Rahu* gets 5th lord Saturn's glance from the 8th house and is stabilized by the placement of five *grahas* in *kendra* houses from its location in the 10th. *Rahu* in the 7th house of the (also *vargottama*) D-10 is disposited by *swakshetra* Mars and aspected by exalted 5th lord Saturn as well as by *vargottama* 3rd lord (in the D-10, not D-9) Jupiter.

Within a year of the onset of his *Rahu* major period, Glen Campbell began his 11-year *Jaimini* Capricorn *Chara dasha*. As the 4th house of the birth chart, the sign of Capricorn receives a glance from exalted DK Moon, as Moon and *swakshetra* natal 5th lord/AK Saturn aspect the 10th house from Capricorn. The musical and instrumental 3rd house from Capricorn holds exalted Venus and is aspected by its dispositor Jupiter, along with *Rahu* and *Ketu*, while the 11th house from Capricorn is activated by glances from Scorpio owner *swakshetra* BK Mars, exalted PK Sun, and AmK Mercury. Glen Campbell's *vargottama* D-9 supports the potential of his Capricorn period, as we find a 1 – 5 *Parivartana yoga* from Capricorn involving Saturn and Venus. The sign of Capricorn is occupied by the Moon and Venus, and strengthened by Saturn's aspect back to its own house. The 10th house from Capricorn holds AmK Mercury and BK Mars, in mutual aspect with natal and local 5th lord/AK Saturn. The 11th house of gains and entertainment is aspected by Jupiter, Moon, and Venus, as well as *Rahu* and *Ketu*, while 11th lord Mars inhabits the 10th.

Glen Campbell's D-10 is just as compelling, as Capricorn ruler Saturn goes to its sign of exaltation in the 10th house (the ascendant of D-10) while the sign of Capricorn is tenanted by DK Moon. The 11th house from Capricorn contains *swakshetra* BK Mars and AmK Mercury, and is activated by the Sun, Moon, and *Rahu*. In keeping with the theme of Glen Campbell's primary skill as a peerless instrumentalist, the 3rd house from Capricorn is aspected by its lord, *vargottama* (in D-10) Jupiter, and Venus. It was during his Capricorn *Jaimini Chara dasha* that Glen Campbell had a series of hit songs and albums, and was awarded five Grammys for his songs "Gentle on My Mind," and "By the Time I Get to Phoenix." Simultaneously, Glen Campbell was honored by the Country Music Association as Top Male Vocalist for the years 1967 and 1968.

Our second chart in this set of two is that of Roy Orbison, who was born the day after Glen Campbell. (April 23, 1936, Vernon, TX, 3:39 p.m. Astro-databank at www.astro.com lists a 3:50 p.m. birth time for Roy Orbison with AA rating. Roy Orbison's biography at his official website www.royorbison.com gives a birth time of 3:30 p.m. Rectification by the author, using dates of events in Roy Orbison's life, and divisional charts, yields a birth time of 3:39 p.m.) Although he played guitar competently enough to accompany himself, Roy Orbison possessed one of the most distinctive singing voices of his generation, a dynamic yet ethereal voice which some music critics referred to as "operatic." Elvis Presley, who believed he could not match the power and elegance of Orbison's voice, never recorded a Roy Orbison song. Elvis referred to Roy Orbison's voice as "the most perfect" and once told a Las Vegas audience that Roy Orbison was "quite simply, the greatest singer in the world" (www.elvis-history-blog.com). At Roy Orbison's induction into the Rock & Roll Hall of Fame in 1987, Bruce Springsteen said, "Everybody knows that nobody sings like Roy Orbison." A songwriter as well as singer, Orbison wrote, sang, and recorded in the late '50s and through the 1960s, when he had 15 top-ten song hits, including "Crying," "Only the Lonely," "Oh Pretty Woman," "Running Scared" and "It's Over." Roy Orbison was the only musical act to open for both Elvis Presley and the Beatles, and according to legend, once received 14 encores from a British audience before the Beatles could take the stage following his performance, as John Lennon and Paul McCartney forcibly restrained him backstage. (https://royorbison.com/roy-orbison-official-biography/)

Michael A. Sugarman

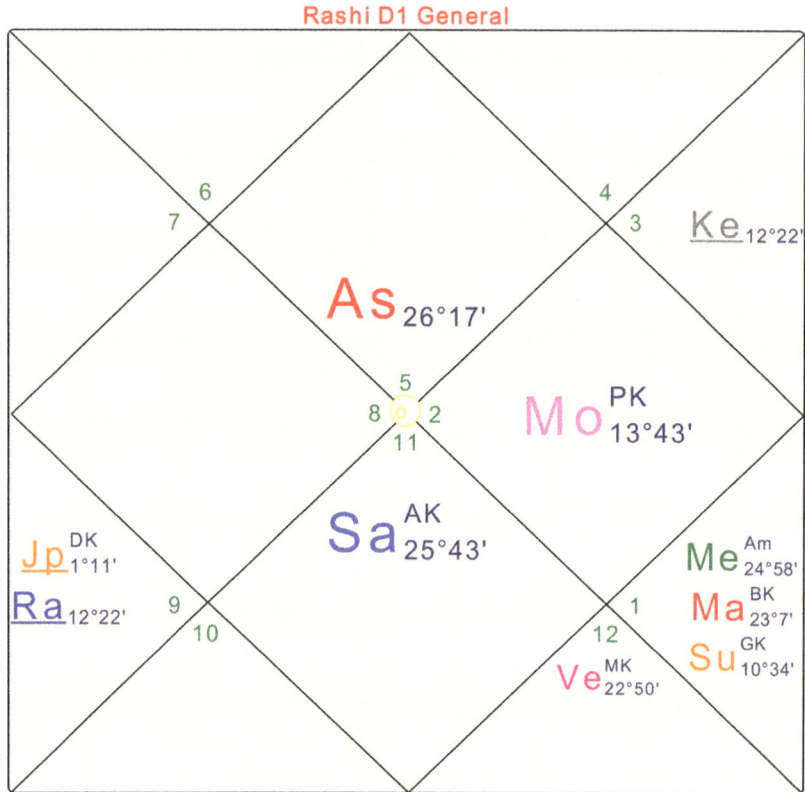

Rashi D1 General

```
+-------------------+-------------------+-------------------+-------------------+
|                   | Su GK 10°34'      | Mo PK 13°43'      | Ke 12°22'         |
|                   | Ma BK 23°7'       |                   |                   |
| Ve MK 22°50'      | Me Am 24°58'      |                   |                   |
+-------------------+-------------------+-------------------+-------------------+
| Sa AK 25°43'      |                                                           |
+-------------------+         Roy Orbison                                       +
|                   |   Thu. 4/23/1936  15:39:00                                |
|                   |         Vernon, TX        | As 26°17'                     |
+-------------------+-------------------+-------------------+-------------------+
| Ra 12°22'         |                   |                   |                   |
| Jp DK 1°11'       |                   |                   |                   |
+-------------------+-------------------+-------------------+-------------------+
```

At 26 degrees 17 minutes, Roy Orbison's Leo chart rises in *Purva Phalguni nakshatra*. Precisely exalted ascendant lord Sun is joined in the 9th house by yoga *karaka* 9th lord Mars and 2nd and 11th lord Mercury. (Notice that Mercury also rules the 2nd house from the Moon.) The Sun's disposition by *swakshetra* Mars in the 9th constitutes a *Raj* yoga known as *Parvata*. As described in *Phaladeepika* Chapter 6 verses 35 & 36, *Parvata* yoga confers wealth, happiness, and the performance of acts of "lasting benefit" to others. Where Jupiter rules and occupies the 3rd house in Glen Campbell's chart, it becomes the owner and occupant of the 5th house in Roy Orbison's chart. From the 5th house Jupiter aspects the three planets in the 9th as well as his ascendant. Roy Orbison did play the guitar with a certain amount of proficiency, but his creativity manifested more through his songwriting and especially his singing. In the context of the change in ascendants and corresponding lords, two other subtle but significant differences occur between the charts of Glen Campbell and Roy Orbison: The exalted Sun, located in a weapon *drekkana* in the chart of Glen Campbell, advances to 10 degrees 34 minutes Aries in Roy Orbison's chart and is no longer in the weapon *drekkana* section of Aries. Glen Campbell's *Krittika* Moon has moved on to *Rohini*, where it is exalted and *vargottama* (in both D-9 and D-10), in the 10th house in the chart of Roy Orbison. Situated 2nd from ascendant ruler Sun, *Rohini* Moon will play an important role in contributing to the beauty of Roy Orbison's voice, as well as his vocal range, said to be somewhere between 3 and 4 octaves. (Every *nakshatra* is assigned one of three directions, i.e., up, sideways, or down; *Rohini*'s direction is upward.) Finally, the quality of Roy Orbison's voice is enhanced by the aspect of exalted 3rd lord Venus to his 2nd house.

A *Jaimini* assessment of Roy Orbison's birth chart reveals the presence of exalted *vargottama* PK Moon in the 10th house, the KL of the chart. BPHS chapter 33 verses 41 -- 45 informs us that the Moon alone in the KL renders one "versed in rhetorics, and singing." AK Saturn creates *Shasha Maha Purusha* yoga in the 10th house from the Moon and KL, and is aspected there by AmK Mercury, *swakshetra* BK Mars and the Sun, as Mercury, Mars, and exalted Sun also aspect the ascendant of the chart. Roy Orbison's chart holds three *Jaimini Raj* yogas which meet criteria for "royal association" as delineated in BPHS chapter 40. These include (40:5), location of the AmK in the 1st, 5th, or 9th (in this case AmK Mercury in the 9th); (40:6), AK in an angle or trine from the ascendant (AK Saturn in the 7th); and notably (40:8), AK residing in an angle or trine or *swakshetra* or exalted, and in aspect to the 9th lord (AK Saturn *swakshetra* in the 7th in *Jaimini* aspect to 9th lord Mars). *Swakshetra* Jupiter and exalted Venus, natural benefics in strength, activate the 2nd, 5th, 8th, and 11th houses from the natal ascendant; notice that the 8th house and sign of Pisces is the 2nd house (voice) from AK Saturn, the 11th house and sign of Gemini is the 2nd house from the KL and Moon, and the sign of Virgo is the 2nd house from the chart's ascendant.

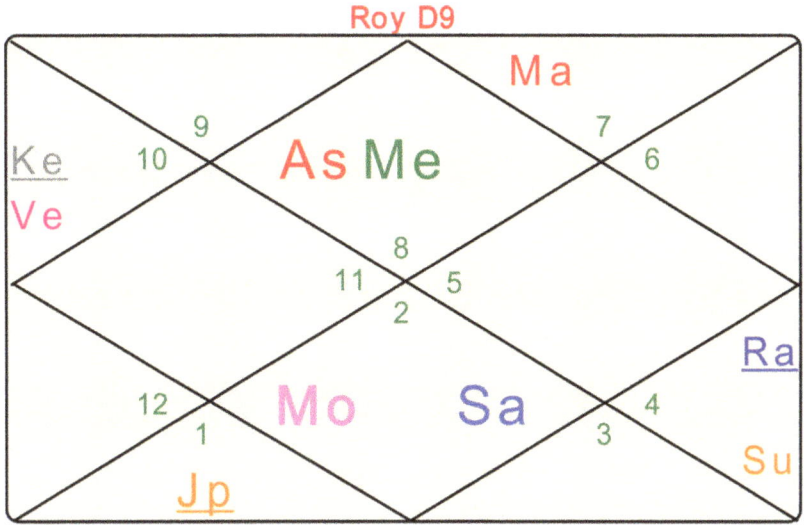

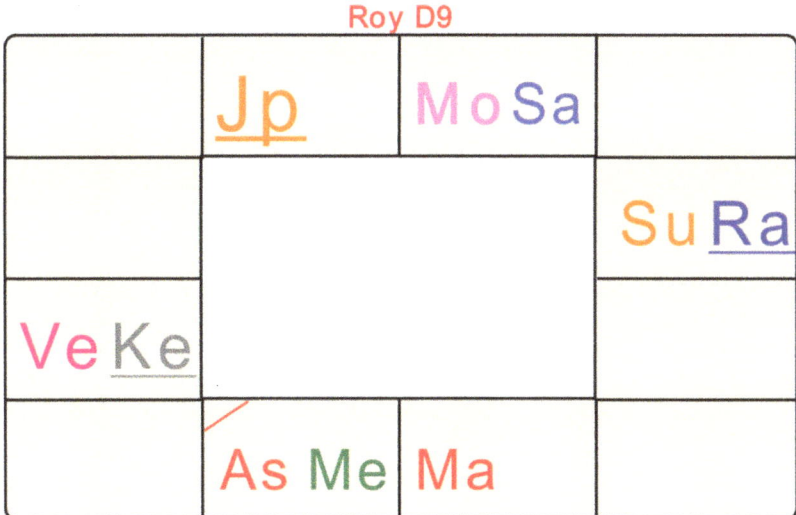

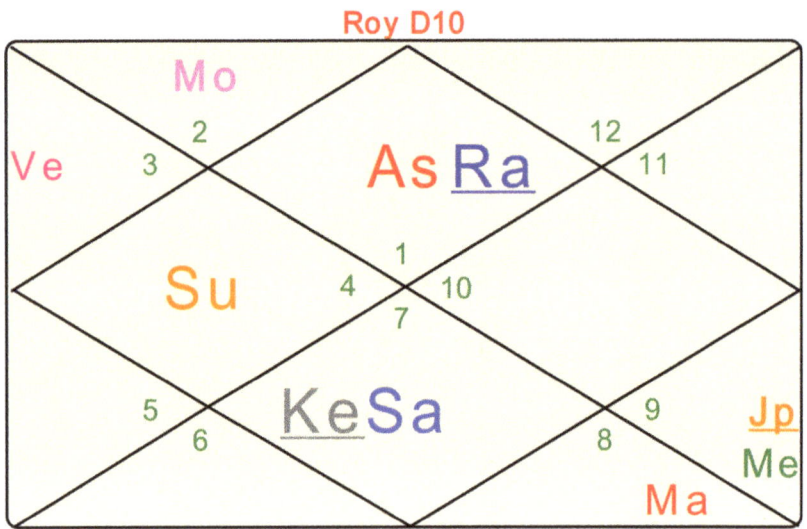

Roy: Vimshottari

Start Date			Age	Dashas	
1/	21/	1947	10.7	Ma	Me
1/	18/	1948	11.7	Ma	Ke
6/	15/	1948	12.1	Ma	Ve
8/	15/	1949	13.3	Ma	Su
12/	21/	1949	13.7	Ma	Mo
7/	**22/**	**1950**	**14.2**	**Ra**	**Ra**
4/	3/	1953	16.9	Ra	Jp
8/	28/	1955	19.3	Ra	Sa
7/	4/	1958	22.2	Ra	Me
1/	20/	1961	24.7	Ra	Ke
2/	8/	1962	25.8	Ra	Ve
2/	8/	1965	28.8	Ra	Su
1/	2/	1966	29.7	Ra	Mo
7/	4/	1967	31.2	Ra	Ma
7/	**22/**	**1968**	**32.2**	**Jp**	**Jp**
9/	9/	1970	34.4	Jp	Sa
3/	22/	1973	36.9	Jp	Me
6/	28/	1975	39.2	Jp	Ke
6/	3/	1976	40.1	Jp	Ve
2/	2/	1979	42.8	Jp	Su
11/	21/	1979	43.6	Jp	Mo
3/	22/	1981	44.9	Jp	Ma
2/	26/	1982	45.8	Jp	Ra
7/	**22/**	**1984**	**48.2**	**Sa**	**Sa**
7/	26/	1987	51.3	Sa	Me
4/	4/	1990	53.9	Sa	Ke

Roy: Chara

Start Date	Age	Dashas
4/ 23/ 1936	-0.0	Leo
4/ 23/ 1940	4.0	Virg
4/ 24/ 1945	9.0	Libr
4/ 24/ 1950	14.0	Sco
4/ 24/ 1955	19.0	Sag
4/ 24/ 1967	31.0	Cap
4/ 24/ 1978	42.0	Aqu
4/ 23/ 1980	44.0	Pis
4/ 24/ 1983	47.0	Ari
4/ 24/ 1995	59.0	Tau
4/ 24/ 2005	69.0	Gem
4/ 24/ 2015	79.0	Can

Roy Orbison's *Vimshottari Rahu* period was his most successful. *Rahu* joins *swakshetra* Jupiter in the 5th house of his birth chart. From *Rahu* and Jupiter, exalted 11th lord Venus inhabits the 4th house and aspects the 10th. The three planets in the natal 9th fall in the 5th house from *Rahu*, and aspect the 11th house. In Roy Orbison's D-9 *Rahu* joins 10th lord Sun, forming *Raj* yoga in the 9th house, where the Sun and *Rahu* are aspected by both planets involved in a 3 – 7 *Parivartana* yoga, Venus, and 3rd lord Saturn. *Rahu* sits prominently in the ascendant of his D-10 *dashamsha* chart, where it benefits from dispositor Mars' *swakshetra* status as well as aspects from exalted 10th lord Saturn and *swakshetra* 9th lord Jupiter. Exalted *vargottama* Moon is located in the 2nd house of voice, while 2nd lord Venus in the 3rd house of artistic expression is aspected by 3rd lord Mercury and Jupiter.

Concurrent with the most successful period of his life, beginning in 1955 and the *Vimshottari* period of *Rahu* -- Saturn, Roy Orbison ran his 12-year Sagittarius *Jaimini Chara dasha*. Sagittarius holds *swakshetra* DK and 5th lord Jupiter as the *kendra* houses are activated by benefics Jupiter and exalted Venus. From Sagittarius in the D-1, AK Saturn rules the 2nd house of voice and falls in the 3rd house of artistry in its sign of Aquarius, where it is aspected by AmK Mercury, *swakshetra* BK Mars and exalted Sun. The 5th house of creativity, the sign of Aries, is strong and well activated by the presence of those same three *grahas*, which also receive the aspect of AK Saturn. A *Jaimini Raj* yoga is created by the *sambandha* of AK Saturn and AmK Mercury. The theme of vocal expression during those twelve years is enhanced by the aspect from exalted PK Moon to the 2nd house. In Roy Orbison's D-9, the second house from Sagittarius is occupied by Venus and aspected by AK Saturn, exalted PK Moon, and AmK Mercury. The 5th house from period sign Sagittarius holds DK Jupiter, in aspect with Mercury.

Roy Orbison's D-10 reinforces the success he enjoyed during his Sagittarius period. The sign of Sagittarius holds its powerful (*vargottama* and *swakshetra*) natal 5th lord Jupiter, and AmK Mercury, as both enjoy *sambandha* with Venus in Gemini. The three natural benefics activate the *kendra* houses from Sagittarius; those houses are also strengthened by activation from their ruling planets. The 2nd house from Sagittarius is aspected by *vargottama* PK Moon as well as by *swakshetra* BK Mars. The 11th house of gains and public acclaim has exalted AK Saturn in *sambandha* with exalted Moon.

We will now move on to the chart of Duke Ellington (April 29, 1899, Washington, D.C., 1:25 a.m. Note: Although no birth time is currently listed for Duke Ellington on the Astro-databank feature at www.astro.com, an earlier version cited Duke Ellington's birth time as 1:25 a.m. with a Rodden rating of A. Rectification by the author confirms a 1:25 a.m. time of birth for Ellington.)

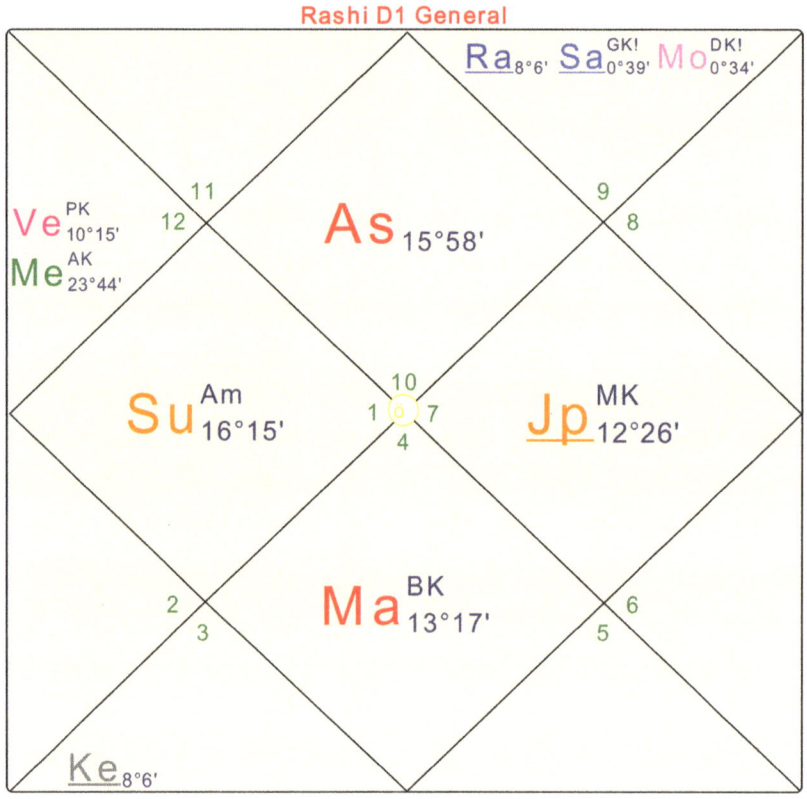

Rashi D1 General

Ve PK 10°15' Me AK 23°44'	Su Am 16°15'		Ke 8°6'
			Ma BK 13°17'
As 15°58'	\multicolumn{2}{c}{**Duke Ellington** Sat. 4/29/1899 1:25:00 Washington, DC}	
Ra 8°6' Sa GK! 0°39' Mo DK! 0°34'		Jp MK 12°26'	

In a long career as an accomplished pianist, composer, arranger and band leader, Duke Ellington was one of the pre-eminent musical figures of the 20th century, acclaimed as "a giant among giants … one of the half-dozen greatest masters of our time" (Schuller, 1989). Duke Ellington composed more than one thousand songs, arias, and extended pieces, or musical "suites." Many of his songs are jazz standards, including "Mood Indigo," "Solitude," "Satin Doll," "Caravan," "Sophisticated Lady," "I Let a Song Go Out of My Heart," and "Don't Get Around Much Anymore." He maintained the Duke Ellington Orchestra, recording, touring, and performing globally, while constantly composing, from 1924 until the end of his life. Among numerous honors conferred upon him, Duke Ellington won 13 Grammy awards as well as a Grammy Lifetime Achievement Award, given in 1966. In 1969, Duke Ellington was awarded the Presidential Medal of Freedom, and in 1999 Duke Ellington's life and musical legacy were honored with a Pulitzer Prize for music. Upon his death in 1974, singer Ella Fitzgerald commented, "It's a very sad day … a genius has passed." (www.dukeellington.com).

The Capricorn chart of Duke Ellington has the *nakshatra* of *Shravana* on the ascendant. At 15 degrees the rising *navamsha* becomes Venus-ruled Taurus, drawing the indications of *Shravana* more decidedly in the direction of music. Recall that *Shravana*'s symbol is the human ear, and is therefore associated with sensitivity to sound, including musical sound. *Shravana* prominent in a chart can confer the subtle ability to tune into one's internal sense of melody, and contributes to the richness and versatility of Duke Ellington's musical imagination. Duke Ellington's chart features a *Parivartana* yoga between houses 3 and 10. As lord of the 10th house of career, Venus resides in the 3rd house of music and artistic expression while 3rd house ruler Jupiter is found in the 10th. There are several aspects of this exchange which are striking: As yoga *karaka*, Venus happens to also rule the 5th house of creativity and is exalted in the 3rd house in Pisces. Notice that as 5th lord, Venus is PK in the *Jaimini* system, and gains strength in Libra in Ellington's D-9. Venus is accompanied by 9th lord Mercury, creating 9 – 10 and 5 – 9 *Raj* yogas in the 3rd house. Mercury in Pisces is debilitated, but that debilitation is cancelled by Jupiter's position in the 10th as well as the location of Venus (exalted where Mercury is debilitated) and Mercury in an angle from the Moon. (The reader is referred to *Phaladeepika* Chapter 7 verses 26 – 30 for annotation of criteria for cancellation of planetary debilitation and qualification for *Neecha Bhanga Raj* yoga.) 9th lord Mercury's placement in *Revati* nakshatra will also contribute to the distinctiveness of Ellington's musical vision. Venus and Mercury aspect the 10th house from the Moon and ascendant ruler Saturn, while we find 3rd lord Jupiter in *Swati*, another *nakshatra* notable for musical enjoyment and proficiency.

Duke Ellington's success and wide appeal is seen through 11th

lord Mars' aspect to 3rd lord Jupiter in the 10th house, reinforced by Jupiter's location in the 11th house from the Moon. Mars' debilitation is cancelled and achieves *Neecha Bhanga Raj* yoga secondary to its location in an angle as well as that of Jupiter, (exalted in Cancer, where Mars is debilitated), and the mutual *kendra* placement of Saturn and the Moon. Emphasis on the 3rd house of the chart is also evidenced by the aspects of Saturn, Mars, and Jupiter to the 3rd house from the Moon. In addition to ascendant lord Saturn's status as lord of the 3rd house from the Moon, and Saturn's very tight conjunction with the Moon, Duke Ellington's keyboard artistry is emphasized through the placement of Saturn and Moon in a weapon *drekkana*, the first of Sagittarius.

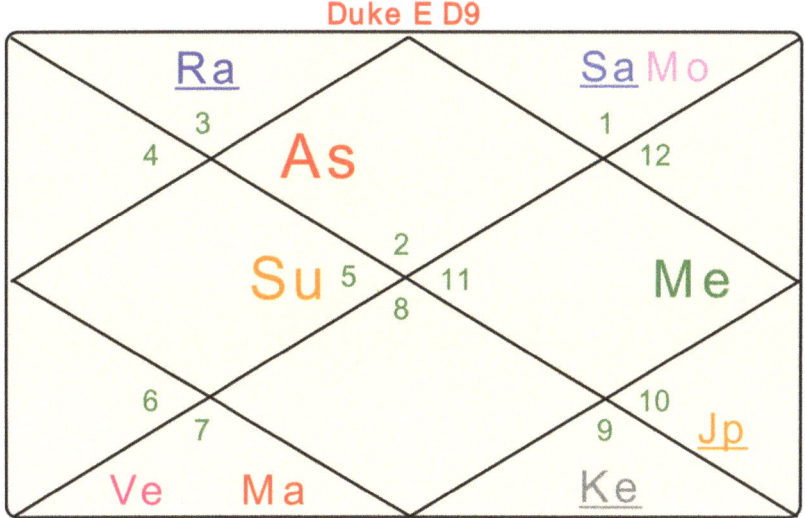

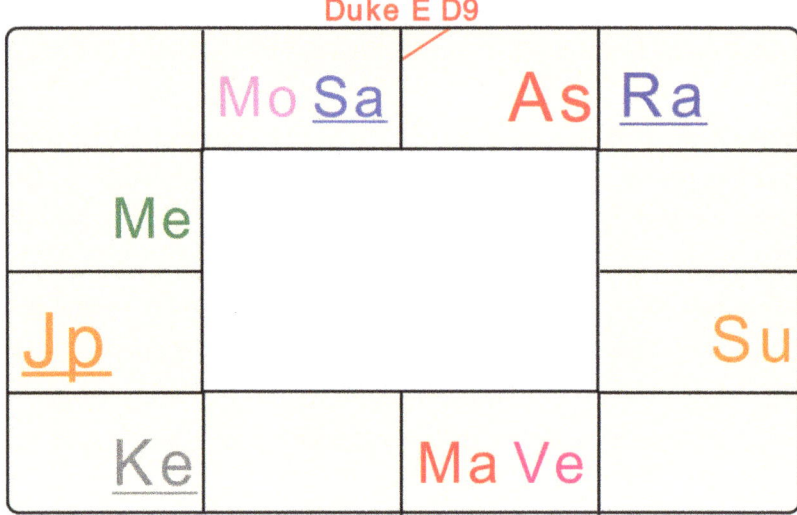

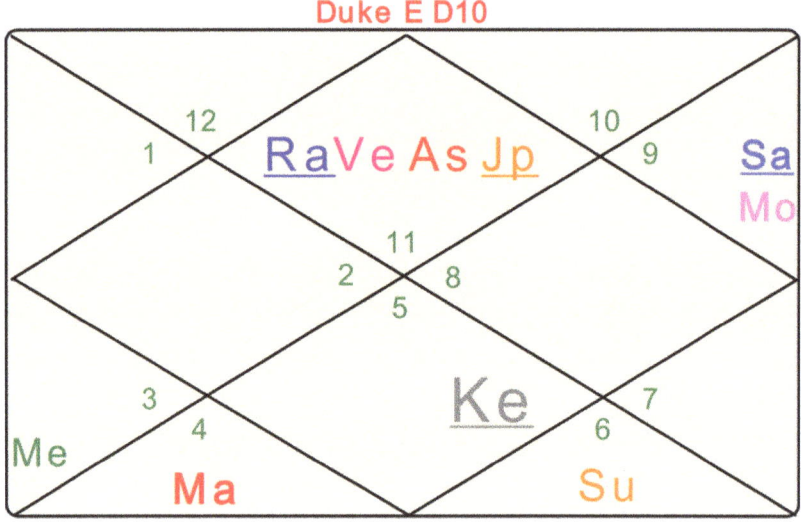

Creativity in the Vedic Astrology Chart

Duke E D10

			Me
Ra As Ve Jp			Ma
			Ke
Sa Mo			Su

Duke : Vimshottari

Start Date			Age	Dashas	
3/	12/	1916	16.9	Ve	Jp
11/	11/	1918 e	19.5	Ve	Sa
1/	10/	1922	22.7	Ve	Me
11/	10/	1924	25.5	Ve	Ke
1/	**10/**	**1926**	**26.7**	**Su**	**Su**
4/	30/	1926	27.0	Su	Mo
10/	29/	1926	27.5	Su	Ma
3/	6/	1927	27.9	Su	Ra
1/	29/	1928	28.8	Su	Jp
11/	16/	1928	29.6	Su	Sa
10/	29/	1929	30.5	Su	Me
9/	5/	1930	31.4	Su	Ke
1/	11/	1931	31.7	Su	Ve
1/	**11/**	**1932**	**32.7**	**Mo**	**Mo**
11/	10/	1932	33.5	Mo	Ma
6/	11/	1933	34.1	Mo	Ra
12/	11/	1934	35.6	Mo	Jp
4/	11/	1936	37.0	Mo	Sa
11/	10/	1937	38.5	Mo	Me
4/	12/	1939	40.0	Mo	Ke
11/	11/	1939	40.5	Mo	Ve
7/	12/	1941	42.2	Mo	Su
1/	**10/**	**1942**	**42.7**	**Ma**	**Ma**
6/	9/	1942	43.1	Ma	Ra
6/	27/	1943	44.2	Ma	Jp
6/	2/	1944	45.1	Ma	Sa
7/	12/	1945	46.2	Ma	Me
7/	9/	1946	47.2	Ma	Ke
12/	5/	1946	47.6	Ma	Ve
2/	4/	1948	48.8	Ma	Su
6/	11/	1948	49.1	Ma	Mo
1/	**10/**	**1949**	**49.7**	**Ra**	**Ra**
9/	23/	1951	52.4	Ra	Jp
2/	16/	1954	54.8	Ra	Sa
12/	23/	1956	57.7	Ra	Me
7/	12/	1959	60.2	Ra	Ke
7/	30/	1960	61.3	Ra	Ve
7/	31/	1963	64.3	Ra	Su
6/	23/	1964	65.2	Ra	Mo
12/	23/	1965	66.7	Ra	Ma
1/	**11/**	**1967**	**67.7**	**Jp**	**Jp**

Duke: Chara

Start Date			Age	Dashas
4/	29/	1899	-0.0	Cap
4/	29/	1900	1.0	Sag
4/	29/	1910	11.0	Sco
4/	29/	1918 e	19.0	Libr
4/	30/	1923	24.0	Virg
4/	29/	1929	30.0	Leo
4/	29/	1933	34.0	Can
4/	29/	1940	41.0	Gem
4/	29/	1949	50.0	Tau
4/	30/	1959	60.0	Ari
4/	30/	1962	63.0	Pis
4/	30/	1967	68.0	Aqu

Duke: Chara

Start Date			Age	Dashas	
4/	30/	1923	24.0	Virg	Libr
10/	29/	1923	24.5	Virg	Sco
4/	29/	1924	25.0	Virg	Sag
10/	29/	1924	25.5	Virg	Cap
4/	29/	1925	26.0	Virg	Aqu
10/	29/	1925	26.5	Virg	Pis
4/	29/	1926	27.0	Virg	Ari
10/	29/	1926	27.5	Virg	Tau
4/	30/	1927	28.0	Virg	Gem
10/	29/	1927	28.5	Virg	Can
4/	29/	1928	29.0	Virg	Leo
10/	29/	1928	29.5	Virg	Virg

1924 was the year that Ellington assumed the leadership of his jazz ensemble; the Duke Ellington Orchestra was maintained until the end of Ellington's life in 1974, and beyond, led by Ellington's son Mercer. From January of 1922 until November 1924, Duke Ellington ran his *Vimshottari* Venus -- Mercury period. As noted, the two planets form *Raj* yogas in the 3rd house of the birth chart: Mercury aspects back to its own 10th house from the Moon and chart lord Saturn.

The placement of Venus in the ascendant of Duke Ellington's D-10 confirms the likelihood of elevation of status in his Venus period; sub-period ruler Mercury is *swakshetra* in Gemini in the 5th house. Both planets benefit from the influence of directional strength Jupiter and ascendant ruler Saturn, as Venus is also aspected by 3rd and 10th lord Mars. The D-10 has an auspicious 1 – 11 *Parivartana* yoga and *sambandha* relationship formed between Saturn and 11th lord Jupiter, as Saturn aspects its sign of Aquarius and occupant Jupiter. In Ellington's Taurus rising D-9, *swakshetra* Venus in the 6th house has Mercury again five houses away in the 10th.

Duke Ellington's 6-year *Jaimini Chara dasha* of Virgo had begun in 1923, as he ran the sub-period of Sagittarius between late April and late October of 1924. The signs of Virgo and Sagittarius create activation of Saturn and DK Moon in addition to the strong *Jaimini Raj* yoga formation of AK Mercury and exalted 5th lord/PK Venus. The signs of Virgo and Gemini are stabilized by activation from their ruling planet as well as the combined Venus – Moon influence. In Ellington's D-10, AmK Sun in Virgo is disposited by AK Mercury in Gemini in the 10th house, as *vargottama* (in D-10) Moon and Saturn reside in Sagittarius. In 1927, in Ellington's Virgo -- Gemini period, the Duke Ellington Orchestra was hired by New York's legendary Cotton Club; this engagement lasted four years and contributed to Ellington's burgeoning status in the realm of big band and jazz music.

Creativity in the Vedic Astrology Chart

Our next chart will be that of singer/songwriter Stevie Nicks (May 26th, 1948, Phoenix, AZ, 3:02 a.m., A), who gained prominence as a member of acclaimed rock and roll band Fleetwood Mac. Ms. Nicks wrote and sang a number of Fleetwood Mac's most memorable songs, including "Rhiannon," "Dreams," "Landslide," "Silver Springs," "Angel," "I Don't Want to Know," "Sara," and "Gold Dust Woman."

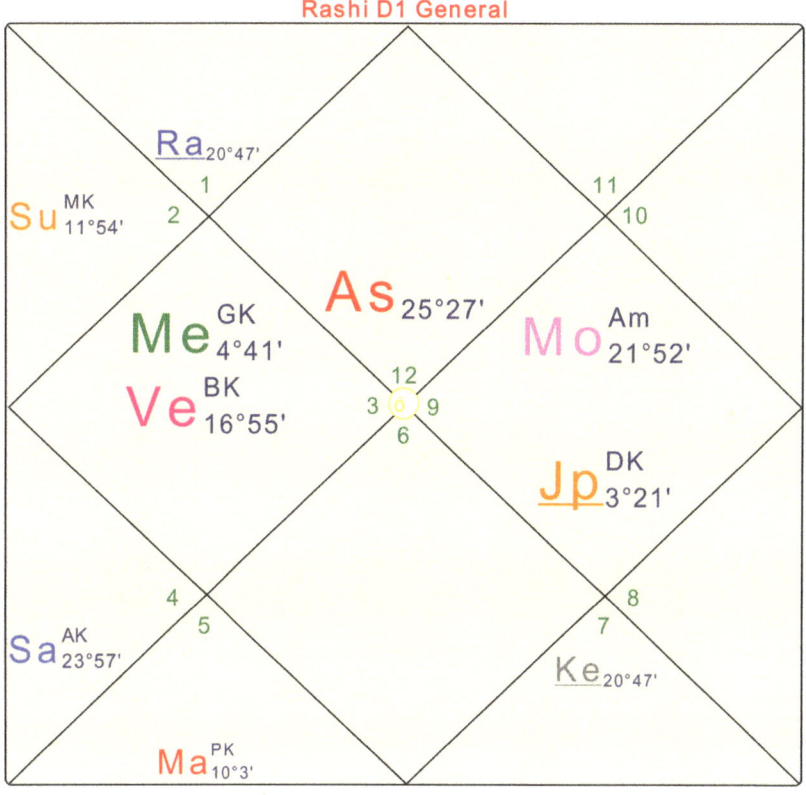

Rashi D1 General

	Su MK 11°54'	Me GK 4°41'
As 25°27'	Ra 20°47'	Ve BK 16°55'
		Sa AK 23°57'
	Stevie Nicks Wed. 5/26/1948 3:02:00 Phoenix, AZ	Ma PK 10°3'
Mo Am 21°52' Jp DK 3°21'	Ke 20°47'	

Upon being given a guitar for her 16th birthday, Stevie Nicks began writing songs. As a singer and songwriter, Ms. Nicks played in several bands during her teens and early twenties. At the end of 1974, Stevie Nicks and her musical partner Lindsey Buckingham were invited to join the British group Fleetwood Mac. Through the remainder of the decade, Fleetwood Mac became one of the most successful rock and roll groups in the world, touring extensively and recording several highly regarded albums. Fleetwood Mac's 1977 album *Rumours* won that year's Grammy award, and at 40 million sales is one of the best-selling albums of all time. Following her tenure with Fleetwood Mac, Stevie Nicks embarked on an equally successful solo career, including world tours and a series of creative partnerships with fellow musicians Sheryl Crow, Tom Petty, Walter Egan, Kenny Loggins and

John Stewart. In 2003, the Stevie Nicks composition "Landslide," as recorded and performed by the Dixie Chicks, was awarded BMI (Broadcast Music, Inc.) song of the year. Although she had been elected to the Rock & Roll Hall of Fame in 1998 as a member of Fleetwood Mac, Stevie Nicks was inducted for the 2nd time, as a solo artist, in 2019.

Stevie Nicks' Pisces chart rises in richly imaginative *Revati nakshatra*. Ruling planet Jupiter forms *Hamsa* yoga in the 10th house in the sign of Sagittarius, where Jupiter is joined by 5th lord Moon. The configuration of Jupiter and the Moon, in opposition *sambandha* with Mercury and Venus, comprises a stellar *Gaja Kesari* yoga, in which both constituents are in aspect with natural benefics and occupy angular houses from the ascendant as well as the Moon. BPHS chapter 36 verses 3 & 4 cites the qualities of splendor, wealth, intelligence, and possession of numerous "laudable virtues" given by the *Gaja Kesari* yoga. A *Saraswati* yoga occurs from the ascendant as well as the Moon. The BPHS version of *Kahala* yoga (36: 9 & 10) is formed in the chart by the placement of 4th lord Mercury and Jupiter in mutual *kendra* houses, accompanied by the ascendant lord in strength. Each of the planets in the 4th house of the chart gains in capability, as Mercury's location in Gemini constitutes *Bhadra* yoga and Venus gets directional strength; notice Venus' exalted status in the D-9 of Ms. Nicks. The collection of mutual influences enjoyed by Jupiter, the Moon, and Mercury creates 1 – 5, 4 – 5, 4 – 10, and 5 – 10 *Raj* yogas across the 4 – 10 axis. The talent of Stevie Nicks as a poetic lyricist and composer of captivating melodies is evidenced by the strength of her 5th lord Moon, whose status is wholly benefic due to its brightness and *sambandha* relationship with all three natural benefics. A strong Mercury – Venus connection favors poetic inspiration (Ms. Nicks is an accomplished poet as well as songwriter), while the mutual aspect between 3rd lord Venus and 5th lord Moon will promote musical expression and creates a Venus – Moon *Raj* yoga as denoted in BPHS chapter 39 verse 41.

Ms. Nicks' chart meets criteria for several *Raj* yogas enumerated in chapter 7 of the *Phaladeepika*. Verse 7 confers royal status on the native when the bright Moon is aspected by a *swakshetra* or exalted planet, while verse 18 promises kingship with "unequalled fame" when Jupiter and Moon occupy a *kendra* house and are aspected by Venus, with no *graha* in its state of debilitation. Of the four *Raj* yogas cited in verse 20, Ms. Nicks' chart qualifies for three: Venus in reception of an aspect from Jupiter; the chart's ascendant ruler in strength and located in a *kendra* house (Jupiter also rules the ascendant taken from the Moon), and a flawless strong Mercury in a *kendra* house aspected by Jupiter. Small wonder that in 2021, *Rolling Stone* magazine released a special issue dedicated exclusively to the life and art of Stevie Nicks, entitled "Tribute to the Queen of Rock & Roll."

Stevie Nicks' chart holds several *Jaimini Raj* yogas as described in BPHS Chapter 40. AmK Moon in strength, as AK dispositor and situated in the 10th house with 10th lord Jupiter qualifies for yogas of "royal association" as described in verses 1, 3, 4, 6 and 15. The verse 6 yoga is emphasized by the location of AK Saturn in the 5th house. The placement of Venus in the 5th house from Ms. Nicks' Aquarius KL, while in aspect to Jupiter and the Moon, gives a *Raj* yoga ("related to royal circles") defined in BPHS 39:11. Between late October 1974 and late May 1975, Stevie Nicks sustained her Cancer -- Cancer *Jaimini Chara dasha*; this was the time during which Ms. Nicks' life and career were transformed as the result of her invitation to join Fleetwood Mac. AK Saturn occupies the 5th house in the sign of Cancer in the birth chart and is aspected by 2nd lord (from Cancer) Sun. The D-9 chart's *Parivartana* yoga, involving Jupiter and exalted Venus, occurs between houses 9 and 11 from the sign of Cancer, and creates a benefic flanking around exalted Sun in the 10th house. The Sun is aspected by Mercury and *swakshetra* AK Saturn, while Saturn, Mercury, and Jupiter activate Cancer and occupant PK Mars. DK Jupiter and the 11th house of gains, awards, and opportunities are aspected by PK Mars, AmK Moon, and *Rahu*. Stevie Nicks' very sturdy D-10 supports the promise of a luminous career and the fortunate turn of events which occurred in her Cancer -- Cancer period. *Swakshetra* AmK/natal 5th lord Moon and directionally strong Mercury sit in the ascendant of Ms. Nicks' D-10, with Sun duplicating its exalted status (from the D-9) in directional strength in the 10th house. The Sun and the 10th house are favorably aspected by *swakshetra* 10th lord PK Mars and BK Venus. From their location in the 5th house in Scorpio, Mars and Venus also aspect the sign of Cancer on the ascendant and residents Moon and Mercury.

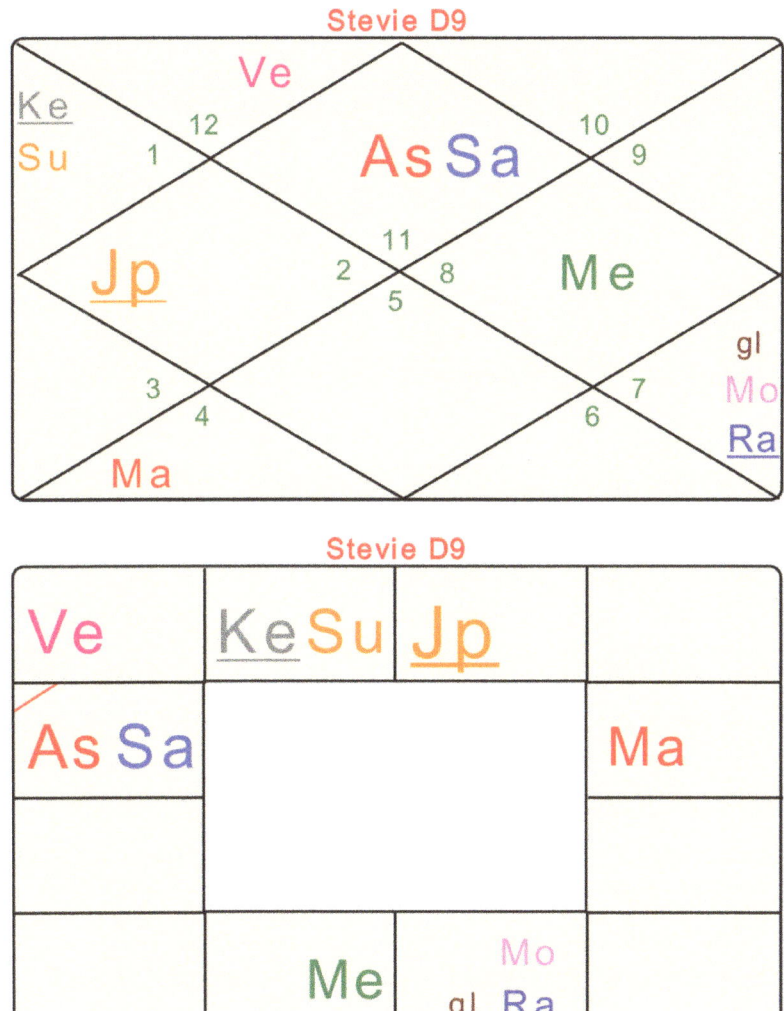

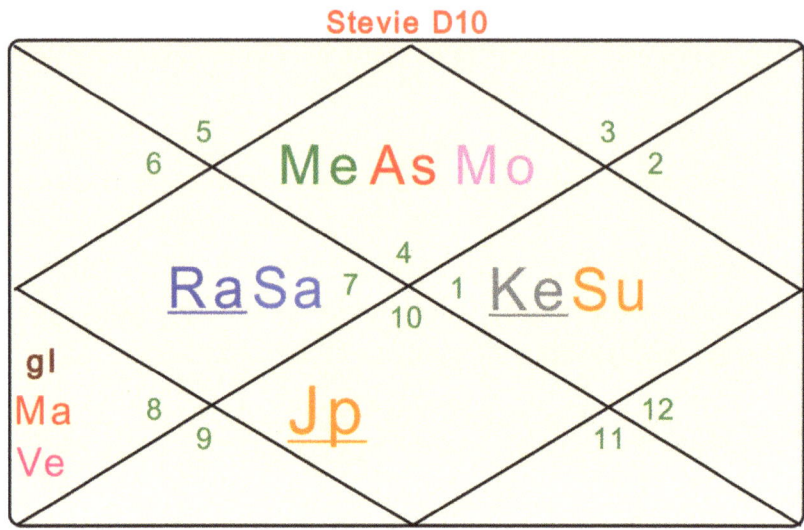

SN: Vimshottari

Start Date			Age	Dashas	
5/	31/	1969	21.0	Mo	Ve
1/	30/	1971	22.7	Mo	Su
7/	31/	1971	23.2	Ma	Ma
12/	27/	1971	23.6	Ma	Ra
1/	14/	1973	24.6	Ma	Jp
12/	21/	1973	25.6	Ma	Sa
1/	30/	1975	26.7	Ma	Me
1/	27/	1976	27.7	Ma	Ke
6/	24/	1976	28.1	Ma	Ve
8/	24/	1977	29.2	Ma	Su
12/	30/	1977	29.6	Ma	Mo
7/	31/	1978	30.2	Ra	Ra
4/	12/	1981	32.9	Ra	Jp
9/	6/	1983	35.3	Ra	Sa
7/	13/	1986	38.1	Ra	Me
1/	29/	1989	40.7	Ra	Ke
2/	17/	1990	41.7	Ra	Ve
2/	16/	1993	44.7	Ra	Su
1/	11/	1994	45.6	Ra	Mo
7/	13/	1995	47.1	Ra	Ma
7/	31/	1996	48.2	Jp	Jp
9/	18/	1998	50.3	Jp	Sa
3/	31/	2001	52.8	Jp	Me
7/	7/	2003	55.1	Jp	Ke
6/	12/	2004	56.0	Jp	Ve
2/	11/	2007	58.7	Jp	Su

SN: Chara

Start Date	Age	Dashas	
1/ 24/ 1973	24.7	Can	Libr
8/ 25/ 1973	25.2	Can	Virg
3/ 26/ 1974	25.8	Can	Leo
10/ 25/ 1974	26.4	Can	Can
5/ 27/ 1975	**27.0**	**Leo**	**Virg**
8/ 26/ 1975	27.2	Leo	Libr
11/ 25/ 1975	27.5	Leo	Sco
2/ 24/ 1976	27.8	Leo	Sag
5/ 26/ 1976	28.0	Leo	Cap
8/ 25/ 1976	28.2	Leo	Aqu
11/ 24/ 1976	28.5	Leo	Pis
2/ 24/ 1977	28.8	Leo	Ari
5/ 26/ 1977	29.0	Leo	Tau
8/ 25/ 1977	29.2	Leo	Gem
11/ 25/ 1977	29.5	Leo	Can
2/ 24/ 1978	29.8	Leo	Leo
5/ 26/ 1978	**30.0**	**Virg**	**Libr**
8/ 26/ 1978	30.2	Virg	Sco
11/ 25/ 1978	30.5	Virg	Sag
2/ 24/ 1979	30.8	Virg	Cap
5/ 27/ 1979	31.0	Virg	Aqu
8/ 26/ 1979	31.2	Virg	Pis
11/ 25/ 1979	31.5	Virg	Ari
2/ 25/ 1980	31.8	Virg	Tau
5/ 26/ 1980	32.0	Virg	Gem
8/ 25/ 1980	32.2	Virg	Can

SN: Chara

Start Date	Age	Dashas
5/ 26/ 1948	-0.0	Pis
5/ 26/ 1951	3.0	Ari
5/ 26/ 1955	7.0	Tau
5/ 26/ 1956	8.0	Gem
5/ 26/ 1968	20.0	Can
5/ 27/ 1975	27.0	Leo
5/ 26/ 1978	30.0	Virg
5/ 26/ 1981	33.0	Libr
5/ 26/ 1989	41.0	Sco
5/ 26/ 2000	52.0	Sag
5/ 26/ 2012	64.0	Cap
5/ 27/ 2018 n	70.0	Aqu

The promise of Ms. Nicks' Cancer -- Cancer period is confirmed by her subsequent 3-year Leo *Chara dasha*, which coincides with the last three years of her *Vimshottari* Mars period, during which time Fleetwood Mac recorded and released two extremely successful albums and performed for large audiences around the world. The sign of Leo in the D-1 contains PK Mars with dispositor Sun obtaining directional strength in the 10th house, where the Sun is aspected by AK Saturn. The presence of all the natural benefics across the 5 – 11 axis confers the wealth and popular acclaim which were enjoyed by Stevie Nicks and Fleetwood Mac during this time. The 5th house from Leo holds natal 5th lord Moon as well as Jupiter serving as 5th lord from Leo. In both her D-9 and D-10 charts, Leo is well fortified by the aspect of its exalted owner. In the D-9, DK Jupiter in Taurus in the 10th house is aspected by PK Mars, AmK Moon and *Rahu*. In her D-10, Jupiter and exalted AK Saturn join the Sun in activation of the sign of Leo, while Saturn, Moon, Jupiter, Mercury, and *Rahu* aspect the 10th house from Leo.

In the context of her *Vimshottari* Mars major period, Stevie Nicks began her Saturn sub-period in late 1973. 9th lord Mars is located in the 6th house of her birth chart, where it gains *lagna* and 10th lord Jupiter's one-way glance. Mars' career capability is enhanced due to the location of its dispositor Sun's location in the 10th house from Mars; the Sun's placement in *Rohini nakshatra* contributes to the musically creative direction which Stevie Nicks' career took during her Mars period. Mars rules the 10th house in both her D-9 and D-10; in the D-9, exalted Sun sits in the 10th from debilitated Mars. In Ms. Nicks' D-10, yoga *karaka* Mars gains *swakshetra* status and is joined in the 5th house by 4th and 11th lord Venus. Sub-period ruler Saturn owns and aspects the 11th house of the birth chart from its location in the 5th house of creative endeavors. The essential strength of Saturn manifests with *Shasha* yogas in both her D-9 and D-10 charts, Saturn as chart lord in the ascendant of her D-9, and as exalted 7th lord in the 4th house of the D-10. The elevated degree of success enjoyed by Fleetwood Mac over the 2nd half of the 1970s can be at least partially attributed to the addition of a band member whose *Jyotish* chart so clearly reflects an extreme level of creative and professional achievement during that time.

Stevie Nicks' D-10 chart features a yoga known as *Chatussagara*, formed when all four *kendra* houses are occupied. The *Chatussagara* yoga is said to confer strength, support, and longevity, all of which have characterized Ms. Nicks' successful career. Notice as well that 3 of the 4 *kendra* houses have planets in strength, while the debilitation of Jupiter gives *Raj* yoga due to Jupiter's angular location from ascendant and Moon, exalted Saturn's *kendra* placement, and *swakshetra* Moon's location in the ascendant. Jupiter and the Moon recreate the birth chart's *Gaja Kesari* yoga in Ms. Nicks' D-10.

Creativity in the Vedic Astrology Chart

The following chart is that of Artur Rubinstein (January 28, 1887, Lodz, Poland, 10:00 p.m., AA), who is celebrated as one of the finest and most accomplished pianists of the modern era, a child prodigy who had his formal performance debut at the age of seven, and who performed with the Berlin Philharmonic Orchestra at age thirteen.

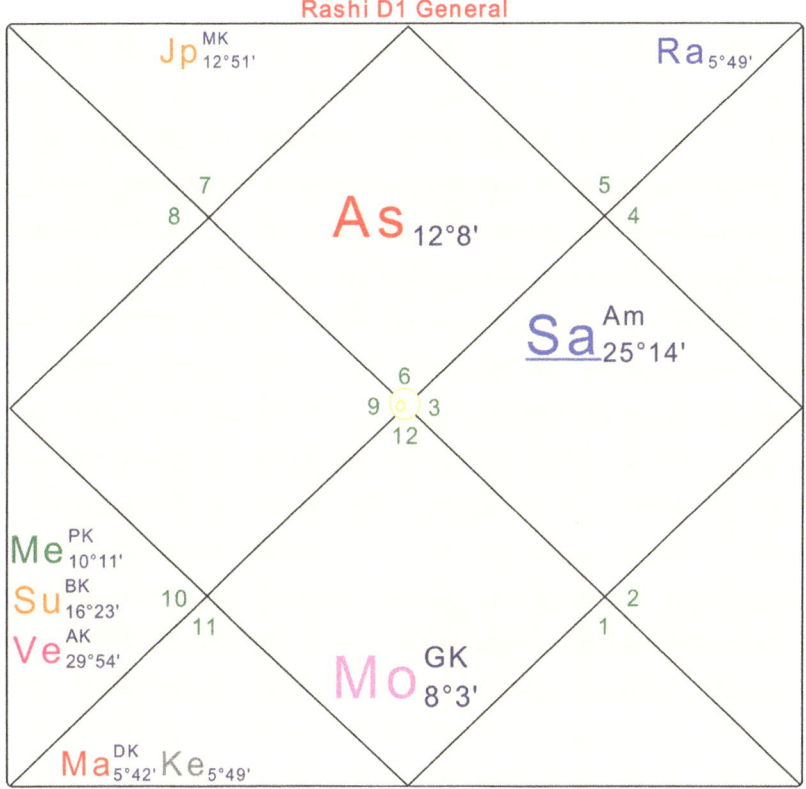

Rashi D1 General

Mo GK 8°3'			Sa Am 25°14'
Ke 5°49' Ma DK 5°42'			
Ve AK 29°54' Su BK 16°23' Me PK 10°11'	☉ Artur Rubinstein Fri. 1/28/1887 22:00:00 Lodz, POL		Ra 5°49'
		Jp MK 12°51'	As 12°8'

At two years of age, Artur Rubinstein displayed perfect pitch and began to play the piano; by the age of four he had gained recognition as a prodigy and had begun to give informal recitals. Mr. Rubinstein enjoyed an extremely long career, as both solo pianist and in accompaniment to many of the world's prominent symphony orchestras. In possession of a vast and eclectic repertoire, Mr. Rubinstein gave thousands of performances, while touring and continuing to record until the age of eighty-nine. His *New York Times* obituary stated, "In the pantheon of 20th century pianists, Mr. Rubinstein's place is assured as one of the titans … What Mr. Rubinstein offered, above all others, was the ability to transmit the joy of music." (*New York Times*, December 21st, 1982). Artur Rubinstein earned four Grammy awards, including a Grammy Lifetime Achievement Award, conferred upon him in 1994. He received the U.S. Presidential Medal of Freedom in 1976, as well as Kennedy Center Honors in 1978. Mr. Rubinstein was similarly awarded with highest national honors by the countries of England, Ireland, Belgium, Portugal, Denmark, France, Italy, and Spain, as well as his native Poland. (For further appreciation of the life and art of Artur Rubinstein, the reader is referred to an excellent essay by music journalist Bradley Bambarger at www.steinway.com/artists.)

Artur Rubinstein's Virgo rising chart gives *Hasta nakshatra* on the ascendant at 12 degrees, which falls within the weapon *drekkana* section of Virgo. Ascendant and 10th lord Mercury joins the Sun in the 5th house in a splendid *Budha Aditya* yoga, which is embellished by the presence of 2nd and 9th lord Venus. Mercury and the Sun reside in *Shravana nakshatra*; here again we are shown the musical and imaginative potential of *Shravana*, especially as we consider this quote from Artur Rubinstein, from his *New York Times* obituary: "At breakfast I might pass a Brahms symphony in my head. Then I am called to the phone, and half an hour later I find it's been going on all the time and I'm in the third movement." Mercury and 5th lord Saturn form a *Maha Parivartana* yoga between houses 5 and 10, as Saturn tenants the 10th house in the sign of Gemini. Saturn also inhabits a weapon *drekkana*, the 3rd of Gemini, and is graced by Jupiter's 9th glance from the 2nd house. The 5th house of the chart contains a *Dharma Karma Adhipati* yoga, formed by 9th lord Venus and 10th lord Mercury, who also comprise a 1 – 9 *Raj* yoga. To reinforce the theme of musical proficiency, we notice that Mars, the ruler of the 3rd house of skills and manual dexterity, is placed in *Dhanishtha nakshatra* in the 6th house. From this position Mars aspects the ascendant as well as the 3rd house from the Moon. The very tight conjunction of Mars and *Ketu* will confer exceptional sensitivity and subtlety to the keyboard artistry of Artur Rubinstein. And, like Saturn, Mars and *Ketu* receive a stabilizing aspect from the planet Jupiter. As Moon ascendant ruler, lord of 10th from Moon, and located in the 10th house from natal ascendant lord Mercury, Jupiter contributes to the dominant musical theme of the chart due to its placement in Libra in *Swati nakshatra*. Rubinstein's chart includes a *Saraswati* (named for the goddess of music and learning) yoga, as all three natural benefics are found in trine or angular houses, or the 2nd. The 5th house from the Moon is activated by Mercury, Venus, and the Sun, as Venus rules the 3rd house from the Moon and Moon itself rules the 5th from the Moon and aspects the ascendant.

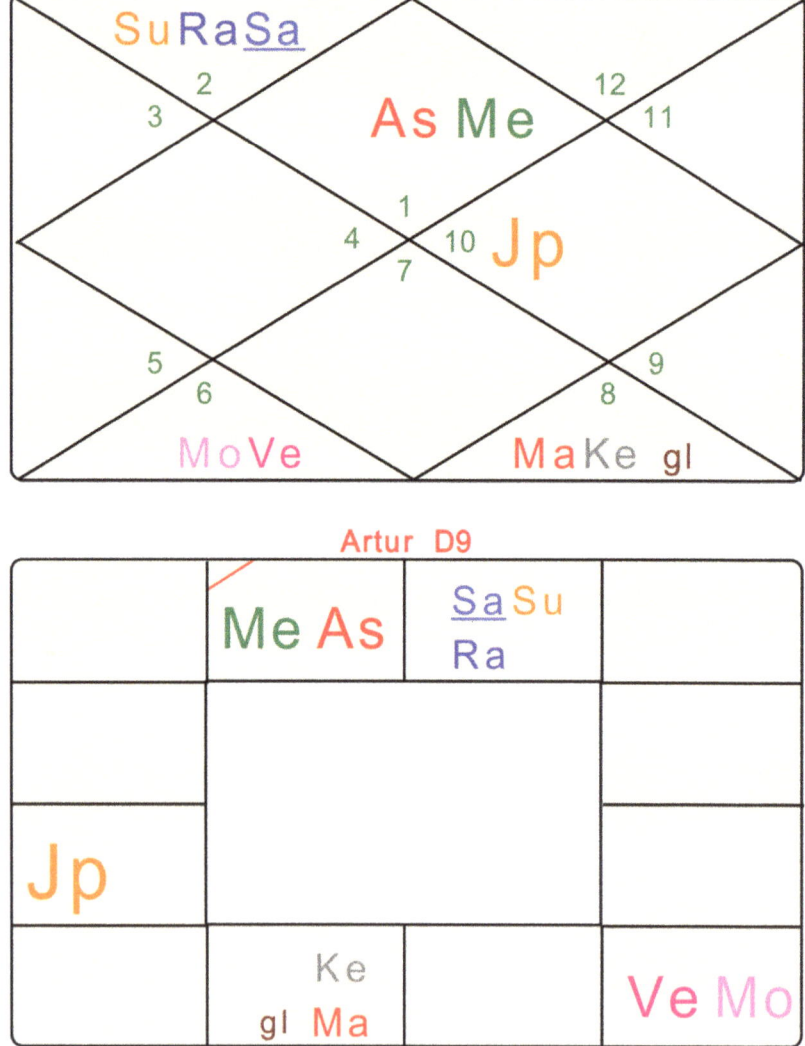

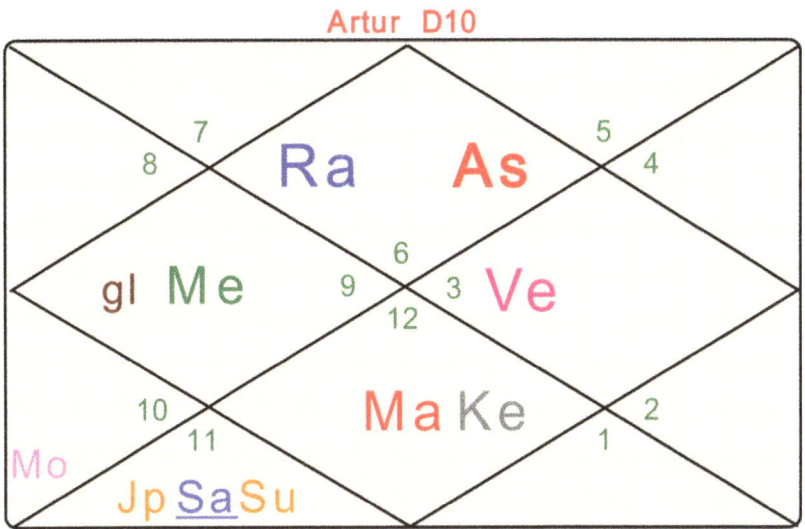

AR: Vimshottari

Start Date			Age	Dashas	
11/	4/	1892	5.8	Sa	Ma
12/	14/	1893	6.9	Sa	Ra
10/	20/	1896	9.7	Sa	Jp
5/	3/	1899	12.3	**Me**	**Me**
9/	30/	1901	14.7	Me	Ke
9/	27/	1902	15.7	Me	Ve
7/	28/	1905	18.5	Me	Su
6/	3/	1906	19.3	Me	Mo
11/	3/	1907	20.8	Me	Ma
10/	30/	1908	21.8	Me	Ra
5/	20/	1911	24.3	Me	Jp
8/	24/	1913	26.6	Me	Sa
5/	4/	1916	29.3	**Ke**	**Ke**
9/	30/	1916	29.7	Ke	Ve
11/	30/	1917	30.8	Ke	Su
4/	7/	1918	31.2	Ke	Mo
11/	6/	1918	31.8	Ke	Ma
4/	4/	1919	32.2	Ke	Ra
4/	21/	1920	33.2	Ke	Jp
3/	28/	1921	34.2	Ke	Sa
5/	7/	1922	35.3	Ke	Me
5/	4/	1923	36.3	**Ve**	**Ve**
9/	3/	1926	39.6	Ve	Su
9/	3/	1927	40.6	Ve	Mo
5/	4/	1929	42.3	Ve	Ma
7/	4/	1930	43.4	Ve	Ra
7/	4/	1933	46.4	Ve	Jp
3/	4/	1936	49.1	Ve	Sa
5/	4/	1939	52.3	Ve	Me
3/	4/	1942	55.1	Ve	Ke
5/	5/	1943	56.3	**Su**	**Su**
8/	22/	1943	56.6	Su	Mo
2/	21/	1944	57.1	Su	Ma
6/	28/	1944	57.4	Su	Ra
5/	22/	1945	58.3	Su	Jp
3/	10/	1946	59.1	Su	Sa
2/	20/	1947	60.1	Su	Me
12/	28/	1947	60.9	Su	Ke
5/	4/	1948	61.3	Su	Ve
5/	4/	1949	62.3	**Mo**	**Mo**
3/	4/	1950	63.1	Mo	Ma

AR: Chara

Start Date	Age	Dashas	
10/ 30/ 1900	13.8	Sco	Sco
1/ 29/ 1901	14.0	Sag	Sco
11/ 29/ 1901	14.8	Sag	Libr
9/ 30/ 1902	15.7	Sag	Virg
7/ 31/ 1903	16.5	Sag	Leo
5/ 31/ 1904	17.3	Sag	Can
3/ 31/ 1905	18.2	Sag	Gem
1/ 29/ 1906	19.0	Sag	Tau
11/ 30/ 1906	19.8	Sag	Ari
9/ 30/ 1907	20.7	Sag	Pis
7/ 30/ 1908	21.5	Sag	Aqu
5/ 31/ 1909	22.3	Sag	Cap
3/ 31/ 1910	23.2	Sag	Sag
1/ 30/ 1911	24.0	Cap	Sag
8/ 31/ 1911	24.6	Cap	Sco
3/ 31/ 1912	25.2	Cap	Libr
10/ 30/ 1912	25.8	Cap	Virg
5/ 31/ 1913	26.3	Cap	Leo
12/ 30/ 1913	26.9	Cap	Can
7/ 31/ 1914	27.5	Cap	Gem
3/ 1/ 1915	28.1	Cap	Tau
9/ 30/ 1915	28.7	Cap	Ari
4/ 30/ 1916	29.2	Cap	Pis
11/ 29/ 1916	29.8	Cap	Aqu
6/ 30/ 1917	30.4	Cap	Cap
1/ 29/ 1918	31.0	Aqu	Pis

Due to the Moon's placement in the *nakshatra* of *Uttara Bhadrapada*, Artur Rubinstein was born in the major period of Saturn, which ran until he was 12 years old; Saturn's 10th house placement, its 5th house rulership and participation in a *Maha Parivartana* yoga, and its stabilization from Jupiter all contribute to Rubinstein's early success and instrumental prowess. Saturn rules the 10th house of his D-9 where it joins 5th lord Sun in the 2nd house in Taurus. Sun and Saturn enjoy *sambandha* with ascendant ruler Mars and the glance of 9th lord Jupiter. Saturn in its sign of Aquarius is joined by Jupiter and Sun in the 6th house of Rubinstein's *vargottama* D-10. His subsequent period of Mercury saw Rubinstein ascend to the level of virtuoso as one of the foremost pianists of his time. Rubinstein's majestic performance with the Berlin Philharmonic occurred late in the year 1900 in his *Vimshottari* Mercury -- Mercury period. In addition to the *Raj* yogas in which Mercury participates, the Mercury period is made more capable by the placement of benefic Jupiter in the 10th house from Mercury. In his D-9 3rd lord Mercury gains directional strength in the ascendant and is disposited by *swakshetra* Mars. There are no aspects to Mercury, either malefic or benefic, while Jupiter again occupies the 10th house from Mercury. In Rubinstein's D-10, Mercury rules the 10th house and locates in the 4th in *sambandha* with 9th lord Venus, re-creating the 9 – 10 *Raj* yoga from the birth chart.

The first eight years of Artur Rubinstein's life saw him run his Virgo *Jaimini Chara dasha*. As we consider this chart from the *Jaimini* perspective, the reader is directed to chapter 39, entitled *Raja* Yogas, of the *Brihat Parashara Hora Shastra* (BPHS). Among the first set of yogas delineated in this chapter, the placement of AK and PK in the 5th house from the ascendant or the KL is cited. Because Rubinstein's AK Venus is at 29 degrees in Capricorn, his KL is Virgo and identical with his natal ascendant. This powerful yoga is highlighted during the Virgo major period and brings additional emphasis to the ascendant due to D-1 *lagna*, KL, and 10th lord Mercury's participation in the yoga as the chart's PK. With 7th house occupant Moon, Rubinstein's AmK Saturn in the 10th activates the *kendra* houses. The chart also meets criteria for "royal association" as narrated in verses 6 and 10 of BPHS Chapter 40; AmK Saturn is found in an angular house while AK Venus is joined by a benefic in a *trikona* house. In Artur Rubinstein's D-9, the sign of Virgo holds Venus and the Moon, while Jupiter in the 5th house is aspected by BK Sun, *swakshetra* DK Mars,

Capricorn ruler natal 5th lord/AmK Saturn and *Rahu/Ketu*. In Rubinstein's *vargottama* D-10, AK Venus prominent in the 10th is activated by dispositor PK Mercury and DK Mars as the birth chart's AK -- PK Raj yoga is recreated.

Concurrent with his *Vimshottari* Mercury – Mercury period, Artur Rubinstein's debut with the Berlin Philharmonic occurred on December 1st, 1900 in his *Jaimini* Scorpio – Scorpio *Chara dasha*. (www.culture.pl/en/artist/arthur-rubinstein). In the birth chart, the powerful AK/PK/BK combination in the 3rd house from Scorpio activates Scorpio itself as well as the 10th house from Scorpio. The 10th house is also aspected by Jupiter; the sign of Leo is therefore influenced by all the natural benefics as well as by its lord. In Artur Rubinstein's D-9, Scorpio holds its ruling planet as both Scorpio and Leo are activated by benefics Jupiter and Mercury. In his D-10, the 5 – 11 axis is influenced by Venus, Mercury, and Mars, including the aspect to the sign of Virgo from its lord PK Mercury.

Our next chart will be that of renowned singer and multi-instrumentalist Andrea Bocelli (September 22, 1958, Pisa, Italy, 5:15 a.m., AA). Born with glaucoma and despite multiple eye surgeries in his youth, Andrea Bocelli lost his eyesight permanently following a sports injury at age twelve. Bocelli sought comfort through music, playing piano by the age of six and later learning to play a variety of instruments, including flute, saxophone, trumpet, trombone, guitar, and drums. (*People*, November 10, 1997). Through his childhood and youth Andrea Bocelli also took pleasure in singing and emulating opera singers, and won a vocal competition at age fourteen. After hearing a recording of Andrea Bocelli in 1992, Luciano Pavarotti helped to advance Bocelli's singing career. In 1994, Bocelli was awarded first prize at the Sanremo Music Festival, from which time his career has risen to great acclaim and international status. Fellow singer Celine Dion is quoted as having said, "If God would have a singing voice, He must sound a lot like Andrea Bocelli." (*The Scotsman*, interview October 27, 2009).

Creativity in the Vedic Astrology Chart

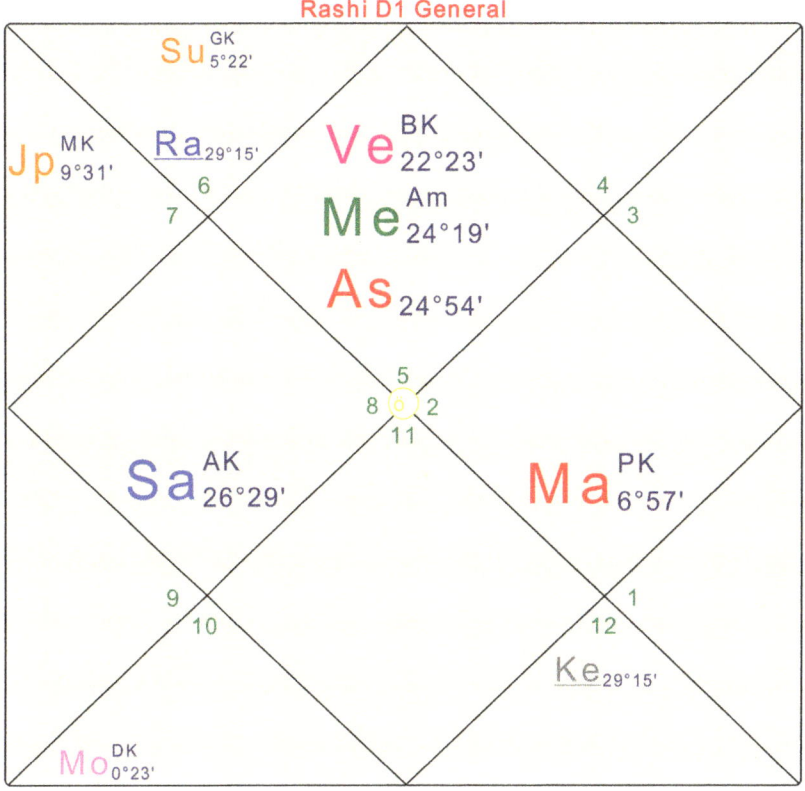

Rashi D1 General

		Ma PK 6°57'	
Ke 29°15'			
	Andrea Bocelli Mon. 9/22/1958 5:15:00 Pisa, IT		Ve BK 22°23' Me Am 24°19' As 24°54'
Mo DK 0°23'			Ra 29°15'
	Sa AK 26°29'	Jp MK 9°31'	Su GK 5°22'

Andrea Bocelli's chart serves to illustrate the creative potential of *Purva Phalguni nakshatra*, which rises within less than a degree of Bocelli's 2nd and 11th lord Mercury, and within 3 degrees of his Venus. Mercury has directional strength and is closely joined in the ascendant by Venus as 3rd and 10th lord. The two natural benefics in the first house form *Camara* yoga and afford Bocelli his career as a vocalist while conferring upon him the exceptional beauty of his voice. Bocelli's ascendant and 2nd lord Mercury therein are aspected by natural malefics Saturn and Mars, causing his blindness (a particular vulnerability of *Purva Phalguni*), but enabling his musical career, as yoga *karaka* Mars rules houses 4 and 9 and gets directional strength in the 10th house, while Saturn rules the 2nd house from Moon. The 2nd house of voice is also activated by a *Parivartana* yoga between ascendant ruler Sun and 2nd lord Mercury, which places Sun in the

2nd house. The Sun is flanked by benefics, forming a positive *Ubhayachari* yoga. From the Sun, voice is emphasized by the presence of 5th lord (from ascendant) Jupiter in the 2nd house in the *nakshatra* of *Swati*. (Recall that *Swati*'s deity is *Vayu*, king of the celestial musicians known as *Gandharvas*.) Bocelli's wide appeal can be seen through the *Kesari* yoga formed by Jupiter and Moon, and by Jupiter's location in the 10th house from the Moon. Notice also that natal 5th lord Jupiter achieves *swakshetra* status in Bocelli's D-9. From the standpoint of Moon ascendant, Mars as 11th lord of mass entertainment has *sambandha* with ascendant and 2nd house ruler Saturn.

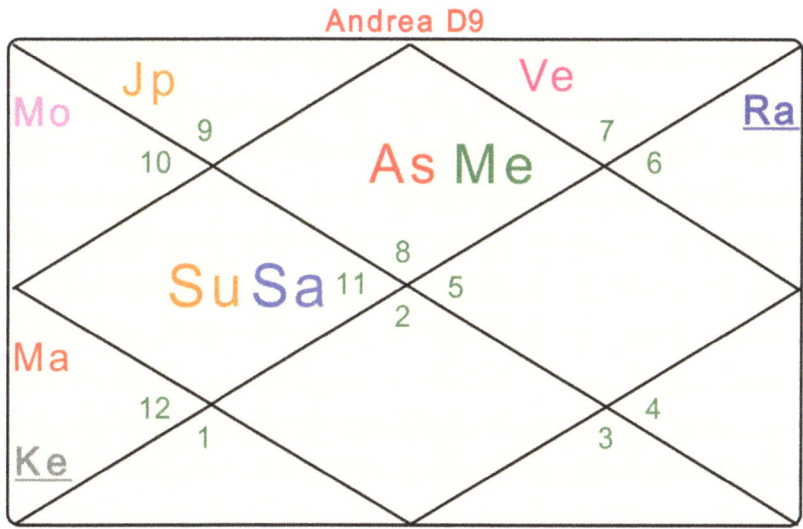

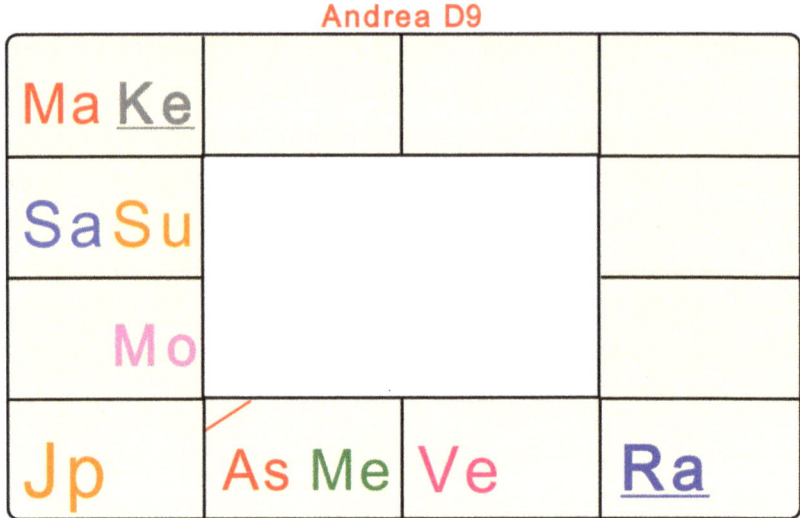

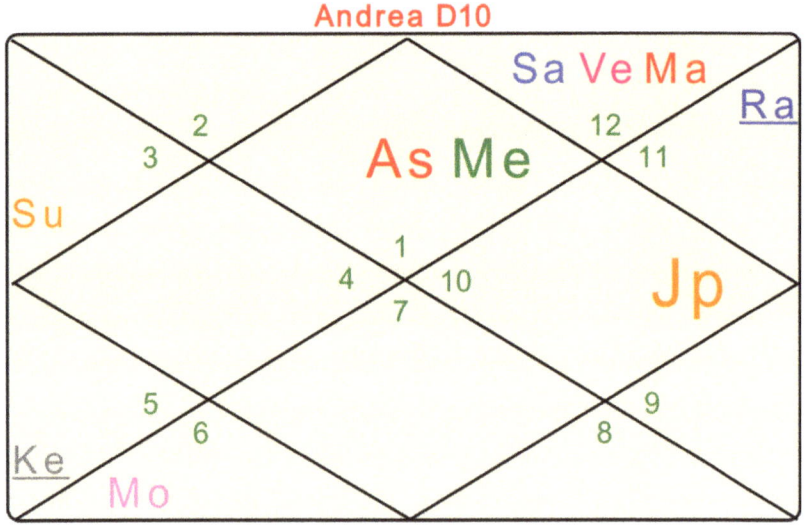

Andrea D10

Ma Sa Ve	Me As		Su
Ra			Ke
Jp			
			Mo

AB: Chara

Start Date	Age	Dashas
9/ 22/ 1958	-0.0	Leo
9/ 22/ 1969	11.0	Virg
9/ 22/ 1970	12.0	Libr
9/ 21/ 1980	22.0	Sco
9/ 21/ 1984	26.0	Sag
9/ 22/ 1994	36.0	Cap
9/ 22/ 1996	38.0	Aqu
9/ 22/ 2001	43.0	Pis
9/ 22/ 2006	48.0	Ari
9/ 22/ 2007	49.0	Tau
9/ 22/ 2010	52.0	Gem
9/ 22/ 2012	54.0	Can

AB: Vimshottari

Start Date			Age	Dashas	
12/	13/	1977	19.2	Ma	Ve
2/	12/	1979	20.4	Ma	Su
6/	20/	1979	20.7	Ma	Mo
1/	19/	1980	21.3	Ra	Ra
10/	1/	1982	24.0	Ra	Jp
2/	23/	1985	26.4	Ra	Sa
12/	31/	1987	29.3	Ra	Me
7/	20/	1990	31.8	Ra	Ke
8/	7/	1991	32.9	Ra	Ve
8/	7/	1994	35.9	Ra	Su
7/	2/	1995	36.8	Ra	Mo
12/	31/	1996	38.3	Ra	Ma
1/	18/	1998	39.3	Jp	Jp
3/	7/	2000	41.5	Jp	Sa
9/	19/	2002	44.0	Jp	Me
12/	25/	2004	46.3	Jp	Ke
12/	1/	2005	47.2	Jp	Ve
8/	1/	2008	49.9	Jp	Su
5/	20/	2009	50.7	Jp	Mo
9/	19/	2010	52.0	Jp	Ma
8/	26/	2011	52.9	Jp	Ra
1/	18/	2014	55.3	Sa	Sa
1/	21/	2017	58.3	Sa	Me
10/	1/	2019	61.0	Sa	Ke
11/	9/	2020 n	62.1	Sa	Ve
1/	10/	2024	65.3	Sa	Su

Andrea Bocelli's ascent to fame and success as a singer took place in his mid-30s, concurrent with his *Rahu* -- Sun period. In his birth chart, (true node) *Rahu* joins the Sun in the 2nd house. *Rahu*'s additional influences are sign dispositor Mercury and *nakshatra* dispositor Mars. *Rahu*'s placement in the 2nd house in *Chitra nakshatra* will contribute to the distinctive nature of Andrea Bocelli's voice while *Rahu*'s connection to Mars in the 10th makes possible his career as a vocalist.

Rahu gains *swakshetra* status in the sign of Aquarius in the 11th house of Andrea Bocelli's D-10 chart. *Rahu*'s D-10 dispositor Saturn is joined in the 12th house by exalted 2nd lord Venus and ascendant ruler Mars as Saturn and Jupiter exchange house rulership in a 10 – 12 *Parivartana* yoga. *Rahu* is fortified in the D-10 by benefic flanking from Jupiter and Venus. Sub-period ruler Sun owns the 10th house in Andrea Bocelli's D-9 and accompanies *swakshetra* 3rd and 4th lord Saturn in the 4th house; notice that his D-9 strongly implies a career related to creative vocal expression as *swakshetra* 2nd and 5th lord Jupiter aspects the 10th house. In his D-10, Sun rules the 5th house, is aspected by chart ruler Mars, and is placed in the 3rd house of artistic expression.

Andrea Bocelli's *Rahu* -- Sun period coincides with the onset of his 2-year Capricorn *Jaimini Chara dasha*. The sign of Capricorn holds *vargottama* DK Moon, as *Jaimini Raj* yoga is created by the aspect of four planets to the Moon, including AK Saturn, AmK Mercury, BK Venus and PK Mars. The 10th house from Capricorn is occupied by Jupiter and is energized by aspects from Mercury, Venus, and Mars. In Andrea Bocelli's D-9, *swakshetra* BK Venus in the 10th house from Capricorn is aspected by the Sun and strong AK Saturn, while the Moon is aspected by AmK Mercury. In his D-10, debilitated Jupiter engages in the 1 – 3 *Parivartana* yoga with Saturn, while Saturn in Pisces is joined by exalted BK Venus and PK Mars. Andrea Bocelli's career is sustained by the strength of his subsequent 5-year *Chara dasha* of Aquarius; Aquarius is the sign of Bocelli's KL. In the birth chart AK and Aquarius ruler Saturn in the 10th house is aspected by DK Moon while the sign of Aquarius is activated by Jupiter. The sign of Aquarius is also stabilized by the presence of four *grahas* in *kendra* houses. In the D-9, Saturn forms *Shasha* yoga in Aquarius where it is joined by the Sun, as AmK Mercury in the 10th house is aspected by DK Moon. AK Saturn and Sun in Aquarius enjoy *Jaimini sambandha* with *swakshetra* BK Venus. In his D-10, Aquarius has *swakshetra Rahu* aspected by AmK Mercury, while Mercury and Jupiter aspect Scorpio, the 10th house from Aquarius.

The next chart for our consideration will be that of Keith Richards (December 18, 1943, Dartford, England, 6:00 a.m., A), acclaimed guitarist, and with Mick Jagger, one of two founding and enduring members of the famously successful rock and roll band the Rolling Stones.

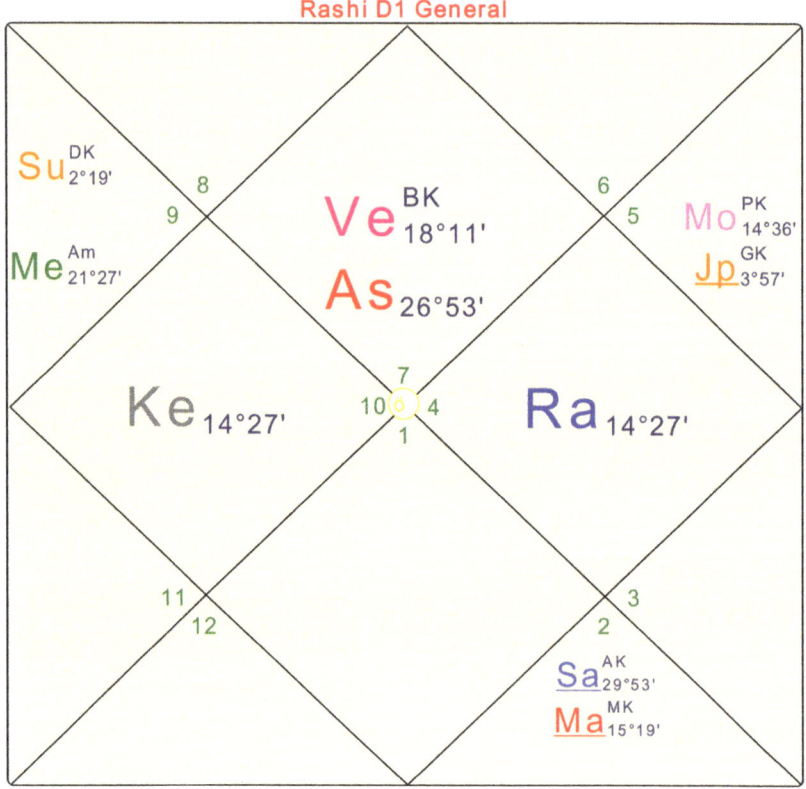

Creativity in the Vedic Astrology Chart

Rashi D1 General

	Ma MK 15°19' Sa AK 29°53'		Ra 14°27'
	ö **Keith Richards** Sat. 12/18/1943 6:00:00 Dartford, UK		Jp GK 3°57' Mo PK 14°36'
Ke 14°27'			
Me Am 21°27' Su DK 2°19'		As 26°53' Ve BK 18°11'	

Recognized for his proficiency on the guitar, Keith Richards cultivated the ability to play both rhythm and lead guitar and experimented with original, idiosyncratic tunings of the instrument. A 2011 *Rolling Stone* magazine survey of the "100 Greatest Guitarists" ranked Keith Richards at number four (*Rolling Stone*, November 22, 2011). In addition to his instrumental skill, Keith Richards has distinguished himself as a songwriter, particularly in his role as co-writer with singer Mick Jagger, of numerous Rolling Stones hit songs.

The centerpiece of Keith Richards' Libra rising chart is his *Malavya* yoga, formed by Venus in *Swati nakshatra* in the ascendant. The planet's strength is reinforced as Venus becomes exalted 5th lord and 10th house resident in his D-9, where a *Parivartana* yoga occurs between Venus and 10th lord Jupiter. Venus is the dominant planet in the D-9; four *grahas* occupy signs of Venus, including D-9 ascendant ruler Mercury, while a fifth, Saturn, is aspected by Venus. There is a prominent *Parivartana* yoga in the birth chart; 11th lord Sun in the 3rd house exchanges with 3rd lord Jupiter's placement in the 11th. This creates a strong *sambandha* between the two houses and their lords, as the Sun in a Jupiter-ruled sign is aspected by Jupiter. The exchange perfectly describes Keith Richards' life and career – playing a musical instrument (3rd house) in a group ensemble with mass appeal and success (11th house). Both planets in the 3rd house of hands and musical expression sit in weapon *drekkanas*. In the 11th house, vargottama 10th lord Moon also falls in a weapon *drekkana* in creative *Purva Phalguni* and forms a *Kesari* yoga with Jupiter. Despite its 8th house location, Mars plays a strongly influential role in the chart. Located in *Rohini nakshatra*, Mars maintains its artistic nature due to its *vargottama* status and the strength of dispositor Venus in both the D-1 and D-9. From the 8th, Mars aspects and energizes both sides of the 3 – 11 exchange. From the Moon, Venus owns houses 3 and 10 and occupies the 3rd. Employing Moon ascendant, the *Parivartana* yoga occurs between the 1st house and the 5th house of creativity, while Mars becomes a yoga *karaka* planet as 4th and 9th lord in the 10th house. In the *Jaimini* system, the 3 – 11 mutual *sambandha* relationship between Moon and Venus is a *Raj* yoga (BPHS 39:41), more so in this case due to the strength of both *grahas*. The Moon – Venus yoga also serves to incline the chart in the direction of artistic creativity, given the status of Venus as BK and Moon as PK. Venus in the ascendant in *Jaimini* aspect to Jupiter and the Moon qualifies for the *Raj* yoga described in BPHS 39:11. BPHS *Kahala* (36: 9 & 10) yoga is formed as the result of the placement of 4th lord Saturn and Jupiter in mutual *kendras*, qualified by the strength of ascendant ruler Venus.

Creativity in the Vedic Astrology Chart

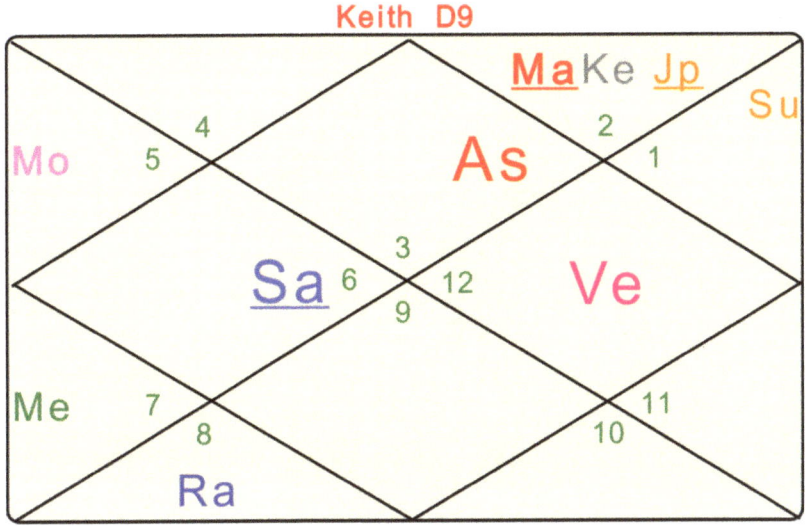

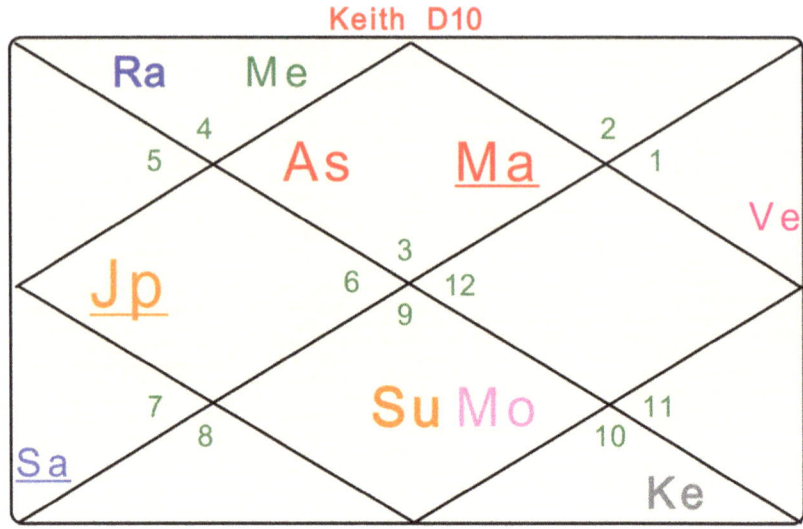

KR: Vimshottari

Start Date	Age	Dashas	
11/ 17/ 1960	16.9	Ve	Ke
1/ 17/ 1962	18.1	Su	Su
5/ 7/ 1962	18.4	Su	Mo
11/ 5/ 1962	18.9	Su	Ma
3/ 13/ 1963	19.2	Su	Ra
2/ 5/ 1964	20.1	Su	Jp
11/ 23/ 1964	20.9	Su	Sa
11/ 5/ 1965	21.9	Su	Me
9/ 12/ 1966	22.7	Su	Ke
1/ 17/ 1967	23.1	Su	Ve
1/ 18/ 1968	24.1	Mo	Mo
11/ 17/ 1968	24.9	Mo	Ma
6/ 18/ 1969	25.5	Mo	Ra
12/ 18/ 1970	27.0	Mo	Jp
4/ 18/ 1972	28.3	Mo	Sa
11/ 17/ 1973	29.9	Mo	Me
4/ 19/ 1975	31.3	Mo	Ke
11/ 18/ 1975	31.9	Mo	Ve
7/ 19/ 1977	33.6	Mo	Su
1/ 17/ 1978	34.1	Ma	Ma
6/ 15/ 1978	34.5	Ma	Ra
7/ 4/ 1979	35.5	Ma	Jp
6/ 9/ 1980	36.5	Ma	Sa
7/ 19/ 1981	37.6	Ma	Me
7/ 16/ 1982	38.6	Ma	Ke
12/ 12/ 1982	39.0	Ma	Ve

KR: Chara

Start Date	Age	Dashas
12/ 18/ 1943	-0.0	Libr
12/ 18/ 1955	12.0	Sco
12/ 17/ 1961	18.0	Sag
12/ 17/ 1969	26.0	Cap
12/ 17/ 1977	34.0	Aqu
12/ 18/ 1986	43.0	Pis
12/ 18/ 1993	50.0	Ari
12/ 18/ 1994	51.0	Tau
12/ 18/ 1999	56.0	Gem
12/ 18/ 2005	62.0	Can
12/ 17/ 2016 n	73.0	Leo
12/ 17/ 2024	81.0	Virg

Although Keith Richards and Mick Jagger had been childhood friends, they had lost touch for some years, but happened to meet again in October 1961. This meeting occurred in Keith's *Vimshottari* Venus – *Ketu* period; notice that his *Ketu* is in the musical and melodic *nakshatra* of *Shravana* in the 4th house. *Ketu*'s influences, 10th lord Moon and yoga *karaka* Saturn, reflect this significant moment of opportunity in Richards' life. The Rolling Stones were subsequently formed and began performing as a band in 1962. Simultaneously, Keith Richards began his Sun *dasha*, the period during which the Rolling Stones first toured and recorded, then ascended to worldwide acclaim as the foremost rock and roll band of that era. In his D-9, the Sun rules the 3rd house and is exalted in the 11th. In Keith's D-10, Sun again rules the 3rd, inhabits an angular house (7th) and sits in *sambandha* with 11th lord Mars.

At the end of 1961, Keith Richards began his 8-year Sagittarius *Jaimini Chara dasha*. Sagittarius is the sign on Keith's 3rd house and features two planets in weapon *drekkanas*. The Sun and Mercury in Sagittarius form a 9 – 10 *Raj* yoga, with Sun as DK and Mercury as the AmK (career) and lord of Keith's Virgo KL, the 10th house from

Sagittarius. In his Gemini rising D-9, AK and natal 5th house ruler Saturn is prominent in the 10th house from Sagittarius while Venus as BK (3rd house significations) is exalted in the 4th, as both *grahas* activate the *kendra* houses in the chart. In Keith's D-10, the *kendra* houses are again well activated, as Sagittarius has DK Sun and PK (5th house significations) Moon, with period sign ruler Jupiter in the 10th house in Virgo and Mars in the sign of Gemini. The sign of Sagittarius is fortified by the aspect of its ruling planet. The 3rd house – 11th house relationship in the birth chart is reinforced from Sagittarius in the D-10 as 3rd lord Saturn goes to its sign of exaltation in the 11th.

Moving on, we will next consider the chart of gifted singer and musician Eva Cassidy (February 2, 1963, Washington, D.C., 9:59:10 p.m., A).

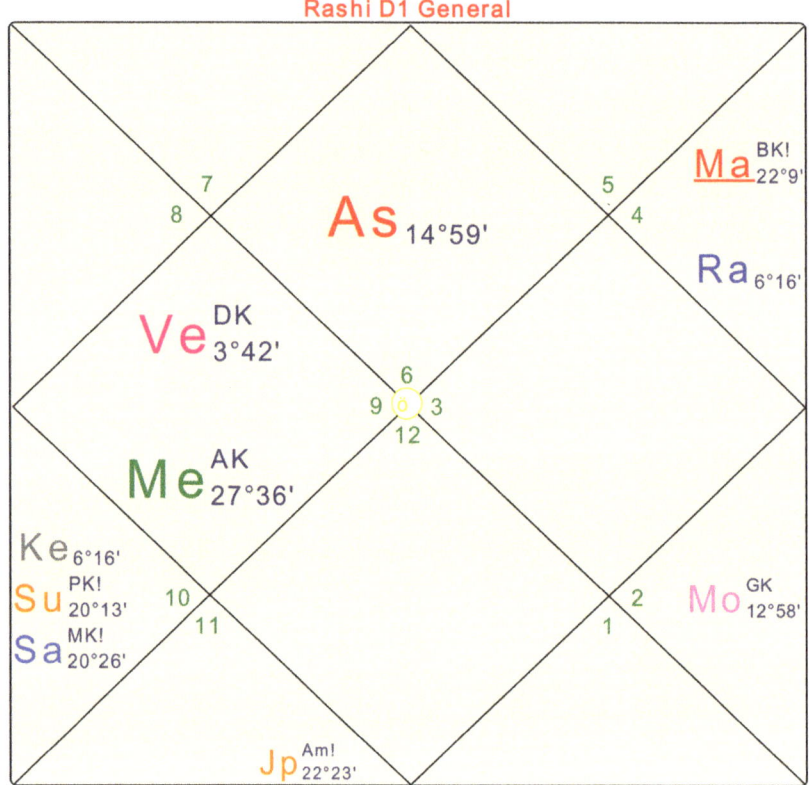

Creativity in the Vedic Astrology Chart

Rashi D1 General

	Mo GK 12°58'		
Jp Am! 22°23'			Ra 6°16' Ma BK! 22°9'
Sa MK! 20°26' Su PK! 20°13' Ke 6°16'	Eva Cassidy Sat. 2/2/1963 21:59:10 Washington, DC		
Me AK 27°36' Ve DK 3°42'			As 14°59'

Eva Cassidy's life and career were tragically cut short by illness at the age of thirty-three and much of the acclaim she has received has been posthumous. Having begun to learn guitar at the age of nine, Ms. Cassidy was a skilled instrumentalist, but she is appreciated primarily for the versatility of her extraordinary voice. As a performer and recording artist in the Washington D.C. area in her late twenties and early thirties, Eva Cassidy gained strong local adulation for her exceptional vocal style. A *Washington Post* article written several weeks after her death in 1996 stated; "she could sing anything – folk, blues, pop, jazz, R&B, gospel – and make it sound like the only music that mattered." (Richard Harrington, *Washington Post*, 11/17/1996). In a 2002 *New York Times* review of several of Eva Cassidy's CDs, music critic Alex Ward wrote of her "silken soprano voice with a wide and seemingly effortless range, unerring pitch and a gift for phrasing that at times was heart-stoppingly eloquent." (*New York Times*, August 12, 2002). In a 2005 survey of its 25 best-selling musicians, on-line seller Amazon ranked Eva Cassidy's recordings at 5th overall, surpassed only by the Beatles, U2, Norah Jones and Diana Krall. To date, Eva Cassidy's CD *Live at Blues Alley* has sold 12 million copies.

Eva Cassidy's Virgo rising chart combines ascendant lord Mercury and 2nd lord of voice Venus in the 4th house, where Venus gains directional strength and the two planets form a 9 – 10 *Dharma Karma Adhipati Raj* yoga as they aspect the 10th house of the chart. The chart features a *Maha Bhagya* yoga (*Phaladeepika* 6: 14 & 15). *Phaladeepika Kahala* yoga is formed secondary to the disposition of Jupiter (*lagna* lord Mercury's dispositor) by *swakshetra* Saturn in a *trikona* house. Notice also that Mercury and Venus escape any direct malefic influence, enabling Mercury to enjoy its status as a natural and temporal benefic for the chart. Venus proceeds to its sign of Taurus in the D-9 ascendant in *Malavya* yoga, while Mercury at 27 degrees attains *vargottama* status. *Hasta nakshatra* rises in the D-1 as *swakshetra* 5th lord Saturn and the Sun occupy the *nakshatra* of *Shravana*. The ascendant degree, in the 2nd *drekkana* of Virgo, as well as the placements of Mercury, Venus, Sun and Saturn all occur in weapon *drekkanas*. Eva Cassidy's Moon, lord of 11th house for the Virgo rising chart, is placed in the 9th house in its exaltation sign of Taurus in *Rohini nakshatra*. (It is worth noting the variety of ways in which *Rohini nakshatra* expressed itself in the life of Eva Cassidy; in addition to music, Ms. Cassidy worked as a propagator in a plant nursery and pursued painting, jewelry design, and sculpture.) Exalted Moon will always give the Moon rulership of 3rd from itself and in this chart, Moon from the 9th aspects the 3rd house from the chart's ascendant. Moon as ascendant is where the clearest indication of the beauty and versatility of Eva Cassidy's voice is evident, as all three natural benefics aspect the 2nd house from the Moon. The 2nd house from the ascendant is aspected by Jupiter, 5th lord Saturn, and 3rd house ruler Mars. From the *Jaimini* system perspective, we find

Mercury and Venus in the KL in the sign of Sagittarius. The BPHS Chapter 33 verses 13 – 18 states that strong Mercury (in this case, *vargottama*) in the KL renders one "skillful in the arts."

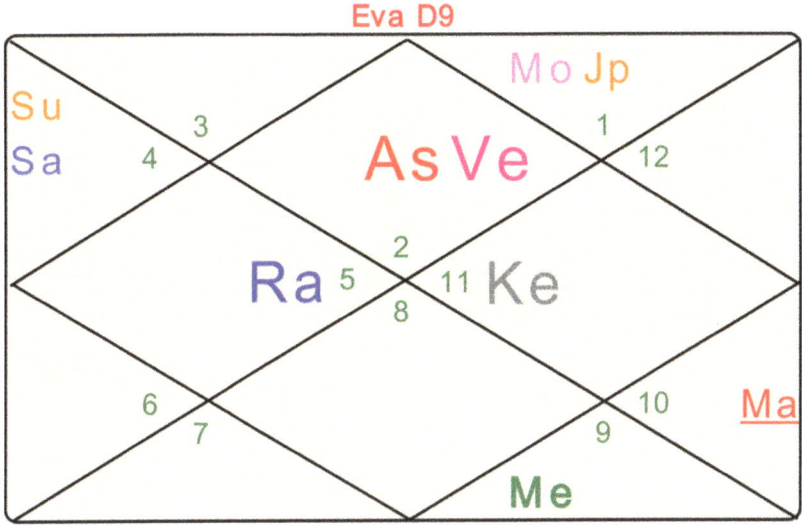

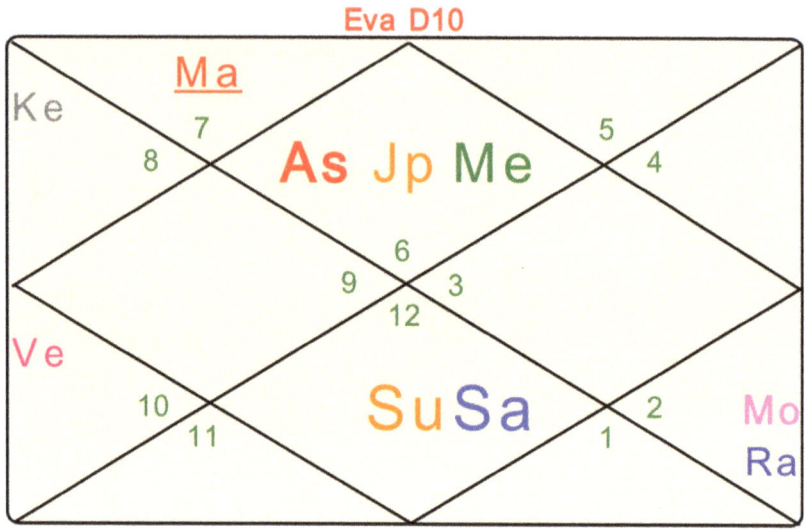

Eva C: Vimshottari

Start Date			Age	Dashas	
10/	9/	1963	0.7	Mo	Jp
2/	7/	1965	2.0	Mo	Sa
9/	8/	1966	3.6	Mo	Me
2/	7/	1968	5.0	Mo	Ke
9/	7/	1968	5.6	Mo	Ve
5/	9/	1970	7.3	Mo	Su
11/	**8/**	**1970**	**7.8**	**Ma**	**Ma**
4/	6/	1971	8.2	Ma	Ra
4/	23/	1972	9.2	Ma	Jp
3/	30/	1973	10.2	Ma	Sa
5/	9/	1974	11.3	Ma	Me
5/	6/	1975	12.3	Ma	Ke
10/	3/	1975	12.7	Ma	Ve
12/	2/	1976	13.8	Ma	Su
4/	8/	1977	14.2	Ma	Mo
11/	**8/**	**1977**	**14.8**	**Ra**	**Ra**
7/	21/	1980	17.5	Ra	Jp
12/	14/	1982	19.9	Ra	Sa
10/	20/	1985	22.7	Ra	Me
5/	9/	1988	25.3	Ra	Ke
5/	27/	1989	26.3	Ra	Ve
5/	27/	1992	29.3	Ra	Su
4/	21/	1993	30.2	Ra	Mo
10/	21/	1994	31.7	Ra	Ma
11/	**8/**	**1995**	**32.8**	**Jp**	**Jp**
12/	26/	1997	34.9	Jp	Sa

Eva : Chara

Start Date			Age	Dashas
2/	2/	1963	-0.0	Virg
2/	3/	1972	9.0	Libr
2/	2/	1974	11.0	Sco
2/	3/	1976	13.0	Sag
2/	2/	1978	15.0	Cap
2/	2/	1990	27.0	Aqu
2/	3/	1991	28.0	Pis
2/	3/	1992	29.0	Ari
2/	3/	1995	32.0	Tau
2/	2/	2002	39.0	Gem
2/	3/	2008	45.0	Can
2/	2/	2010	47.0	Leo

Eva Cassidy's career as a recording and performing artist began to rise in her mid-20s, during the *Vimshottari* period of *Rahu* -- Venus. Ms. Cassidy released her first CD in 1992, shortly before the end of her Venus sub-period. In the birth chart, *Rahu* joins 3rd lord Mars in the 11th house. Mars achieves *Neecha Bhanga Raj* yoga as the result of its *sambandha* with Saturn, Jupiter's placement in the 10th house from the Moon, and Mars' exaltation in the D-9. *Rahu* is disposited by the exalted Moon, and *nakshatra* disposited and aspected by *swakshetra* 5th lord Saturn. In the D-9, *Rahu* in the 4th house is disposited by 3rd house occupant Sun and is aspected by exalted Mars and 11th lord Jupiter. Career rise and wider appreciation for her musical skills is evident in the Venus sub-period, as *Malavya* yoga Venus locates in the 10th house from *Rahu* in the ascendant of the D-9. In her *vargottama* D-10, *Rahu* joins exalted and *vargottama* (for the D-10) Moon in the 9th house, as dispositor Venus is found in the 5th house in Capricorn. Notably, both *Rahu* and Venus in the D-10 are aspected by Jupiter and 3rd lord Mars while *Rahu* is also influenced by the aspect of natal and local 5th lord Saturn.

On her 27th birthday in 1990, Eva Cassidy began a one-year

Jaimini Chara dasha of Aquarius. In her birth chart, Aquarius has AmK Jupiter, while AK Mercury and DK Venus occupy the 11th house of gains and awards, and aspect the 2nd house from Aquarius. The following period of Pisces, also of one year's duration, brought increased recognition and performance opportunities for Ms. Cassidy as Venus and Mercury are found in the 10th house in Sagittarius, the chart's KL, and aspect the sign of Pisces as well as Gemini and Virgo. *Vargottama* AK Mercury remains in the 10th house from Pisces in the D-9. In Eva Cassidy's Virgo rising D-10 the *kendra* houses are activated by four *grahas*, including AK Mercury, AmK Jupiter, PK Sun and natal 5th lord Saturn, all categorized as *Jaimini Raj* yoga-forming *grahas*. The D-10 chart becomes strongly capable with ruling planet AK Mercury in the ascendant in *Bhadra* yoga, where Mercury and AmK Jupiter achieve directional strength. The D-10 angular *dwishwabhava* signs gain strength secondary to activation from their lords. Notice that the ascendant is occupied by the chart ruler in *Maha Purusha* yoga in both Ms. Cassidy's D-9 and D-10 charts.

Eva Cassidy was to enjoy her highest degree of musical success, with a CD release, the formation of her band, and celebrated concerts during the last 4 ½ years of her life. This period began at age twenty-nine with Eva Cassidy's 3-year Aries *dasha*. From Aries, Mercury and Venus inhabit the fortunate 9th house and aspect the 3rd house of musical and artistic expression. *Swakshetra* natal 5th lord Saturn and PK Sun reside in the 10th house from Aries and are aspected by her exalted Moon. The Moon and AmK Jupiter locate in Aries in her D-9, while sign ruler and BK Mars attains exaltation and directional strength in the 10th from Aries, where it is aspected by *swakshetra* DK Venus. Eva Cassidy's exceptional vocal skills are displayed during this Aries period as *swakshetra* Venus in the 2nd house from Aries gains the influence of exalted BK Mars. Located in the 10th house from Aries in Ms. Cassidy's D-10, Venus is found in mutual aspect with exalted *vargottama* (in D-10) Moon, creating Venus – Moon *Raj* yoga, while her 2nd house Moon is also aspected by BK Mars. Finally, the 3rd house from Aries is strongly activated by aspects from Saturn, the Sun, and the combined influence of Jupiter and Mercury.

Readers who may wish to learn more about her are directed to www.evacassidy.org, a well maintained and comprehensive appreciation of the life and art of Eva Cassidy.

Our next chart will be that of Brian Wilson (June 20, 1942, Inglewood, CA, 3:45 a.m., AA) singer, songwriter and musical arranger and producer for the pop music band the Beach Boys. The consistent beauty and originality of his melodies and vocal and instrumental arrangements, as well as his innovative production and recording techniques, serve to justify Brian Wilson's reputation as a musical genius. Brian Wilson wrote, arranged, and produced the great majority of the Beach Boys' hit songs and albums through the 1960s and into the 1970s. His crowning achievement is the album *Pet Sounds*, released in 1966 and critically acknowledged as one of the best pop music LPs ever created. In several *Rolling Stone* magazine surveys of the top 500 LPs of the pop music era, *Pet Sounds* is ranked number two, while British music publications *Uncut*, *Mojo* and *New Musical Express* all list *Pet Sounds* at number one. Paul McCartney is quoted: "I figure no one is educated musically 'til they've heard *Pet Sounds*. I love the orchestra, the arrangements – it may be going overboard to say it's the classic of the century – but to me it certainly is a total, classic record that is unbeatable in many ways." Beatles producer George Martin stated, "If there is one person that I have to select as a living genius of pop music, I would choose Brian Wilson." (quotes from www.brianwilson.com).

Michael A. Sugarman

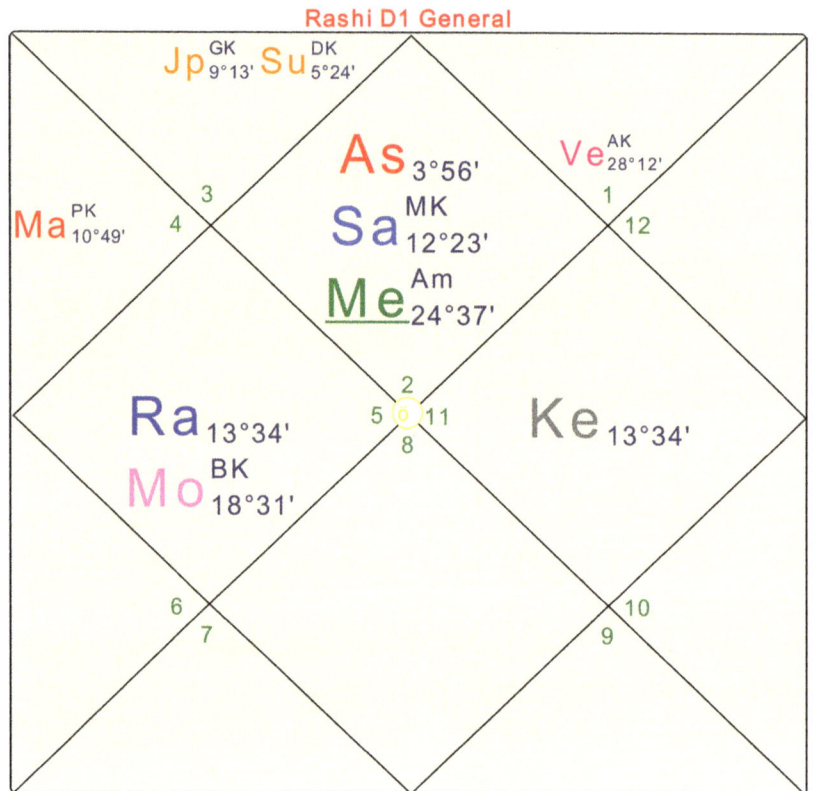

Rashi D1 General

	As 3°56' Sa MK 12°23' Me Am 24°37'	Su DK 5°24'	
Ve AK 28°12'		Jp GK 9°13'	
		Ma PK 10°49'	
Ke 13°34'	Brian Wilson Sat. 6/20/1942 3:45:00 Inglewood, CA	Ra 13°34' Mo BK 18°31'	

The chart of Brian Wilson features a *mala* (necklace) of natural benefics across the ascendant, the configuration known as *Shubha* yoga, formed in this chart by ascendant lord Venus in the 12th, Mercury in the 1st and Jupiter in the 2nd house. BPHS chapter 36 verses 1 -- 2 assigns the qualities of virtuosity, eloquence, beauty, and longevity to the *Shubha* yoga. Mercury obtains directional strength in the ascendant, while Jupiter in the 2nd house achieves *swakshetra* status in Brian Wilson's D-9. We locate chart lord Venus and the ascendant degree in *Krittika nakshatra*; recall that the quality of creative genius is known as one of *Krittika*'s gifts and is consistent with Brian Wilson's well-deserved reputation in the realm of popular music. As ruler of the 9th and 10th houses, yoga *karaka* Saturn occupies *Rohini nakshatra*. Saturn is joined in the ascendant by 5th lord Mercury, as the two planets constitute a 5 -- 9 *Raj* yoga and a 5 -- 10 *Dharma Karma Adhipati*

Raj yoga. In Taurus, Mercury and Saturn are in the sign of a great friend and reside in the 10th house from the Moon. The collective influence of *Krittika nakshatra*, Saturn in *Rohini* and a strong 5th lord Mercury creates Brian Wilson's seemingly inexhaustible reservoir of musical inspiration. As 3rd lord in the 4th house in creative *Purva Phalguni*, enjoying directional strength and sitting in the 5th house from ascendant ruler Venus, Brian Wilson's Moon makes its own contribution to the theme of musical innovation in the chart. Notice also that the 3rd house from the Moon is activated by aspects from owner Venus, 5th lord (from Moon) Jupiter, and Mars. The 5th house from the Moon is similarly activated by aspects from its ruler Jupiter and Moon's dispositor Sun. At 28 degrees of Aries ascendant lord Venus is in a weapon *drekkana*, as is 3rd lord Moon in the 2nd *drekkana* of Leo; Brian Wilson did all his composing on the piano, and during the years that he performed with the Beach Boys, played the Fender electric bass.

Brian Wilson's KL is the sign of Sagittarius, the 8th house of his birth chart. The 5th house from the KL occupied by Venus in aspect to the Moon and/or Jupiter comprises a *Raj* yoga as described in BPHS chapter 39 verse 11 ("related to royal circles"); Venus as AK lends this yoga more strength. The presence of Venus in the 5th and Moon's status as natal 3rd lord and BK will also incline the chart in the direction of artistic and musical creativity.

Creativity in the Vedic Astrology Chart

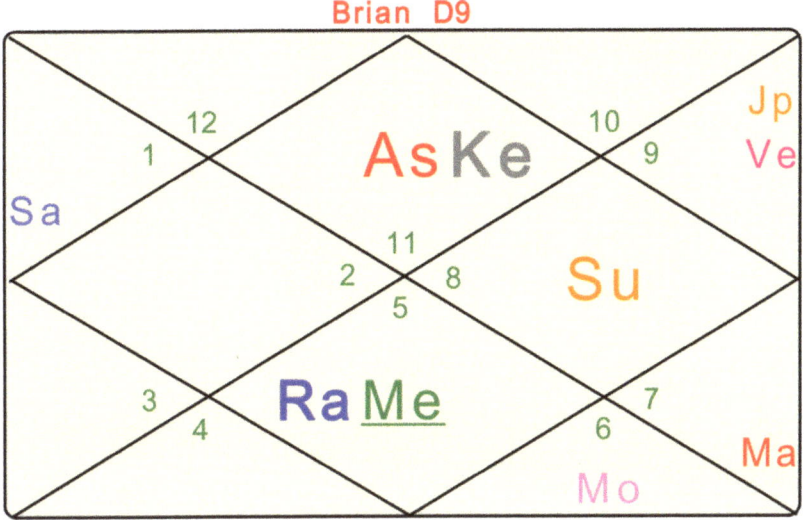

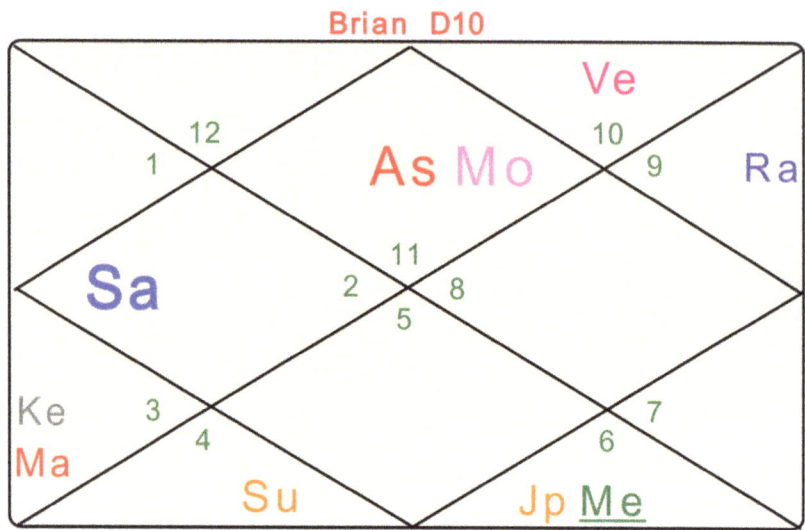

BW: Vimshottari

Start Date			Age	Dashas	
7/	17/	1957	15.1	Su	Sa
6/	29/	1958	16.0	Su	Me
5/	5/	1959	16.9	Su	Ke
9/	10/	1959	17.2	Su	Ve
9/	9/	1960	18.2	Mo	Mo
7/	11/	1961	19.1	Mo	Ma
2/	9/	1962	19.6	Mo	Ra
8/	11/	1963	21.1	Mo	Jp
12/	10/	1964	22.5	Mo	Sa
7/	11/	1966	24.1	Mo	Me
12/	10/	1967	25.5	Mo	Ke
7/	10/	1968	26.1	Mo	Ve
3/	11/	1970	27.7	Mo	Su
9/	10/	1970	28.2	Ma	Ma
2/	6/	1971	28.6	Ma	Ra
2/	24/	1972	29.7	Ma	Jp
1/	30/	1973	30.6	Ma	Sa
3/	11/	1974	31.7	Ma	Me
3/	8/	1975	32.7	Ma	Ke
8/	5/	1975	33.1	Ma	Ve
10/	4/	1976	34.3	Ma	Su
2/	8/	1977	34.6	Ma	Mo
9/	10/	1977	35.2	Ra	Ra
5/	23/	1980	37.9	Ra	Jp
10/	16/	1982	40.3	Ra	Sa
8/	22/	1985	43.2	Ra	Me
3/	11/	1988	45.7	Ra	Ke
3/	29/	1989	46.8	Ra	Ve
3/	29/	1992	49.8	Ra	Su
2/	21/	1993	50.7	Ra	Mo
8/	23/	1994	52.2	Ra	Ma
9/	10/	1995	53.2	Jp	Jp
10/	28/	1997	55.4	Jp	Sa
5/	11/	2000	57.9	Jp	Me
8/	17/	2002	60.2	Jp	Ke
7/	24/	2003	61.1	Jp	Ve
3/	24/	2006	63.8	Jp	Su
1/	10/	2007	64.6	Jp	Mo
5/	11/	2008	65.9	Jp	Ma
4/	17/	2009	66.8	Jp	Ra
9/	10/	2011	69.2	Sa	Sa

BW: Chara		
Start Date	Age	Dashas
6/ 20/ 1942	-0.0	Tau
6/ 19/ 1953	11.0	Ari
6/ 19/ 1956	14.0	Pis
6/ 20/ 1965	23.0	Aqu
6/ 20/ 1971	29.0	Cap
6/ 20/ 1979	37.0	Sag
6/ 20/ 1985	43.0	Sco
6/ 19/ 1988	46.0	Libr
6/ 20/ 1994	52.0	Virg
6/ 20/ 1998	56.0	Leo
6/ 20/ 2000	58.0	Can
6/ 20/ 2011	69.0	Gem

Under Brian Wilson's guidance and leadership, the Beach Boys formed as a band in 1961, soon after the onset of his 10-year Moon period, as the band began to perform and record prolifically in the early 1960s. In his D-1, directional strength Moon as 3rd lord aspects the 10th house of career; the Moon gains prominence in the ascendant of his D-10. In the D-9, the Moon participates in a *Gaja Kesari* yoga with *swakshetra* Jupiter and Venus.

In the *Jaimini Chara dasha* scheme, Brian Wilson ran his Pisces period from 1956 to 1965. From the sign of Pisces, PK Mars in the 5th house of creativity is aspected by Saturn and natal 5th lord/AmK Mercury. In his D-10 Pisces is activated by Mars, Mercury, and Jupiter. From the sign of Pisces in Wilson's D-10, the *Parivartana* yoga between Saturn and Venus becomes a favorable exchange between houses 3 and 11 as the two *grahas* aspect each other in *Jaimini sambandha*. The placement of Jupiter and Mercury in Virgo ensures that the *kendra* houses are activated by their own lords. In Brian Wilson's D-9, AK Venus and *swakshetra* Jupiter occupy the 10th house from Pisces as BK Moon is located in the 7th house in Virgo. The *dwishwabhava* signs in Brian Wilson's D-9 are activated by

Venus and the Moon while those in the D-10 benefit from the shared influence of Jupiter and Mercury.

The following 6-year period of Aquarius granted Wilson as much if not more critical success; this was the time during which Brian Wilson wrote, arranged, produced, and performed on a series of successful LPs, beginning with *Pet Sounds*. Aquarius is the sign on the 10th house of the birth chart; AK Venus in Aries in the 3rd house is aspected there by BK Moon. The sign of Aquarius and 10th therefrom are aspected by AK Venus and PK Mars, while Jupiter and DK Sun inhabit the 5th house. Aquarius is the sign on the ascendant of both the D-9 and D-10; in the D-9 DK Sun gains directional strength in the 10th house. The D-9 ascendant is aspected by PK Mars and ascendant ruler Saturn, while the 5th and 11th houses are activated by Jupiter, Venus, and the Moon. In his D-10, BK Moon in the ascendant is aspected by DK Sun as the 10th house of the chart is aspected by the Sun and AK Venus. The 5th house of the D-10 holds a *Chaya Graha Raj* yoga as 10th lord PK Mars is joined by *Ketu*. As in the D-9, the 5 – 11 axis of the chart is activated, in this case by Mars, Jupiter and *swakshetra* AmK/5th lord Mercury. At the age of 81, Brian Wilson continues to write music, arrange, record, produce and perform before highly appreciative audiences.

The next chart for our study will be that of legendary Italian violinist and composer Niccolo Paganini (October 27, 1782, Genoa, Italy, 10:30 a.m., DD, rectified and verified by the author). Niccolo Paganini is known as one of the most skilled and influential violinists who ever lived, a prodigy who began learning the mandolin at age five, violin at seven, and performing by age eleven. Paganini is said to have mastered the guitar as well, and to have never travelled without a guitar, although he rarely performed on the instrument. (A guitar presented as a gift from Paganini to composer Hector Berlioz and signed by both gentlemen is on display at the Musee de la Musique in Paris.) As a young violin student, a succession of teachers each determined that Paganini's skill had quickly exceeded their own and that they had nothing to offer him. Niccolo Paganini performed and toured extensively, first in Italy and later throughout Europe, to wide acclaim as the greatest violinist of his era. Paganini's technique is described as having been powerful and fiery, while maintaining exquisite technical control of the instrument. Paganini was known to occasionally cut notches into three of his violin strings before performing a piece known as "Witches' Dance," causing each of the strings to break mid-performance, and Paganini to complete the piece on one string. Paganini's Wikipedia page states that he possessed exceptional reach and was capable of spanning 3 octaves on the violin, across all 4 strings. A proficient composer as well as instrumentalist, Niccolo Paganini is best known for his twenty-four violin "Caprices" as well as a set of violin concertos. (In addition to his Wikipedia page, readers are directed to the PBS informational page www.thirteen.org where an informative biography of violinist Niccolo Paganini can be found.)

Creativity in the Vedic Astrology Chart

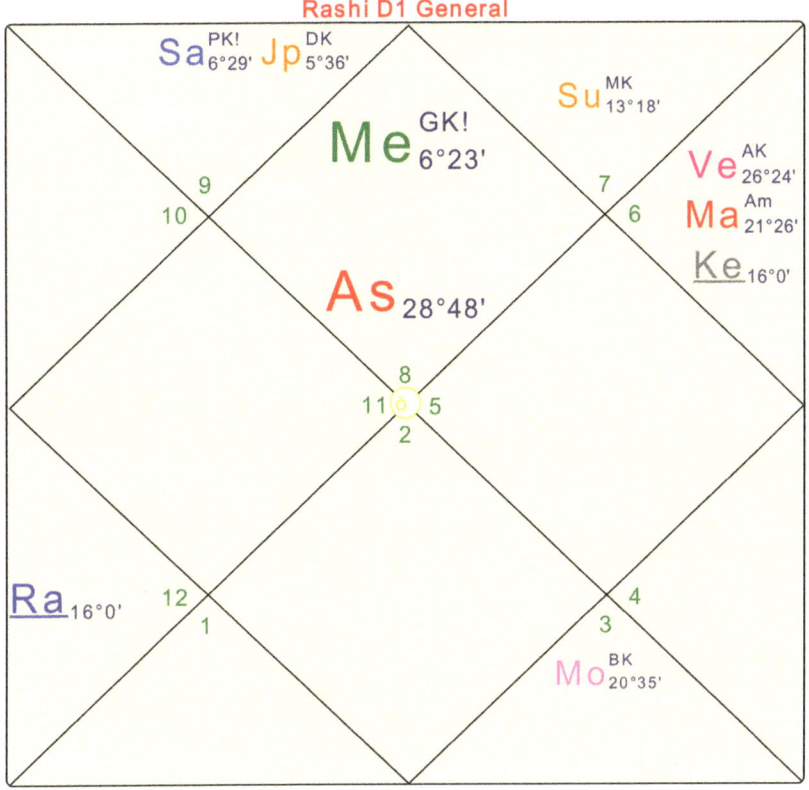

Rashi D1 General

Ra 16°0'			Mo BK 20°35'
	☉ **Niccolo Paganini** Sun. 10/27/1782 10:30:00 Genoa, IT		
Sa PK! 6°29' Jp DK 5°36'	As 28°48' Me GK! 6°23'	Su MK 13°18'	Ve AK 26°24' Ma Am 21°26' Ke 16°0'

Paganini's Scorpio rising chart locates ascendant lord Mars in the 11th house of awards and popular entertainment in the sign of Virgo and *nakshatra* of *Hasta*. Recall that *Hasta* can confer manual dexterity, and notice that Mars lies within 6 degrees of *Ketu*, also in *Hasta* but at 16 degrees *Ketu* is in the middle, weapon *drekkana* section of Virgo. Mars and *Ketu* in *Hasta* are joined in Virgo by debilitated Venus in *Chitra nakshatra*. The debilitation of Venus is cancelled by the location of dispositor Mercury in the ascendant and the placement of Venus and Jupiter in angular houses from the Moon. Given the presence of several criteria for cancellation and Jupiter's *swakshetra* status, the debilitation of Venus is elevated to *Neecha Bhanga Raj* yoga. Paganini's instrumental skill is enhanced by Mars' association with *Ketu*, while Venus will confer beauty and creativity secondary to its status as lord of the 5th house from the Moon and placement in *Chitra*. Venus, Mars, and *Ketu* in the 11th are aspected by 3rd lord Saturn, who also happens to inhabit a weapon *drekkana* (1st of Sagittarius) with 2nd and 5th lord Jupiter. The mutual activation of houses 3 and 5, as we are seeing consistently, is classic for musical creativity, and occurs twice over in this chart, as the 3rd lord from the Moon resides in the 5th house. *Swakshetra* 5th lord Jupiter aspects the 3rd house from the Moon. Paganini's 10th lord Sun is placed in the 12th house in musical *Swati nakshatra*. The Sun's debilitation is cancelled by the location of dispositor Venus, Sun's exaltation lord Mars, and Saturn (exalted where Sun is debilitated) in *kendra* houses from the Moon. The Sun is fortified by *Shubha Ubhayachari* yoga, as it is flanked by benefics Mercury and Venus. *Swakshetra* Jupiter and Moon create a *Kesari yoga*, the *Phaladeepika* 7:7 *Raj* yoga, and a 5th lord -- 9th lord *Raj* yoga. Benefits and numerous accolades were granted to Paganini as the result of the 1 – 11 *Parivartana* yoga between ascendant lord Mars and Mercury, as Mercury obtains directional strength in the ascendant.

The chart of Niccolo Paganini includes the *Jaimini Raj* yoga configured by the *sambandha* of four (or more) *grahas* with the Moon; the chart is also graced by the mutual relationship of Venus and the Moon. No less significant is the placement of PK Saturn and 5th lord/DK Jupiter in the 5th house from Paganini's KL of Leo. The sign of Sagittarius and occupants Saturn and Jupiter are activated by *Jaimini* aspects from Venus, Mars, and the Moon, as the 11th house from his KL is similarly influenced.

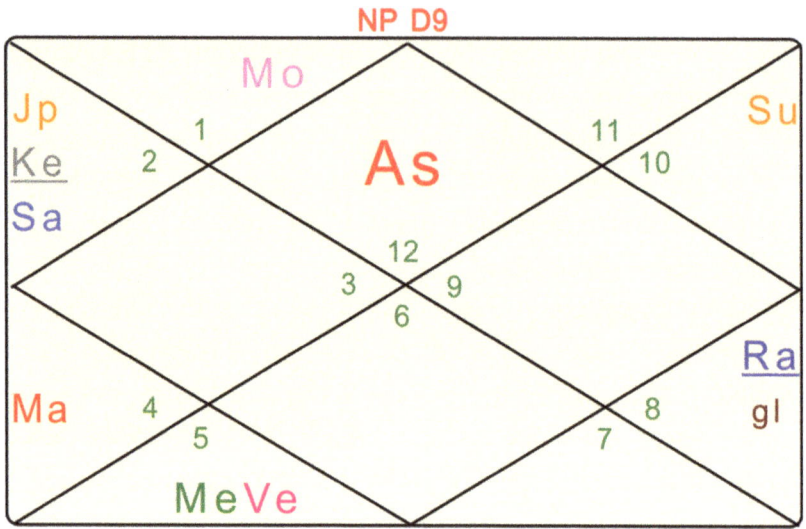

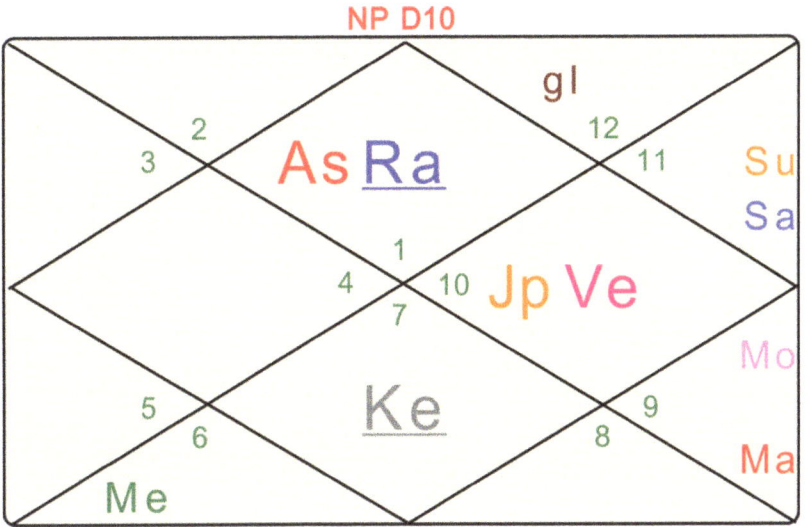

NP: Vimshottari

Start Date	Age	Dashas	
1/ 13/ 1789	6.2	Jp	Ke
12/ 20/ 1789	7.1	Jp	Ve
8/ 20/ 1792	9.8	Jp	Su
6/ 8/ 1793	10.6	Jp	Mo
10/ 8/ 1794	11.9	Jp	Ma
9/ 14/ 1795	12.9	Jp	Ra
2/ 7/ 1798	**15.3**	**Sa**	**Sa**
2/ 11/ 1801	18.3	Sa	Me
10/ 22/ 1803	21.0	Sa	Ke
11/ 30/ 1804	22.1	Sa	Ve
1/ 30/ 1808	25.3	Sa	Su
1/ 11/ 1809	26.2	Sa	Mo
8/ 13/ 1810	27.8	Sa	Ma
9/ 22/ 1811	28.9	Sa	Ra
7/ 29/ 1814	31.7	Sa	Jp
2/ 8/ 1817	**34.3**	**Me**	**Me**
7/ 8/ 1819	36.7	Me	Ke
7/ 4/ 1820	37.7	Me	Ve
5/ 5/ 1823	40.5	Me	Su
3/ 10/ 1824	41.4	Me	Mo
8/ 10/ 1825	42.8	Me	Ma
8/ 7/ 1826	43.8	Me	Ra
2/ 23/ 1829	46.3	Me	Jp
6/ 1/ 1831	48.6	Me	Sa
2/ 8/ 1834	**51.3**	**Ke**	**Ke**
7/ 7/ 1834	51.7	Ke	Ve

NP: Chara

Start Date	Age	Dashas	
11/ 28/ 1802	20.1	Libr	Libr
10/ 28/ 1803	21.0	Virg	Libr
8/ 28/ 1804	21.8	Virg	Sco
6/ 28/ 1805	22.7	Virg	Sag
4/ 28/ 1806	23.5	Virg	Cap
2/ 27/ 1807	24.3	Virg	Aqu
12/ 28/ 1807	25.2	Virg	Pis
10/ 28/ 1808	26.0	Virg	Ari
8/ 28/ 1809	26.8	Virg	Tau
6/ 28/ 1810	27.7	Virg	Gem
4/ 29/ 1811	28.5	Virg	Can
2/ 27/ 1812	29.3	Virg	Leo
12/ 28/ 1812	30.2	Virg	Virg
10/ 28/ 1813	31.0	Leo	Virg
8/ 28/ 1814	31.8	Leo	Libr
6/ 29/ 1815	32.7	Leo	Sco
4/ 28/ 1816	33.5	Leo	Sag
2/ 26/ 1817	34.3	Leo	Cap
12/ 28/ 1817	35.2	Leo	Aqu
10/ 28/ 1818	36.0	Leo	Pis
8/ 29/ 1819	36.8	Leo	Ari
6/ 28/ 1820	37.7	Leo	Tau
4/ 28/ 1821	38.5	Leo	Gem
2/ 27/ 1822	39.3	Leo	Can
12/ 28/ 1822	40.2	Leo	Leo
10/ 28/ 1823	41.0	Can	Gem

NP: Chara				
Start Date			Age	Dashas
10/	27/	1782	-0.0	Sco
10/	27/	1792	10.0	Libr
10/	28/	1803	21.0	Virg
10/	28/	1813	31.0	Leo
10/	28/	1823	41.0	Can
10/	28/	1824	42.0	Gem
10/	28/	1829	47.0	Tau
10/	28/	1833	51.0	Ari
10/	28/	1838	56.0	Pis
10/	28/	1841	59.0	Aqu
10/	29/	1843	61.0	Cap
10/	28/	1844	62.0	Sag

Paganini's career ascended during his 19-year Saturn period, which took him from ages 15 to 34. Saturn as 3rd and 4th lord is closely joined in a planetary war (Saturn is the winner) by 2nd and 5th lord Jupiter as the two *grahas* oppose 9th lord Moon and are aspected by ascendant ruler Mars. In Paganini's D-10, Saturn rules the 10th house and locates in the 11th in its own sign of Aquarius, while in his D-9 11th lord Saturn is joined in the 3rd house in Venus-owned Taurus by 1st and 10th house ruler Jupiter and *Ketu*.

Between ages 21 and 31 Niccolo Paganini ran his *Jaimini* Virgo *Chara dasha*. Following a series of enthusiastically received concerts in the city of Milan in 1812 and 1813, Paganini became a national sensation and embarked on a set of successful tours of Italy. The Virgo -- Virgo period, from late December 1812 until late October 1813, activates all the *Jaimini Raj* yoga-forming planets in the chart, with AK Venus and AmK Mars in the sign of Virgo, while 5th lord/ DK Jupiter and PK Saturn are in Sagittarius opposite BK Moon in Gemini. In his D-10, exalted Mercury sits in mutual aspect with BK Moon and AmK Mars in Sagittarius. Natal 5th lord/DK Jupiter and AK Venus occupy the sign of Capricorn in the 5th house. Simultaneously, Paganini sustained his *Vimshottari* Saturn – *Rahu* period. Located in the 5th house of his D-1, *Rahu* benefits from a variety of influences, including dispositor Jupiter and *nakshatra* dispositor Saturn, as well as Venus and ascendant ruler Mars. *Rahu*'s D-9 placement in the 9th house again falls under the influence of Jupiter and Saturn. *Rahu* is favorably placed in the ascendant of the D-10 and gains the aspect of *swakshetra* 10th and 11th lord Saturn. Natural benefics Jupiter and Venus in the 10th house of the D-10 ensured Paganini's success during his *Rahu* sub-period.

Paganini continued to enjoy wide acclaim over the course of his subsequent 10-year Leo *Chara dasha*; we see that the 5 – 11 axis from Leo is strongly activated. As the chart's KL, the sign of Leo is occupied by AK Venus and Mercury in Paganini's D-9. Leo benefits from the combined influence of Venus and the Moon as well as the aspect from its lord; the Sun also aspects the 10th house and residents Jupiter, Saturn, and *Ketu*. In his D-10, the 5 – 11 axis is activated by the Moon, Mars, and Mercury, while the signs of Leo and Taurus are influenced by natural benefics Jupiter and Venus in their respective status as natal 5th lord and AK. The sign of Taurus is also enabled by the activation from its lord Venus.

Our next chart will be that of globally renowned operatic soprano Leontyne Price (February 10th, 1927, Laurel, MS, 6:15 a.m., AA). Leontyne Price was born to a musical family and began taking piano lessons at age six. At nine years old Leontyne was accompanied by her mother to Jackson, Mississippi to hear a performance of Marian Anderson, whose voice and dignified, regal presentation left an enduring impression on the young girl. Leontyne Price studied music education and voice in college, followed by 3 ½ years' attendance at the Julliard School of Music, during which time she became increasingly fascinated with opera. In early 1952 Leontyne Price performed in a Julliard production of the Giuseppe Verdi opera *Falstaff*. Later the same year she won the role of Bess in a Broadway revival of Gershwin's *Porgy and Bess*, which included several hundred performances and tours of the U.S. and Europe. Ms. Price's operatic career ascended through the 1950s, featuring acclaimed roles in the operas of Mozart, Puccini, Strauss, and Verdi in New York, Chicago, San Francisco, London, Salzburg, Vienna, and Milan. Of her performance as *Aida* at La Scala in 1960, an Italian music critic wrote, "our great Verdi would have found her the ideal *Aida*."

Creativity in the Vedic Astrology Chart

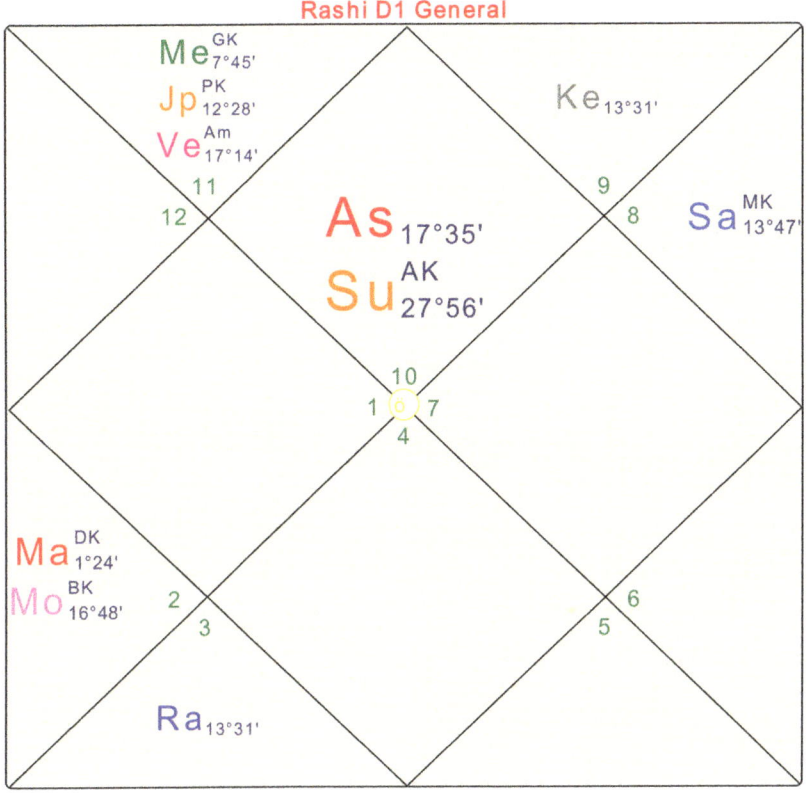

Rashi D1 General

		Ma DK 1°24' Mo BK 16°48'	Ra 13°31'
Ve Am 17°14' Jp PK 12°28' Me GK 7°45' Su AK 27°56' As 17°35'	ö	**Leontyne Price** Thu. 2/10/1927 6:15:00 Laurel, MS	
Ke 13°31'	Sa MK 13°47'		

In January of 1961 Leontyne Price made her debut at the New York Metropolitan Opera in Verdi's *Il Trovatore*. The performance received a standing ovation of forty-two minutes, one of the longest in Metropolitan Opera history. Leontyne Price was awarded the Presidential Medal of Freedom in 1964, Kennedy Center Honors in 1980, and the National Medal of Arts in 1985. Over a long and rich recording career, Ms. Price won 13 Grammy Awards and a Grammy Lifetime Achievement Award, conferred upon her in 1989. She has received numerous honorary degrees, including those granted by Columbia University, Harvard, and Yale. In a 2013 essay for the BBC, British music critic Hugh Canning describes Leontyne Price as "possessor of the most sumptuously beautiful soprano voice of the recording era," who "shone as Bess." Canning poses the rhetorical question,

"Has there ever been a more gorgeous account of 'Summertime' than Price's?" (Hugh Canning, *BBC Music*, July 17, 2013).

At 17 degrees, the Capricorn rising chart of Leontyne Price has *Shravana nakshatra* on the ascendant with 8th lord Sun in *Dhanishtha*. A *Saraswati* yoga is formed in the 2nd house by the three natural benefic planets, with no direct affliction to the house, and serves perfectly to illustrate the beauty and power of the voice of Ms. Price. The placement of all three *grahas* in *Shatabhisha nakshatra*, including Venus as 10th lord and Jupiter as ruler of the 12th, confirms the likelihood of vocal expression in a visual, theatrical media, specifically opera. The combination of 9th lord Mercury and yoga *karaka* Venus creates 9 – 10 and 5 – 9 *Raj* yogas, enhanced and stabilized by the presence of 3rd and 12th lord Jupiter. Ms. Price's Moon is exalted in the 5th house, where it participates in *Chandra Mangala* yoga with 4th and 11th lord Mars, and once again we find an influential *graha* in *Rohini nakshatra*. The angular relationship between the Moon and Jupiter gives a fully-formed *Gaja Kesari* yoga, as Jupiter is accompanied in the 10th house from the Moon by benefics Venus and Mercury. The placement of 4th lord Mars and Jupiter in mutual *kendras*, with *lagna* lord Saturn in strength (*vargottama*) gives BPHS *Kahala* yoga. Located in the 11th, ascendant and 2nd house ruler Saturn has *sambandha* with the Moon and 11th lord Mars. Certainly, the strong 11th house influence carried by Leontyne Price's Saturn can be seen as contributing to the high level of success and international acclaim which she achieved. In both the *Parashara* and *Jaimini* systems of *Jyotish*, the ascendant of the chart is fortified by the aspect of its ruling planet.

Chapter 6, verses 14 and 15 of the *Jyotish* classic *Phaladeepika* narrates the structure and conference of benefits of the yoga known as *Maha Bhagya* ("great fortune"). This yoga is configured in a female chart when the native is born between sunset and sunrise while the ascendant, Sun and Moon occur in even signs. The chart of Leontyne Price meets each of these criteria, amplified by the even sign placement of ascendant ruler Saturn. The *Maha Bhagya* yoga is said to confer immense popularity in the context of a stellar reputation, generosity, longevity, and to render the native a "ruler of the earth."

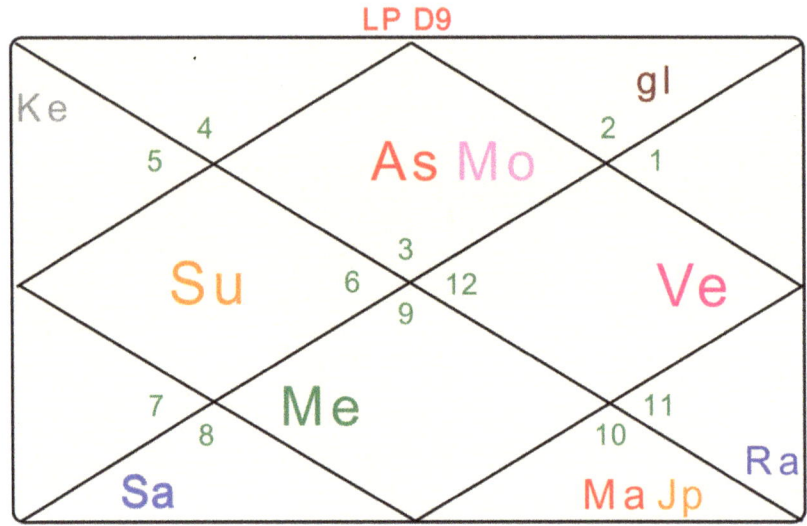

Creativity in the Vedic Astrology Chart

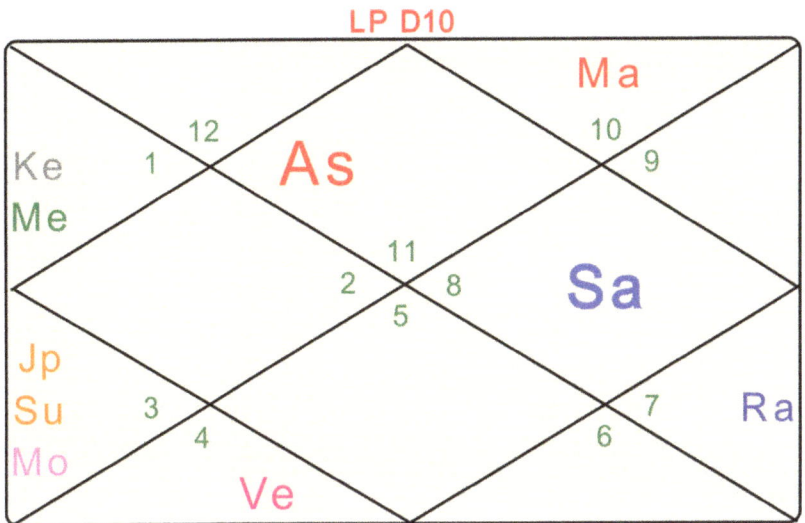

In the D-9 of Leontyne Price, 2nd lord Moon in the ascendant enjoys *sambandha* with chart lord Mercury while 5th and 12th lord Venus is exalted in the 10th house. The 2nd house of voice is activated by aspects from 10th lord Jupiter and exalted 11th lord Mars. In her D-10, we find 2nd lord Jupiter in the 5th house of creativity and aspecting the ascendant; Jupiter and Moon replicate the birth chart's *Kesari* yoga. It is notable that in both the D-9 and D-10 charts there is a connection between the 10th and 12th houses, emphasizing the theme of visual expression in the career of Leontyne Price. In addition to 12th lord Venus' placement in the 10th house of the D-9, the D-10 of Ms. Price features a 10 – 12 *Parivartana* yoga between Saturn and Mars. In the birth chart, 3rd and 12th lord Jupiter accompanies 10th lord Venus and aspects the 10th house. (The role of the 12th house in charts of visual and theatrical artistry will be explored more fully in the final chapter.)

Secondary to AK Sun's location in the sign of Capricorn at nearly 28 degrees, the KL of Leontyne Price's chart is the sign of Virgo. Even though neither house is occupied, the 2nd and 11th houses from the KL are strongly activated, as the 2nd is aspected by five *grahas* while the 11th gains the cumulative influence of six – all except Sun, *Rahu*, and *Ketu*. This pattern is consistent with the wealth and acclaim which Leontyne Price attained in her life, including the high degree of support (including financial support) from family, friends, and benefactors. It is observed that Ms. Price ran a 7-year Virgo *Chara dasha* from ages 14 to 21. This was the time during which Leontyne Price's musical skills became increasingly evident to her family and community, as she was encouraged to study music more formally. In her D-9, BK Moon in Gemini occupies the 10th house from AK Sun; the Sun, Moon, Mercury, and exalted AmK/5th lord Venus all enjoy mutual activation in *dwishwabhava* signs. Notice as well the location of PK Jupiter in the 5th house of education from Virgo; Jupiter's debilitation in the D-9 is cancelled by its association with exalted Mars, the aspect from dispositor Saturn, and the Moon's placement in the ascendant.

LP: Vimshottari

Start Date	Age	Dashas	
6/ 20/ 1933	6.4	Ma	Jp
5/ 27/ 1934	7.3	Ma	Sa
7/ 6/ 1935	8.4	Ma	Me
7/ 2/ 1936	9.4	Ma	Ke
11/ 28/ 1936	9.8	Ma	Ve
1/ 28/ 1938	11.0	Ma	Su
6/ 5/ 1938	11.3	Ma	Mo
1/ 4/ 1939	11.9	Ra	Ra
9/ 16/ 1941	14.6	Ra	Jp
2/ 10/ 1944	17.0	Ra	Sa
12/ 17/ 1946	19.8	Ra	Me
7/ 5/ 1949	22.4	Ra	Ke
7/ 24/ 1950	23.4	Ra	Ve
7/ 24/ 1953	26.4	Ra	Su
6/ 17/ 1954	27.3	Ra	Mo
12/ 17/ 1955	28.8	Ra	Ma
1/ 4/ 1957	29.9	Jp	Jp
2/ 22/ 1959	32.0	Jp	Sa
9/ 4/ 1961	34.6	Jp	Me
12/ 11/ 1963	36.8	Jp	Ke
11/ 16/ 1964	37.8	Jp	Ve
7/ 18/ 1967	40.4	Jp	Su
5/ 5/ 1968	41.2	Jp	Mo
9/ 4/ 1969	42.6	Jp	Ma
8/ 11/ 1970	43.5	Jp	Ra
1/ 4/ 1973	45.9	Sa	Sa

LP: Chara

Start Date	Age	Dashas
2/ 10/ 1931	4.0	Sco
2/ 9/ 1937	10.0	Libr
2/ 9/ 1941	14.0	Virg
2/ 10/ 1948	21.0	Leo
2/ 10/ 1955	28.0	Can
2/ 9/ 1957	30.0	Gem
2/ 10/ 1965	38.0	Tau
2/ 10/ 1974	47.0	Ari
2/ 10/ 1975	48.0	Pis
2/ 10/ 1976	49.0	Aqu
2/ 10/ 1979	52.0	Cap
2/ 10/ 1981	54.0	Sag

From July of 1950 to July 1953, between ages 23 and 26, Leontyne Price ran her *Vimshottari Rahu – Venus* period. Over the course of those three years, Ms. Price made her first appearances in the operas of Strauss and Verdi and sang the role of Bess. *Rahu*'s primary influences are 2nd house occupants Mercury and Jupiter. *Rahu* attains *swakshetra* status in the 9th house of her D-9 and is placed in the 9th house of her D-10 as well. Sub-period ruler Venus is the birth chart's yoga *karaka* 5th and 10th lord, and a participant in several yogas. Venus is exalted in the 10th house of Ms. Price's D-9, and as the 9th lord of her D-10, has *sambandha* opposite exalted 10th house ruler Mars. In her D-10, the placement of sub-period lord Venus in the 10th house from *Maha dasha* lord *Rahu* will also contribute to Leontyne Price's career elevation during this time.

Leontyne Price's 3-year *Rahu – Venus* period occurs in the context of her Leo *Jaimini Chara dasha*, which ran from ages 21 to 28, spanning the years 1948 to 1955. The 7-year Leo period included Ms. Price's college graduation and subsequent Julliard matriculation, followed by her successful entry into the world of high opera. In the birth chart, AK Sun aspects its own sign of Leo as well as the 10th

LP: Chara

Start Date			Age	Dashas	
3/	12/	1952	25.1	Leo	Ari
10/	11/	1952	25.7	Leo	Tau
5/	12/	1953	26.2	Leo	Gem
12/	11/	1953	26.8	Leo	Can
7/	12/	1954	27.4	Leo	Leo
2/	10/	1955	28.0	Can	Gem
4/	12/	1955	28.2	Can	Tau
6/	12/	1955	28.3	Can	Ari
8/	12/	1955	28.5	Can	Pis
10/	11/	1955	28.7	Can	Aqu
12/	11/	1955	28.8	Can	Cap
2/	10/	1956	29.0	Can	Sag
4/	11/	1956	29.2	Can	Sco
6/	11/	1956	29.3	Can	Libr
8/	11/	1956	29.5	Can	Virg
10/	11/	1956	29.7	Can	Leo
12/	11/	1956	29.8	Can	Can
2/	9/	1957	30.0	Gem	Tau
10/	11/	1957	30.7	Gem	Ari
6/	11/	1958	31.3	Gem	Pis
2/	10/	1959	32.0	Gem	Aqu
10/	11/	1959	32.7	Gem	Cap
6/	11/	1960	33.3	Gem	Sag
2/	9/	1961	34.0	Gem	Sco
10/	11/	1961	34.7	Gem	Libr
6/	11/	1962	35.3	Gem	Virg

and occupants exalted BK Moon and directionally strong DK Mars, while natal 5th lord/AmK Venus, PK Jupiter and Mercury occupy the 7th house of independent career from Leo. In her D-10, the 10th house from Leo is aspected by its owner Venus, exalted DK Mars, and *Rahu*, while the 11th house of awards and popular recognition has Jupiter, Sun, and the Moon. In the D-9 of Leontyne Price, the 10th house from Leo is activated by Jupiter and exalted Mars, while the 11th house is reinforced by the presence of the Moon and aspects from Mercury, exalted AmK Venus, and AK Sun.

Our analysis of the chart of opera star Leontyne Price would not be complete without a brief consideration of January 27th, 1961, the date of Ms. Price's triumphant debut with the New York Metropolitan Opera as Leonora in Verdi's *Il Trovatore*. Having begun her *Vimshottari* Jupiter major period in early 1957, the onset of her 2 ½ year Saturn sub-period had taken place in February of 1959, and it was during her Jupiter – Saturn period that her Metropolitan Opera debut occurred. It can be taken as a basic astrological principle that the angular or *kendra* houses represent themes of stability, support, recognition, and achievement. As sub-period ruler but more importantly as the chart's ascendant lord, Saturn is stabilized by the presence of five *grahas* in *kendra* houses from its 11th house placement, four of which aspect the 10th house from Saturn. Saturn's strength persists in the D-9 and D-10 charts secondary to its *vargottama* status in both, reinforced by its participation in *Parivartana* yoga with exalted dispositor Mars. In Ms. Price's D-10, the *Parivartana* yoga occurs between houses 10 and 12, with 12th lord Saturn in the 10th house and exalted 10th lord Mars in the 12th in reception of Saturn's 3rd aspect. This arrangement constitutes a strong *sambandha* relationship between the houses of career (10) and theatrical performance (12) and helps to explain the timing of a career pinnacle, recalled by Ms. Price as "a height that is practically indescribable … a glorious experience." (Kennedy Center Honors Interview with Robert Jacobson, *Opera News*, 1981).

An overwhelming response such as that which occurred to Leontyne Price's Metropolitan Opera debut in January of 1961 would necessarily be reflected through activation of the 11th house of gains, awards, and popular adulation. Concurrent with Ms. Price's *Vimshottari* Saturn sub-period, her *Jaimini Chara dasha* in early 1961 is Gemini – Sagittarius. From the sign of Gemini, the 11th house is enlivened by aspects from the Mercury/PK Jupiter/AmK Venus combination, as well as that from MK Saturn. Eleventh house activation is even more striking from sub period sign Sagittarius; in addition to the three natural benefics, the 11th is aspected by exalted BK Moon and DK Mars. Notice that the sign of Libra is one of two signs in the chart (Cancer is the other) which is activated by its own lord as well as by all the natural benefics. Leontyne Price's Gemini rising D-9 has natal and local 5th lord/AmK Venus in exaltation in the 10th house and in mutual aspect with AK Sun, D-9 ascendant ruler Mercury and BK Moon. As the reflection sign to Gemini, the Sagittarius sub-period serves to reinforce the inherent strength of her D-9, with AK Sun's placement in the 10th house. In her D-10, PK Jupiter, AK Sun, and BK Moon combine in the sign of Gemini as sign ruler Mercury sits 11 houses away in Aries. Although Leontyne Price had come to the attention of Metropolitan Opera Director Rudolf Bing as early as 1952, Ms. Price declined invitations to join the Met until 1960, with the onset of her very capable *Jaimini* Sagittarius sub-period, and in the latter segment of her *Vimshottari* Saturn sub-period. The *New York Times* review of Leontyne Price's Metropolitan Opera debut, written by the *Times'* esteemed music critic Harold C. Schonberg, stated, "Her voice, warm and luscious, has enough volume to fill the house with ease, and she has a good technique to back up the voice itself. She even took the trills as written, and nothing in the part as Verdi wrote it gave her the least bit of trouble … Voice is what counts, and voice is what Miss Price has." (Harold C. Schonberg, *New York Times*, January 28th, 1961).

The final chart for our consideration in the music section will be that of Wolfgang Amadeus Mozart (January 27, 1756, Salzburg, Austria, 8:00 p.m., AA). Mozart is universally acclaimed as a peerless musical genius and prodigy, having begun to play the clavier at four years old and composing short pieces on the instrument by the age of five. By age seven Mozart had taught himself to play the violin. Although he did not live to see his 36th birthday, Mozart's legacy is unparalleled in the history of music. Mozart created more than 800 musical works in virtually every genre of his time, including opera, string quartets and concertos, choral pieces and symphonies, the first of which he composed at the age of eight. Over the course of extensive tours of Europe, Mozart performed as a child prodigy in many imperial courts of the time. Known as one of the most prolific composers of all time, the music of Mozart possesses qualities of melodic beauty, elegance, and rich harmonic texture. The composer Franz Joseph Haydn said of Mozart, "posterity will not see such a talent again in 100 years."

Creativity in the Vedic Astrology Chart

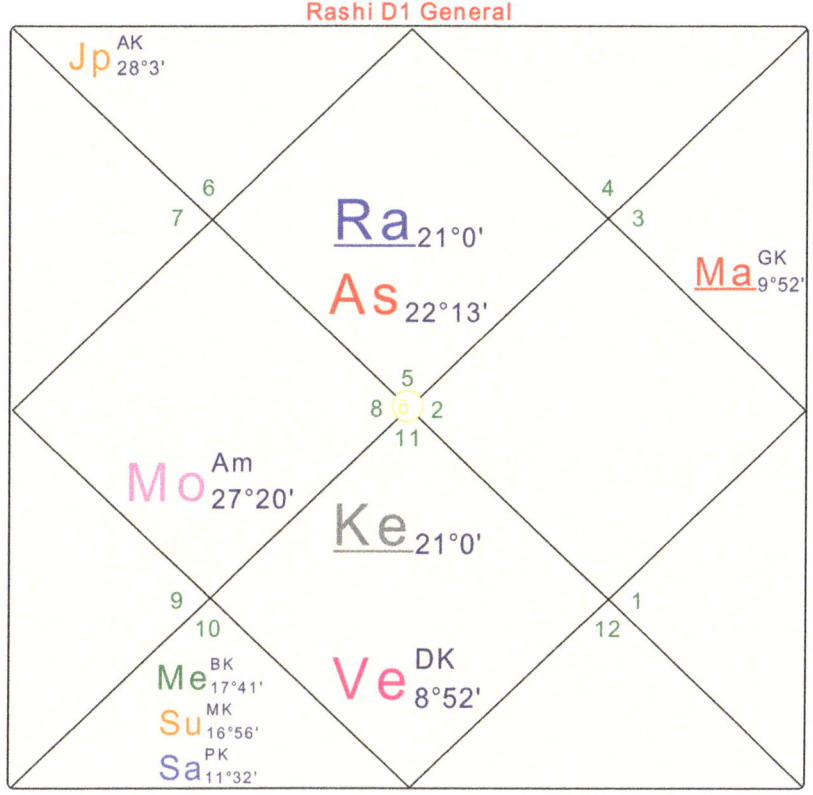

Rashi D1 General

			Ma GK 9°52'
Ke 21°0' Ve DK 8°52'	Ö Wolfgang Amadeus Mozart Tue. 1/27/1756 20:00:00 Salzburg, AUS		
Me BK 17°41' Su MK 16°56' Sa PK 11°32'			Ra 21°0' As 22°13'
	Mo Am 27°20'		Jp AK 28°3'

Among the most compelling features of the chart of Wolfgang Amadeus Mozart is the presence of three planets -- ascendant lord Sun, Mercury, and Saturn -- in the *nakshatra* of *Shravana*. In several previous charts, including those of Duke Ellington, Artur Rubinstein, Leontyne Price, and Eva Cassidy, we have seen the musical and creative gifts that *Shravana nakshatra* is capable of conferring, especially an internal sense of melody, and this is clearly also the case in the chart of Mozart. The Sun and Mercury gain strength as they are disposited in the 6th house by the presence of *swakshetra* 6th and 7th lord Saturn. The 6th house would not normally be directly associated with music, musical creativity, and the creative process in general, but notice that this combination occurs in the 3rd house from the Moon and is aspected by an especially potent 5th lord Jupiter. At 28 degrees of Virgo, Jupiter achieves *vargottama* status in the D-9. Notice that

Jupiter also rules the 5th house from the Moon, and from its location in the 2nd house, throws its 7th aspect to that house (8th from natal *lagna*) which happens to be the 3rd from ascendant lord Sun. Jupiter's 9th aspect activates the 10th house of career and 5th from the Sun. As 9th lord of highest *dharma* as well as *Chandra lagna* lord, Mars also plays a crucial role in the chart, aspecting both 5th house and lord Jupiter as well as the 3 planets in the 6th house. Secondary to Mozart's legendary ability to compose at a rapid pace, Mars' activation of the 5th house and its lord is no doubt instrumental in this regard. The location of the ascendant degree and *Rahu* in the nakshatra of *Purva Phalguni* becomes an "embarrassment of riches" in the chart of Mozart, as well as the aspect of 3rd and 10th lord Venus to the ascendant and *Rahu* therein. Mozart's debilitated Moon achieves *Neecha Bhanga Raj* yoga secondary to its *dig bala* placement in the 4th, and that of Venus in *kendra* locations from the Moon and the ascendant.

The chart's potential for creativity is enhanced by a *Jaimini Maha Raj* yoga, in which (as described in BPHS chapter 39 verses 6 -- 7) houses 1 and 5 from the KL are occupied by the AK and PK, whether the two *grahas* combine in either house or reside separately in each. In Mozart's chart, this yoga becomes especially auspicious, as both 1st and 5th houses from his Virgo KL contain planets in strength. The sign of Virgo holds *vargottama* AK and natal 5th lord Jupiter as the 5th house contains *swakshetra* PK Saturn. Saturn is joined in the 5th by KL lord/BK Mercury, and natal ascendant lord Sun. There is additional activation of that 5th house as the three occupying *grahas* enjoy mutual aspect with AmK Moon.

In *Vimshottari dasha*, Mozart began his *Ketu* major period shortly before he began to play the clavier and compose short musical pieces. The influences on *Ketu* all reflect musical and creative potential: 3rd and 10th lord Venus, dispositor Saturn as lord of 3rd house from the Moon, and *nakshatra* dispositor 5th lord Jupiter. In both his D-9 and D-10, *Ketu* forms a *Chaya Graha Raj* yoga in the 7th house of the chart. In the D-9 the yoga occurs with 4th and 5th lord Saturn as *Ketu's* dispositor Mars inhabits the 3rd. In the D-10 *Ketu* joins 9th lord Mars in the 7th.

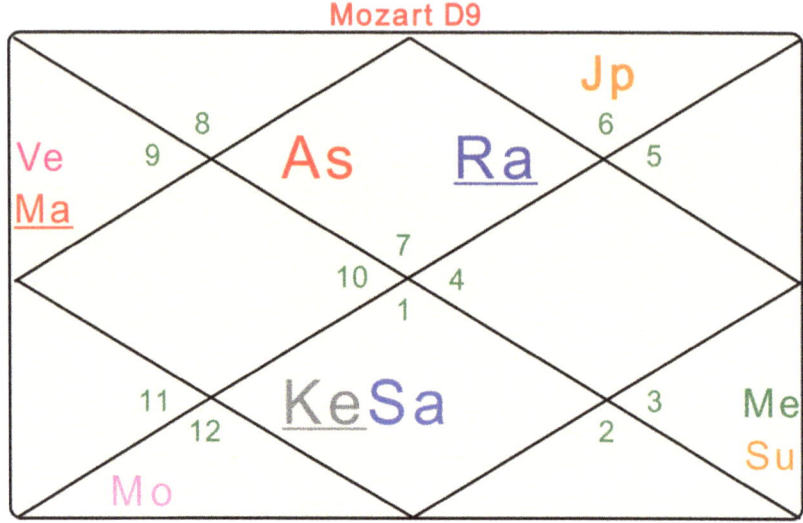

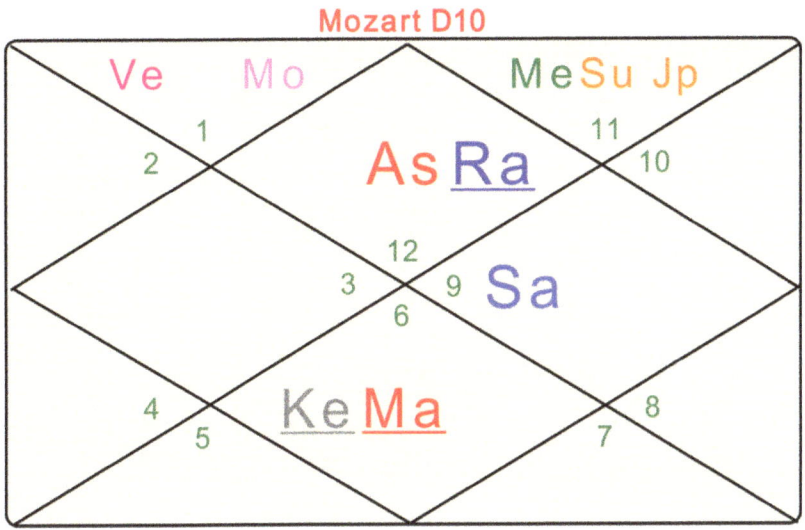

WAM: Vimshottari

Start Date	Age	Dashas	
1/ 13/ 1761	5.0	Ke	Su
5/ 21/ 1761	5.3	Ke	Mo
12/ 20/ 1761	5.9	Ke	Ma
5/ 18/ 1762	6.3	Ke	Ra
6/ 5/ 1763	7.4	Ke	Jp
5/ 11/ 1764	8.3	Ke	Sa
6/ 20/ 1765	9.4	Ke	Me
6/ 17/ 1766	**10.4**	**Ve**	**Ve**
10/ 17/ 1769	13.7	Ve	Su
10/ 17/ 1770	14.7	Ve	Mo
6/ 17/ 1772	16.4	Ve	Ma
8/ 17/ 1773	17.6	Ve	Ra
8/ 17/ 1776	20.6	Ve	Jp
4/ 18/ 1779	23.2	Ve	Sa
6/ 17/ 1782	26.4	Ve	Me
4/ 17/ 1785	29.2	Ve	Ke
6/ 17/ 1786	**30.4**	**Su**	**Su**
10/ 5/ 1786	30.7	Su	Mo
4/ 6/ 1787	31.2	Su	Ma
8/ 11/ 1787	31.5	Su	Ra
7/ 5/ 1788	32.4	Su	Jp
4/ 23/ 1789	33.2	Su	Sa
4/ 5/ 1790	34.2	Su	Me
2/ 10/ 1791	35.0	Su	Ke
6/ 18/ 1791	35.4	Su	Ve
6/ 17/ 1792	**36.4**	**Mo**	**Mo**

WAM: Chara		
Start Date	Age	Dashas
1/ 27/ 1756	-0.0	Leo
1/ 27/ 1763	7.0	Virg
1/ 27/ 1771	15.0	Libr
1/ 27/ 1775	19.0	Sco
1/ 27/ 1778	22.0	Sag
1/ 27/ 1787	31.0	Cap
1/ 27/ 1799	43.0	Aqu
1/ 28/ 1800	44.0	Pis
1/ 28/ 1806	50.0	Ari
1/ 29/ 1808	52.0	Tau
1/ 28/ 1817	61.0	Gem
1/ 29/ 1824	68.0	Can

The timing of young Mozart's rise to acclaim and public notoriety coincides with the onset of his Virgo *Jaimini Chara dasha*, which began at the age of seven. The sign of Virgo activates Mozart's *Maha Raj* yoga described above; the 3rd and 5th houses from Virgo are strongly featured. Note as well the presence of 6 *grahas* in *dwishwabhava* signs in Mozart's D-9, including all the natural benefic planets. Virgo is tenanted by his *vargottama* AK Jupiter and is dispositied by 10th lord Mercury in strength in its own sign of Gemini. Although PK Saturn is not in a dual sign in Mozart's D-9, Saturn does aspect the sign of Scorpio, the 3rd house from Virgo.

This concludes our first section, dedicated to the theme of creativity in the realm of music. In summary, musical proficiency will typically be seen through activation of the 3rd house of the chart and its lord. As the house of skills, the 3rd is the house of the ears and sense of hearing, as well as that of the hands and manual dexterity. When there is some connection between the 3rd house and the 5th house of creative inspiration in the chart, by occupation, aspect, *sambandha*, and/or exchange of lords, including as seen from the Moon, artistic and musical innovation is more likely to manifest in the life of the chart's owner. A strong and influential 5th house ruler is seen in the charts of composers George Gershwin, Duke Ellington, Niccolo Paganini and Wolfgang Amadeus Mozart, as well as songwriters Roy Orbison, Stevie Nicks, Keith Richards, and Brian Wilson. The prevalence of musical *nakshatras* like *Shravana*, *Dhanishtha* and *Swati* is noted, along with creative *nakshatras* of *Krittika, Rohini, Punarvasu, Purva Phalguni, Hasta, Chitra, Shatabhisha*, and *Revati*. Exceptional instrumental prowess is seen by the occupation of multiple planets in weapon *drekkanas* in the charts of George Gershwin, Glen Campbell, Duke Ellington, Stevie Nicks, Artur Rubinstein, Andrea Bocelli, Keith Richards, Eva Cassidy, and Niccolo Paganini. As we conclude our section on the charts of musicians, the reader is encouraged to bring words to life, and to discover musical enjoyment and inspiration by listening to any of the works of the musicians whose lives and charts we have analyzed.

Let us now proceed to the next section, which is a consideration of the charts of dancers and the ways in which the artistry, beauty and elegance of dance are seen to manifest in the Vedic astrology chart.

Chapter 3

Dance

This section, devoted to the theme of dance in the Vedic astrology chart, begins, most appropriately, with the chart of Martha Graham (May 11, 1894, Pittsburgh, PA, 6:01 a.m., A). Martha Graham is considered the foremost dancer, choreographer and teacher of her era, and the leading exponent of modern dance in her time.

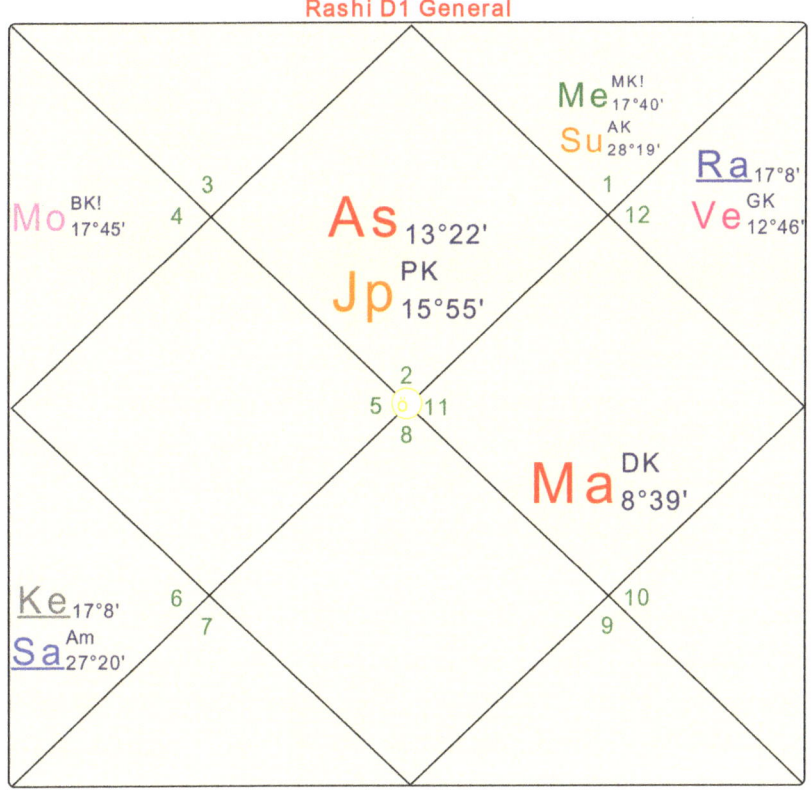

Rashi D1 General

Ve GK 12°46' Ra 17°8'	Me MK! 17°40' Su AK 28°19'	As 13°22' Jp PK 15°55'	
Ma DK 8°39'	\multicolumn{2}{c	}{**Martha Graham** Fri. 5/11/1894 6:01:00 Pittsburgh, PA}	Mo BK! 17°45'
			Sa Am 27°20' Ke 17°8'

Ms. Graham first became enthralled with dance at the age of ten, and began formal study of dance at age nineteen, but (due to her father's objections) did not begin to dance professionally until her early twenties. Nevertheless, Martha Graham's career lasted for more than 70 years, during which she actively performed as a dancer until the age of seventy-five. In 1926, she founded her own dance company as well as the Martha Graham School of Dance, both of which are still in existence. Among numerous teaching roles, Martha Graham taught dance at the Eastman School of Music in Rochester NY, then at Bennington College in Vermont. Ms. Graham is credited with having created and choreographed 181 ballets in her career. In 1938, Martha Graham became the first dancer to perform at the White House, and in 1976 was the first dancer to be awarded the

Presidential Medal of Honor. Martha Graham was honored by the Kennedy Center in 1978, and in 1998 was named by *Time* magazine as the "Dancer of the Century." (Please see www.marthagraham.org for in-depth appreciation of the life and career of Martha Graham.)

As mentioned in the introductory chapter, activation of the 11th house will be seen as a primary feature in the charts of dancers and choreographers. Although the 3rd house can be regarded as the house of general artistic expression, the 11th house will more specifically apply to the art of dance. As the house of the calves, shins, and ankles, the 11th is the house of highest *dharma* (9th) from the 3rd house of non-specific artistry and is the reflection house from the 5th house of creativity.

The chart of Martha Graham offers strong 11th house emphasis. There is a *Parivartana* yoga between houses 1 and 11, with ascendant lord Venus in its sign of exaltation in the 11th. As we saw repeatedly in musical charts, creative *Rohini nakshatra* is again in evidence here, as the rising *nakshatra* as well as that occupied by 11th lord Jupiter. Because of the Moon's placement in the 3rd house, Venus becomes lord of the 11th house from Moon as Jupiter locates in that 11th house. 10th lord Saturn in the 5th house of creative inspiration enjoys 11th lord Jupiter's one-way aspect and has 2-way *sambandha* with ascendant lord Venus. Saturn's location in the *nakshatra* of *Chitra* plays a role in conferring Ms. Graham a sense of artistic design and skill as a choreographer; we also attribute at least some of Martha Graham's innovation in the realm of dance, and especially modern dance, to Saturn's participation in a *Chaya Graha Raj* yoga. Saturn in the 5th is also aspected by 7th and 12th lord Mars. In keeping with the theme of dance, Mars rules the 12th house of the feet, but is also lord of the 5th house from the Moon. Mars' location in a *pakshi* or bird *drekkana* will grace the planet with lightness and movement. In Martha Graham's Taurus rising D-9, *vargottama* 11th lord Jupiter remains in the ascendant and aspects *vargottama* 10th lord Saturn and 5th lord Mercury in Mercury's exaltation sign of Virgo. The 11th house of the D-9 is further activated by an aspect from 12th lord Mars. A similar theme follows in her *vargottama* D-10, where Jupiter repeats as 11th lord and aspects the 10th house and its *swakshetra* lord Saturn in *Shasha* yoga. Ascendant lord Venus repeats its exaltation status in the 11th house of the D-10 opposite exalted 5th lord Mercury.

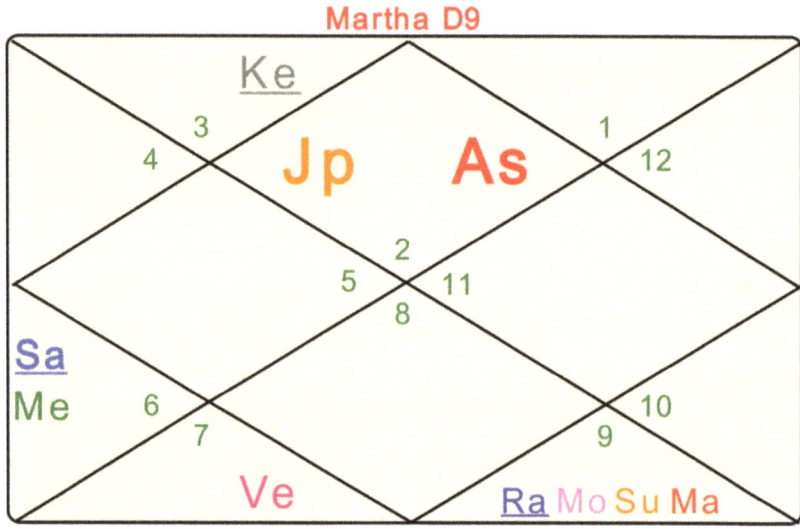

Creativity in the Vedic Astrology Chart

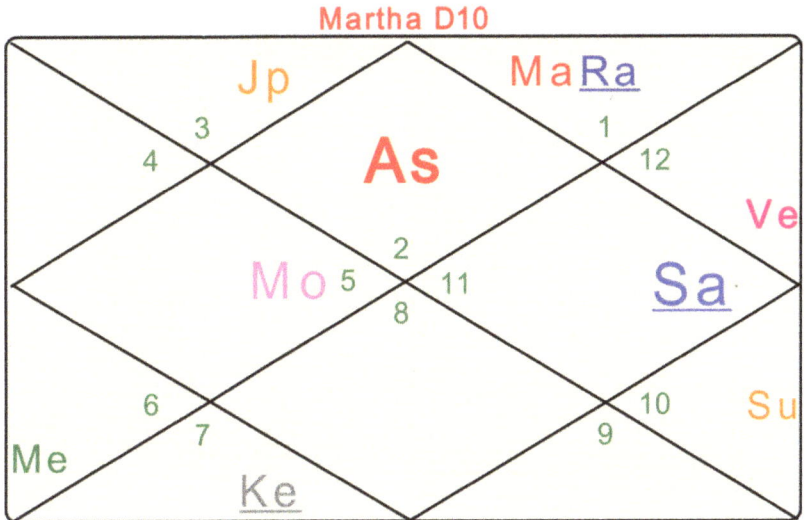

MG: Vimshottari

Start Date			Age	Dashas	
4/	10/	1907	12.9	Me	Sa
12/	18/	1909	15.6	Ke	Ke
5/	16/	1910	16.0	Ke	Ve
7/	16/	1911	17.2	Ke	Su
11/	21/	1911	17.5	Ke	Mo
6/	21/	1912	18.1	Ke	Ma
11/	17/	1912	18.5	Ke	Ra
12/	6/	1913	19.6	Ke	Jp
11/	12/	1914	20.5	Ke	Sa
12/	22/	1915	21.6	Ke	Me
12/	18/	1916	22.6	Ve	Ve
4/	18/	1920	25.9	Ve	Su
4/	18/	1921	26.9	Ve	Mo
12/	18/	1922	28.6	Ve	Ma
2/	17/	1924	29.8	Ve	Ra
2/	17/	1927	32.8	Ve	Jp
10/	18/	1929	35.4	Ve	Sa
12/	18/	1932	38.6	Ve	Me
10/	19/	1935	41.4	Ve	Ke
12/	18/	1936	42.6	Su	Su
4/	6/	1937	42.9	Su	Mo
10/	6/	1937	43.4	Su	Ma
2/	11/	1938	43.8	Su	Ra
1/	6/	1939	44.7	Su	Jp
10/	25/	1939	45.5	Su	Sa
10/	6/	1940	46.4	Su	Me
8/	12/	1941	47.3	Su	Ke
12/	18/	1941	47.6	Su	Ve
12/	18/	1942	48.6	Mo	Mo
10/	19/	1943	49.4	Mo	Ma
5/	19/	1944	50.0	Mo	Ra
11/	18/	1945	51.5	Mo	Jp
3/	20/	1947	52.9	Mo	Sa
10/	18/	1948	54.4	Mo	Me
3/	19/	1950	55.9	Mo	Ke
10/	19/	1950	56.4	Mo	Ve
6/	18/	1952	58.1	Mo	Su
12/	18/	1952	58.6	Ma	Ma
5/	16/	1953	59.0	Ma	Ra
6/	4/	1954	60.1	Ma	Jp
5/	11/	1955	61.0	Ma	Sa

MG: Chara

Start Date			Age	Dashas
5/	11/	1894	-0.0	Tau
5/	11/	1904	10.0	Ari
5/	12/	1914	20.0	Pis
5/	11/	1924	30.0	Aqu
5/	12/	1929	35.0	Cap
5/	12/	1933	39.0	Sag
5/	12/	1938	44.0	Sco
5/	12/	1948	54.0	Libr
5/	12/	1953	59.0	Virg
5/	12/	1958	64.0	Leo
5/	12/	1962	68.0	Can
5/	12/	1974	80.0	Gem

In 1914 at the age of twenty, Martha Graham began her 10-year Pisces *Jaimini Chara dasha*. As the 11th house of the chart, the sign of Pisces holds exalted Venus in *sambandha* with *vargottama* AmK Saturn in the role of lord of the 11th house from Pisces. The 5th house of creativity has *swakshetra* BK Moon in mutual aspect with PK Jupiter and DK Mars. In Ms. Graham's D-10, ascendant lord Venus achieves *vargottama* status and repeats its location in the 11th house of dance. In both D-1 and D-9, *vargottama* (in D-9) PK Jupiter resides in the 3rd and aspects the 5th and 11th houses from Pisces. In Ms. Graham's D-9, the *dwishwabhava* signs become activated by the presence of AK Sun, DK Mars, and BK Moon in Sagittarius in the 10th house from Pisces, as well as by AmK Saturn and natal/local exalted 5th lord Mercury. In her D-10 Venus has *Jaimini sambandha* with the two other natural benefics. The promise of career achievement during periods and/or sub-periods of *dwishwabhava* signs is enhanced by the aspects of PK Jupiter and 5th lord/AmK Mercury to each of their respective signs in the D-10, as well the yoga-forming combined influence of the two *grahas*. Martha Graham's Sagittarius KL confirms a life committed to the art of dance, as 11th lord Venus and 3rd lord AmK Saturn activate the *dwishwabhava* houses; exalted AK Sun and natal 5th lord Mercury occupy the 5th house while the 11th is aspected by PK Jupiter and DK Mars. In addition to the occupation of Sagittarius by the Sun, Moon, and Mars, (and *Rahu*), *swakshetra* Venus tenants the 11th house from KL Sagittarius in Ms. Graham's D-9 and enjoys mutual aspect with PK Jupiter.

Martha Graham's 20-year *Vimshottari* Venus period began two years after the onset of her Pisces *dasha*. In addition to *lagna* lord Venus' strength in her D-1 and D-10 charts, Venus in Libra in the 6th house is the *swakshetra* ascendant lord of her D-9 and dispositor of 11th lord Jupiter. The simultaneity of the two timing systems during her twenties proved foundational and served to establish Martha Graham's pre-eminence in the field of dance for the rest of her life.

Creativity in the Vedic Astrology Chart

Our next dance chart will be that of Michael Ryan Flatley (July 16, 1958, Chicago, IL, 11:55 a.m., A). Michael Flatley is the world-renowned dancer and choreographer who is best known for the creation and production of shows *Lord of the Dance*, *Riverdance*, and *Feet of Flames*. Michael Flatley began pursuing the study of dance at age eleven and at age seventeen won the World Irish Dance Championship for his age category. Michael Flatley is particularly recognized for his tap-dancing speed and prowess; his taps have been timed at 30 per second, a world record. Michael Flatley's shows have been performed in as many as 60 different countries around the world, before an estimated 60 million people. In 1988 Michael Flatley received a National Heritage Fellowship, and in 2001 the Irish Dancing Commission awarded Michael Flatley its first Honorary Fellowship.

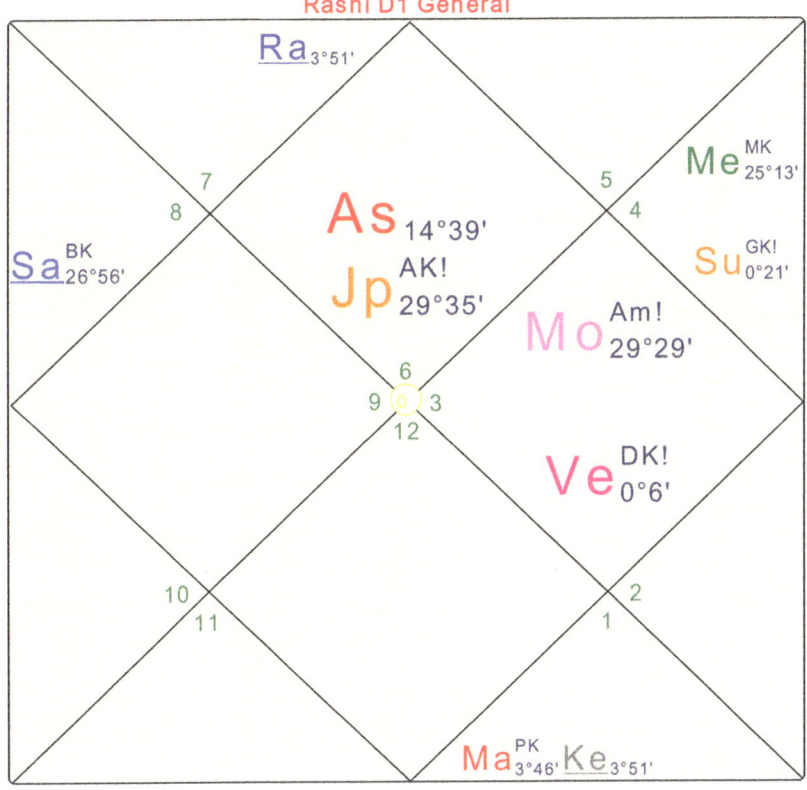

Rashi D1 General

	Ma PK 3°46' Ke 3°51'		Ve DK! 0°6' Mo Am! 29°29'
			Su GK! 0°21' Me MK 25°13'
	ö Michael Ryan Flatley Wed. 7/16/1958 11:55:00 Chicago, IL		
	Sa BK 26°56'	Ra 3°51'	Jp AK! 29°35' As 14°39'

Michael Ryan Flatley's Virgo rising chart locates ascendant and 10th lord Mercury in the 11th house. Mercury participates in a *Parivartana* yoga with 11th lord Moon, who joins 9th lord Venus in the 10th house. *Swakshetra* 3rd lord Mars serves as an activating force in this chart as Mars aspects the 11th house and occupants Mercury and 12th lord (feet) Sun; notice also that Mars resides in the 11th house from the Moon. At 3 degrees Mars is placed in the *laghu* (quick and light) *nakshatra* of *Ashwini*, so Mars' extensive 11th house influence, including that on 12th lord Sun, is responsible for the speed and agility of Michael Flatley's footwork. From the 8th house Mars aspects its own 3rd house and occupant 5th lord Saturn. The chart contains an especially potent *Kesari* yoga, formed by 4th and 7th lord Jupiter in the ascendant and 11th lord Moon in the 10th house. This yoga takes on additional strength secondary to the extremely tight proximity of the two planets' longitudes, as they sit within six minutes of each other.

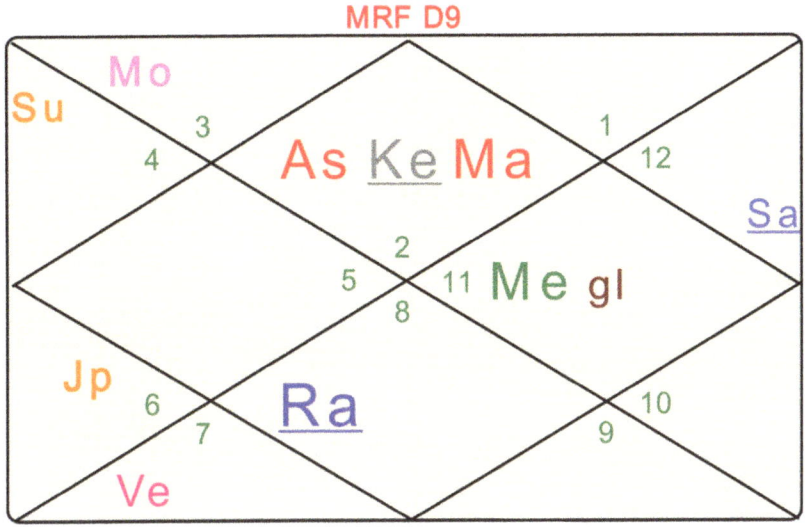

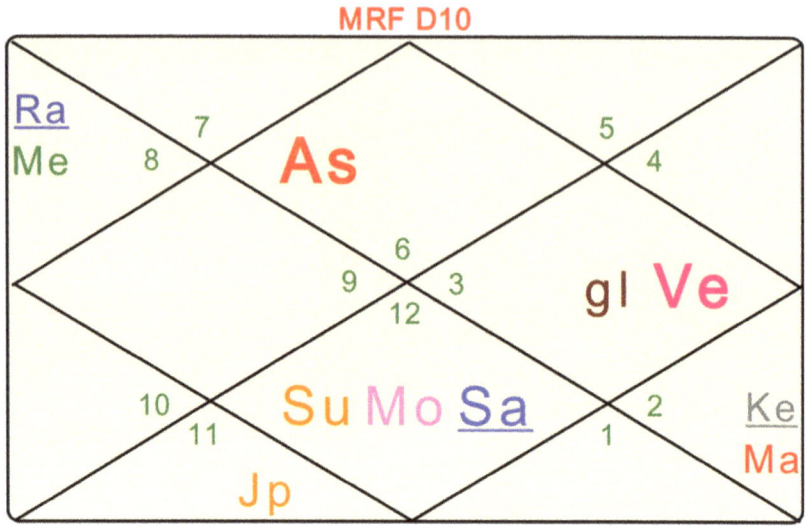

MRF: Vimshottari

Start Date	Age	Dashas	
12/ 18/ 1969	11.4	Sa	Ve
2/ 17/ 1973	14.6	Sa	Su
1/ 30/ 1974	15.5	Sa	Mo
8/ 31/ 1975	17.1	Sa	Ma
10/ 9/ 1976	18.2	Sa	Ra
8/ 16/ 1979	21.1	Sa	Jp
2/ 26/ 1982	23.6	Me	Me
7/ 25/ 1984	26.0	Me	Ke
7/ 22/ 1985	27.0	Me	Ve
5/ 22/ 1988	29.8	Me	Su
3/ 28/ 1989	30.7	Me	Mo
8/ 28/ 1990	32.1	Me	Ma
8/ 25/ 1991	33.1	Me	Ra
3/ 13/ 1994	35.7	Me	Jp
6/ 18/ 1996	37.9	Me	Sa
2/ 26/ 1999	40.6	Ke	Ke
7/ 26/ 1999	41.0	Ke	Ve
9/ 24/ 2000	42.2	Ke	Su
1/ 30/ 2001	42.5	Ke	Mo
8/ 31/ 2001	43.1	Ke	Ma
1/ 27/ 2002	43.5	Ke	Ra
2/ 14/ 2003	44.6	Ke	Jp
1/ 21/ 2004	45.5	Ke	Sa
3/ 1/ 2005	46.6	Ke	Me
2/ 26/ 2006	47.6	Ve	Ve
6/ 28/ 2009	50.9	Ve	Su

MRF: Chara		
Start Date	Age	Dashas
7/ 16/ 1958	-0.0	Virg
7/ 16/ 1960	2.0	Libr
7/ 16/ 1968	10.0	Sco
7/ 16/ 1973	15.0	Sag
7/ 16/ 1982	24.0	Cap
7/ 16/ 1984	26.0	Aqu
7/ 16/ 1987	29.0	Pis
7/ 16/ 1993	35.0	Ari
7/ 16/ 2005	47.0	Tau
7/ 16/ 2006	48.0	Gem
7/ 17/ 2007	49.0	Can
7/ 16/ 2008	50.0	Leo

Michael Flatley won his World Irish Dance Championship and saw his dance career begin to flourish during his Sagittarius *Jaimini Chara dasha*. From the sign of Sagittarius, AK Jupiter in the 10th house occupies the chart's KL while AmK Moon joins DK Venus in the 7th. Secondary to their *vargottama* status, Jupiter and the Moon continue to aspect the *kendra* houses from Sagittarius in the D-9, in addition to BK Saturn, as the 11th house has *swakshetra* DK Venus in *Jaimini sambandha* with Mercury and PK Mars. In the D-10 AK Jupiter, PK Mars, and *Ketu* aspect the 11th from Sagittarius; we again find strong activation of the *dwishwabhava* signs by the Sun, AmK Moon, natal/local 5th lord/BK Saturn and DK Venus. Michael Flatley's chart is elevated by the presence of several *Jaimini Raj* yogas; these include activation of the *dwishwabhava* signs (in both D-1 and D-10) by Venus and the Moon. The placement of both AK and AmK in *kendra* houses in the D-1 meets *Raj* yoga criteria described in BPHS chapter 40 verse 6; verse 8 criteria are met by AK Jupiter's location in the 1st house in aspect with 9th lord Venus.

Beginning at age twenty-three, Michael Flatley ran his successful 17-year *Vimshottari* Mercury period. In addition to Mercury's status as 10th lord in the 11th house in the birth chart, 5th lord Mercury occupies the 10th house in the D-9. Mercury's dispositor 10th lord Saturn in the 11th has sambandha with 11th lord Jupiter in the 5th house. In his *vargottama* D-10, ascendant and 10th lord Mercury in the 3rd house of artistry is opposed by 3rd lord Mars. The 11th house from Mercury, the chart's ascendant, is aspected by 11th lord Moon, 12th lord Sun and 5th and 6th lord Saturn from the 7th house.

The following chart is that of Alessandra Ferri (May 6, 1963, Milan, Italy, 1:15 p.m., AA), Italian ballet dancer who performed with the Royal Ballet, American Ballet Theatre, and La Scala Theatre Ballet. Allesandra Ferri became principal dancer with both the Royal Ballet and American Ballet, where she danced under the direction of Mikhail Baryshnikov. She was awarded the title of *prima ballerina assoluta* during her association with La Scala. Theatrical magazine *Playbill* offered this description in honor of Alessandra Ferri's final performance with American Ballet Theatre in 2007: "Ethereal, sensual, soulful and blessed with a flawless technique, she has long been one of American Ballet Theatre's brightest lights, creating magic in roles as demanding as Giselle, Manon, and Juliet, and in ballets as diverse as Jerome Robbins's *Other Dances* and Antony Tudor's *Pillar of Fire*." (Valerie Gladstone, *Playbill*, June 11, 2007).

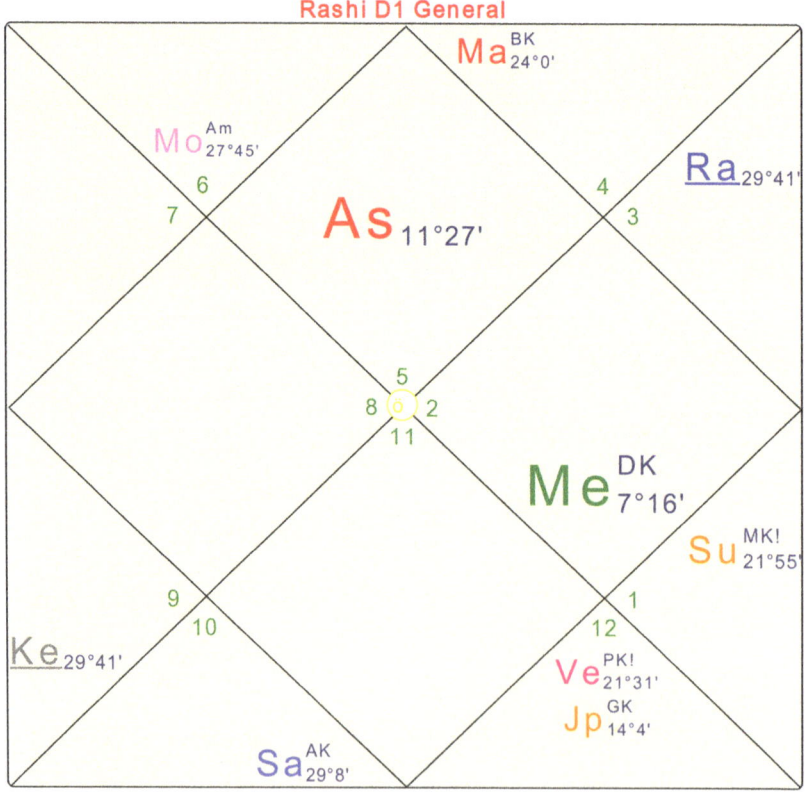

Jp GK 14°4' Ve PK! 21°31'	Su MK! 21°55'	Me DK 7°16'	Ra 29°41'
Sa AK 29°8'	Rashi D1 General ö Allessandra Ferri Mon. 5/6/1963 13:15:00 Milan, IT		Ma BK 24°0' As 11°27'
Ke 29°41'			Mo Am 27°45'

The chart of Alessandra Ferri is straightforward in its activation of the 11th house, as 11th lord Mercury occupies the 10th house of career in Venus-owned Taurus in the physically vital *nakshatra* of *Krittika*. The potential for strength and essential vitality is reinforced by the placement of ascendant lord Sun in its exaltation sign in the 9th house, as the Sun is surrounded by natural benefics, forming an unblemished *Shubha Ubhayachari* yoga. Mercury's dispositor 10th lord Venus is exalted in the 8th house of the chart. Despite its placement in the 8th, Venus gains strength due to its accompaniment by *swakshetra* dispositor Jupiter. Jupiter, bright waxing Moon in *Chitra nakshatra*, and Venus constitute an elegant *Gaja Kesari* yoga across the 2 – 8 axis as the Virgo Moon rules the 11th house from itself. The Moon in Alessandra Ferri's chart warrants special consideration, as it forms additional *Raj* Yogas. *Phaladeepika* 7:7 avers that the bright Moon in aspect to a *swakshetra* or exalted planet confers royalty; in this case both criteria are met, and by natural benefics. *Phaladeepika* 7:13 states that the *vargottama* Moon in aspect with a "strong planet," while the ascendant of the chart is devoid of malefics, renders the native "an emperor" with a "well-formed body." Dance is also indicated in the birth chart by the placement of yoga *karaka* planet Mars in the 11th house from the Moon, where it is aspected by two *swakshetra* planets, Saturn (lord of 5 from Moon) and natal 5th lord Jupiter. Mars aspects the 11th house from ascendant ruler Sun as well as its lord Saturn. The debilitation of Mars is cancelled by Jupiter's location in a *kendra* from the Moon, in Jupiter's role as the *graha* exalted in Cancer, as well as Saturn's aspect to Mars. In Ms. Ferri's D-9, 11th lord Venus aspects the ascendant as the 11th house is aspected by Jupiter and 10th lord Mars, while in her D-10, debilitated 11th lord Mercury joins *swakshetra* 5th lord Jupiter in the 5th house. Mercury's debilitation in her D-9 is cancelled by the position of Venus in an angle and by Jupiter's 5th glance.

Alessandra Ferri's Virgo KL holds *vargottama* AmK Moon, ruler of the 11th house from Virgo. Along with Moon, the KL and *kendra* houses therefrom are aspected by *swakshetra* natal 5th lord Jupiter and exalted PK Venus, as well as *Rahu* and *Ketu*. The yoga-forming Venus – Moon relationship becomes especially potent due to the Moon's brightness and Venus' exalted status. *Swakshetra* AK Saturn in the 5th house from Virgo is aspected by DK Mercury, while the 11th house from Virgo is occupied by BK Mars in *Jaimini* aspect with Mercury.

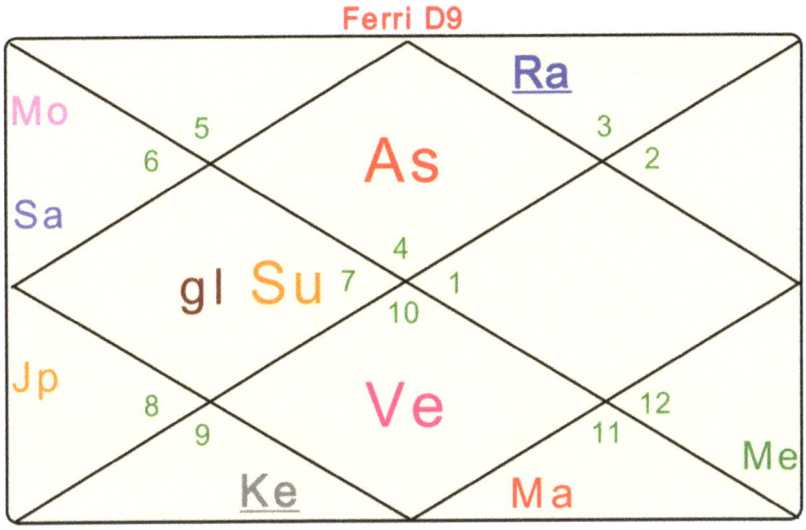

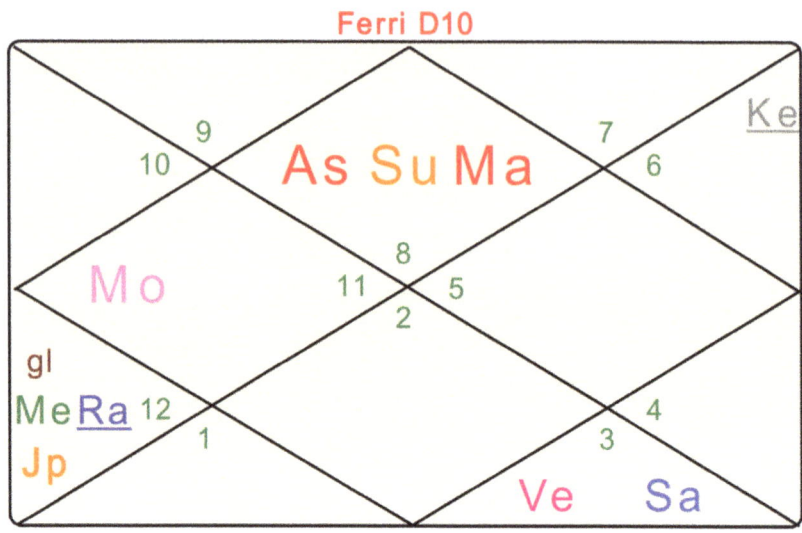

Ferri D10

Ferri: Vimshottari

Start Date			Age	Dashas	
6/	11/	1967	4.1	Ma	Mo
1/	10/	1968	4.7	Ra	Ra
9/	22/	1970	7.4	Ra	Jp
2/	14/	1973	9.8	Ra	Sa
12/	22/	1975	12.6	Ra	Me
7/	11/	1978	15.2	Ra	Ke
7/	29/	1979	16.2	Ra	Ve
7/	29/	1982	19.2	Ra	Su
6/	23/	1983	20.1	Ra	Mo
12/	22/	1984	21.6	Ra	Ma
1/	9/	1986	22.7	Jp	Jp
2/	27/	1988	24.8	Jp	Sa
9/	10/	1990	27.3	Jp	Me
12/	16/	1992	29.6	Jp	Ke
11/	22/	1993	30.5	Jp	Ve
7/	23/	1996	33.2	Jp	Su
5/	11/	1997	34.0	Jp	Mo
9/	10/	1998	35.3	Jp	Ma
8/	17/	1999	36.3	Jp	Ra
1/	9/	2002	38.7	Sa	Sa
1/	12/	2005	41.7	Sa	Me
9/	22/	2007	44.4	Sa	Ke
10/	31/	2008	45.5	Sa	Ve
1/	1/	2012	48.7	Sa	Su
12/	13/	2012	49.6	Sa	Mo
7/	14/	2014	51.2	Sa	Ma

AF: Chara				
Start Date			Age	Dashas
5/	6/	1963	-0.0	Leo
5/	6/	1967	4.0	Virg
5/	6/	1971	8.0	Libr
5/	5/	1976	13.0	Sco
5/	6/	1977	14.0	Sag
5/	5/	1980	17.0	Cap
5/	6/	1992	29.0	Aqu
5/	6/	2000	37.0	Pis
5/	6/	2012	49.0	Ari
5/	6/	2015 n	52.0	Tau
5/	6/	2025	62.0	Gem
5/	6/	2036	73.0	Can

We see that Allesandra Ferri's *Rahu* occupies her 11th house of dance, and that she ran the 18-year *Rahu* period during her formative years, when she studied at La Scala, then at the Royal Ballet school in London. By the time her *Rahu* period ended in 1986 she had moved to New York and begun performing with the American Ballet Theatre. Ms. Ferri enjoyed sustained career success and fame over the sixteen years of her *Vimshottari* Jupiter major period. Jupiter's noted participation in *Raj* yogas with Venus and especially (11th lord from itself) Moon contributed to this success. The one-way glance of Saturn to Jupiter confers upon Ms. Ferri the tendency to apply herself diligently to her craft; this Saturn aspect to Jupiter is repeated in both her D-9 and D-10. In her Cancer rising D-9, 6th and 9th lord Jupiter and yoga *karaka* 5th and 10th lord Mars activate the 11th house, as 11th lord Venus aspects the ascendant from the 7th house. *Swakshetra* and *vargottama* (in D-10) Jupiter achieves eminently influential status in Alessandra Ferri's D-10, as it joins 11th lord Mercury in the 5th. From the 5th house, Jupiter and Mercury aspect the 11th while Jupiter aspects the chart's ascendant and lord Mars as well as 10th lord Sun. It is noteworthy that Alessandra Ferri retired in 2007, during the *dasha* of a planet (Saturn), which is located in the 8th house of her D-10.

Between ages 14 and 17, Alessandra Ferri ran her Sagittarius

Jaimini Chara dasha; this was the period during which she left Milan and La Scala, moved to London, and began her association with the Royal Ballet. Sagittarius activates the chart's *Gaja Kesari* yoga, as well as its Virgo KL and resident AmK Moon in yoga-forming *sambandha* with *swakshetra* 5th lord Jupiter and exalted PK Venus. From the sign of Sagittarius in her D-9, *Raj* yoga is obtained as *vargottama* AmK Moon and AK Saturn occupy the 10th house. In Ms. Ferri's D-10 the *kendra* houses from Sagittarius are activated by *swakshetra* and *vargottama* (in the D-10) natal/local 5th lord Jupiter, as well as DK Mercury, PK Venus, AK Saturn, and *Rahu/Ketu*. The *dwishwabhava* signs here gain activation by all three natural benefics including their lords.

During her subsequent 12-year Capricorn period, Alessandra Ferri achieved career prominence initially with the Royal Ballet, then in New York with the American Ballet Theatre. In the D-1 Capricorn holds *swakshetra* AK Saturn. The 11th house from Capricorn is activated by aspects from Saturn, Scorpio owner BK Mars, and exalted MK/natal ascendant lord Sun. The 3 – 9 axis from Capricorn is influenced by the *Gaja Kesari* yoga. In her D-10, *swakshetra* Mars and Sun occupy the 11th house from Capricorn in the chart's ascendant, while the 3 – 9 axis is activated by Jupiter, DK Mercury, PK Venus, AK Saturn, and *Rahu/Ketu*. AmK Moon aspects the 10th house from Capricorn. In Ms. Ferri's D-9, PK Venus in Capricorn aspects its own sign of Taurus five houses away. Jupiter sits in Scorpio in the 11th from Venus, as the two planets aspect each other in *Jaimini sambandha*, while the 10th house is occupied by the Sun and aspected by BK Mars.

The next chart for our consideration will be that of Fred Astaire (May 10, 1899, Omaha, NE, 9:16 p.m., AA), the renowned dancer and movie star who is regarded as one of the greatest dancers in the history of film, if not the greatest outright. Fred Astaire appeared in thirty-one musicals and is best known for the ten films in which he appeared and danced with Ginger Rogers. Films such as *Top Hat*, *Swing Time*, *Shall We Dance*, and *Flying Down to Rio*, are classic, primarily for their elegant, intricate, and highly polished dance sequences. Astaire was known for his perfectionism as a performer, for his insistence upon extended rehearsals, which included repetition of sequences hundreds of times over, up to 18 hours per day for weeks at a time. Fred Astaire enjoyed a long career, dancing professionally until the age of seventy, and acting in his last film at age eighty-two. Mr. Astaire was a Kennedy Center honoree in 1978 and was conferred the American Film Institute's Lifetime Achievement award in 1981. In 1999 Fred Astaire was ranked 5th on the American Film Institute's list of the 25 greatest male film stars in the history of American cinema.

Creativity in the Vedic Astrology Chart

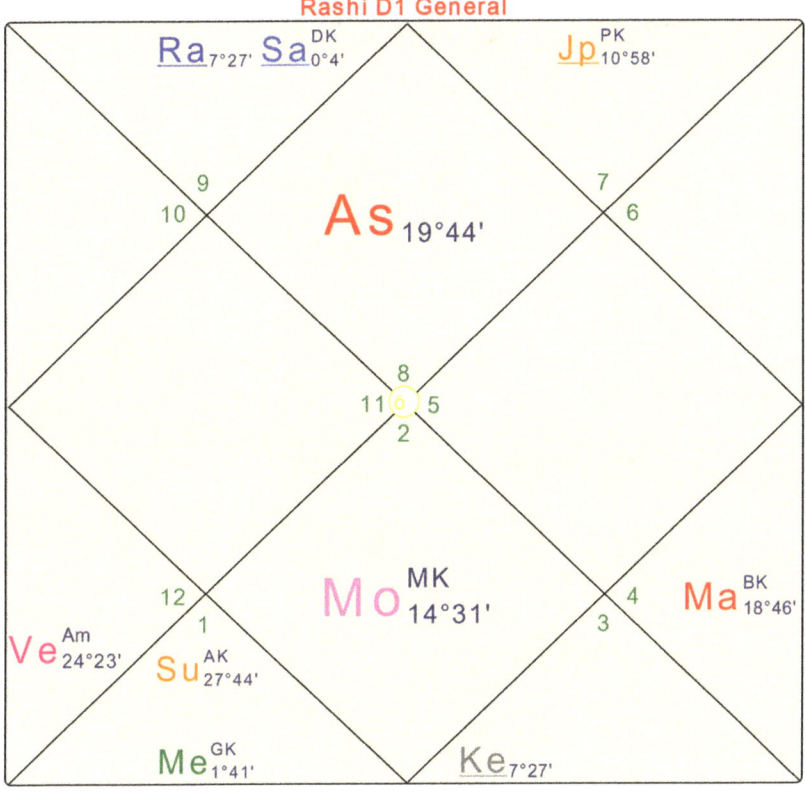

Rashi D1 General

	Me GK 1°41'	Mo MK 14°31'	Ke 7°27'
Ve Am 24°23'	Su AK 27°44'		
			Ma BK 18°46'
		Fred Astaire Wed. 5/10/1899 21:16:00 Omaha, NE	
Ra 7°27' Sa DK 0°4'	As 19°44'	Jp PK 10°58'	

Fred Astaire's Scorpio rising chart locates ascendant lord Mars in the 9th house in its debilitation sign of Cancer. Mars' debilitation is cancelled by dispositor Moon's placement in a *kendra* and in fact a *Parvata* (*Phaladeepika* 6:35) yoga is formed by the Moon's exaltation and placement in an angular house. Mars achieves *Neecha Bhanga Raj* yoga secondary to its 9th house location, the Moon's placement in a *kendra*, and the Moon's exalted *vargottama* status. Note that the Moon is placed in creatively abundant *Rohini* as the ascendant is graced by 9th lord Moon's aspect. Mr. Astaire's Moon gains strength as it maintains its exalted status in both his D-9 and D-10. The chart also features a perfectly formed *Lakshmi* yoga (*Phaladeepika* 6:21) as the result of 9th lord Moon's exaltation in a *kendra* with exalted Venus in a *trikona* house. At 24 degrees, Venus is within 3 degrees and approaching its point of highest exaltation. An interesting pattern of disposition emerges in the chart of Fred Astaire, as ascendant lord Mars' dispositor Moon achieves exaltation 11 houses away, while this configuration repeats from his Taurus Moon. This comprises a remarkable lineage of planetary strength and no doubt contributes to Fred Astaire's exceptional skill and devotion to the art of dance. The chart's *Parvata* yoga is consequently strengthened by the additional formation of *Phaladeepika Kahala* yoga (6:35). A *Parivartana* yoga occurs between houses 5 and 12, with 2nd and 5th lord Jupiter going to the 12th house of the chart. As noted in the introduction, and as will be seen more thoroughly in the final chapter, the 12th house will figure prominently in the charts of theatrical/film actors, directors, etc. This is the case in the chart of Fred Astaire, where we see the ruler of the 5th house of creativity in the 12th house of film and visual presentation while from the 5th house 12th lord Venus aspects the 11th house of dance. In keeping with the theme of dance, Fred Astaire's natal 11th lord Mercury accompanies exalted 10th lord Sun in the 6th house as the two planets enjoy *sambandha* status with 5th lord Jupiter. Mercury's enduring strength is evident from its placement in *Ashwini nakshatra* and its *vargottama* status in the D-9 and D-10. 10th house ruler Sun in *Krittika* reinforces the theme of physical vitality. In Libra, Jupiter resides in the *nakshatra* of *Swati*, notable for conferring skill in music and dance. As lord of the 11th house from the Moon, Jupiter aspects the 10th house from Moon, as do yoga *karaka* 9th and 10th lord (from Moon) Saturn and 12th lord (from Moon) Mars. The placement of 10th lord Sun and 11th lord Mercury together in the 6th house of service, hard work and persistent repetition is consistent with descriptions of Fred Astaire's tireless rehearsal habits. This theme is re-emphasized by *lagna* and 6th lord Mars' one-way glance to Jupiter as a constituent in the 6 – 11 *Parivartana* yoga from the Moon.

Fred Astaire's D-10 warrants special attention. The chart features three *Parivartana* yogas as well as occupation of three separate *kendra* houses by the natural benefics. We find ascendant lord Saturn in the 12th house of film with 12th lord Jupiter in the ascendant, while the rulers of houses 4 and 9, Mars and Mercury respectively, also exchange. Finally, Venus as 5th lord exchanges with Moon as ruler of the 7th. The mutual aspect between Jupiter in the ascendant and 5th and 10th lord Venus in the 7th house recreates the 12th lord -- 5th lord *sambandha* we observed in Mr. Astaire's birth chart. 11th lord Mars is strongly activated in the D-10 by its mutual glance with *lagna* lord Saturn and by 3rd and 12th lord Jupiter's glance to Mars; the 11th house of the D-10 is also enlivened by the aspect from exalted Moon. In Fred Astaire's D-9 11th lord Venus occupies the 3rd house of artistic expression, as Venus' dispositor Saturn goes to the 5th house with Mercury, from which location both planets influence the 11th house.

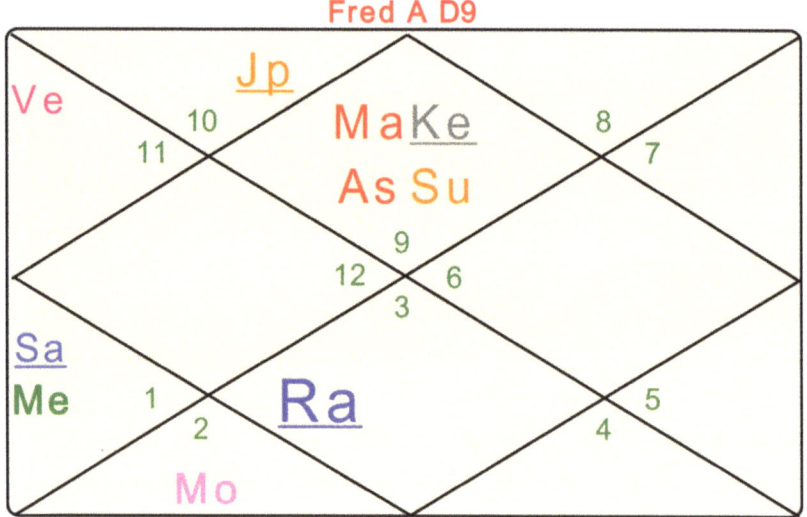

Creativity in the Vedic Astrology Chart

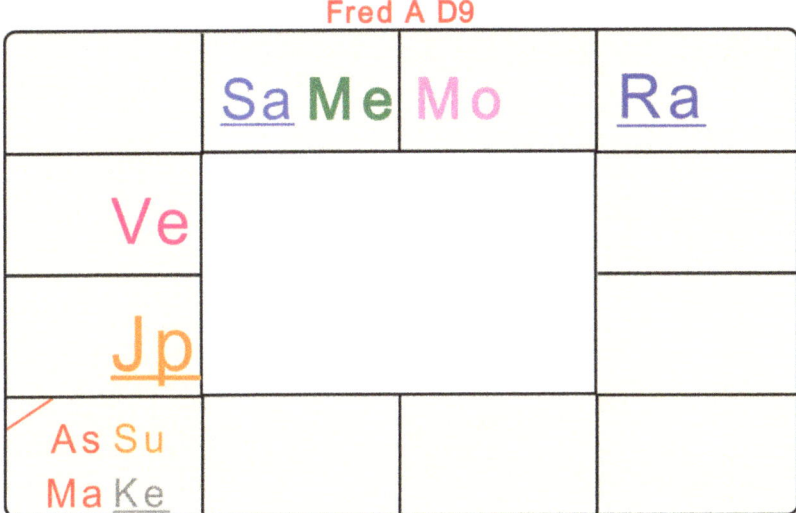

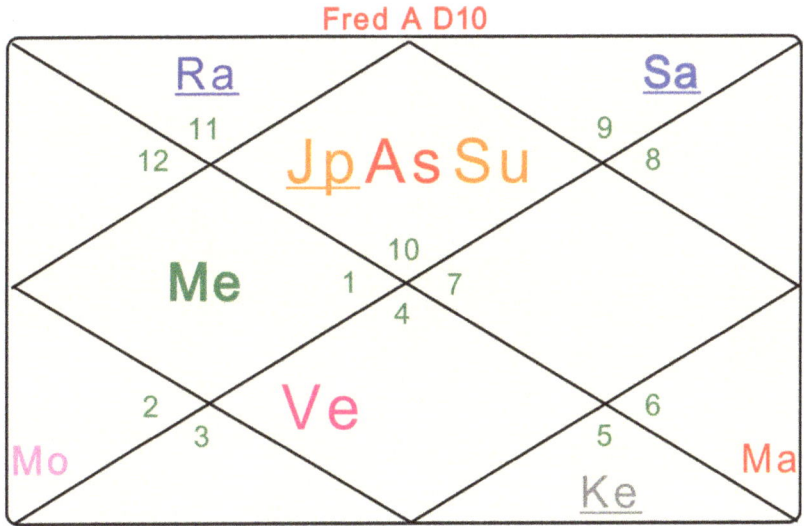

Fred A D10

	Me	Mo	
Ra			Ve
As Jp Su			Ke
Sa			Ma

Fred: Chara

Start Date	Age	Dashas
5/ 11/ 1912	13.0	Virg
5/ 11/ 1917	18.0	Leo
5/ 11/ 1921	22.0	Can
5/ 12/ 1923	24.0	Gem
5/ 11/ 1933	34.0	Tau
5/ 12/ 1943	44.0	Ari
5/ 11/ 1946	47.0	Pis
5/ 12/ 1951	52.0	Aqu
5/ 11/ 1953	54.0	Cap
5/ 11/ 1954	55.0	Sag
5/ 11/ 1964	65.0	Sco
5/ 11/ 1972	73.0	Libr

Fred : Vimshottari

Start Date			Age	Dashas	
5/	20/	1912	13.0	Ma	Mo
12/	19/	1912	13.6	Ra	Ra
9/	1/	1915	16.3	Ra	Jp
1/	25/	1918	18.7	Ra	Sa
12/	1/	1920	21.6	Ra	Me
6/	20/	1923	24.1	Ra	Ke
7/	7/	1924	25.2	Ra	Ve
7/	8/	1927	28.2	Ra	Su
6/	1/	1928	29.1	Ra	Mo
12/	1/	1929	30.6	Ra	Ma
12/	19/	1930	31.6	Jp	Jp
2/	6/	1933	33.7	Jp	Sa
8/	20/	1935	36.3	Jp	Me
11/	25/	1937	38.5	Jp	Ke
11/	1/	1938	39.5	Jp	Ve
7/	2/	1941	42.1	Jp	Su
4/	20/	1942	42.9	Jp	Mo
8/	20/	1943	44.3	Jp	Ma
7/	26/	1944	45.2	Jp	Ra
12/	19/	1946	47.6	Sa	Sa
12/	22/	1949	50.6	Sa	Me
8/	31/	1952	53.3	Sa	Ke
10/	10/	1953	54.4	Sa	Ve
12/	10/	1956	57.6	Sa	Su
11/	22/	1957	58.5	Sa	Mo
6/	23/	1959	60.1	Sa	Ma

As a performing duo Fred Astaire and his sister Adele made their Broadway debut in 1917. This occurred during Fred's *Vimshottari Rahu* -- Jupiter period and at the outset of his 4-year Leo *Jaimini Chara dasha*. In the birth chart *Rahu* joins 3rd and 4th lord Saturn in the 2nd house and is disposited by Jupiter in the 12th. Jupiter has (*Parashara*) *sambandha* with 10th lord Sun and 11th lord Mercury from the 6th, and is activated by Mars' one-way aspect. Jupiter's potency is confirmed by the continued success achieved by Fred Astaire during his 16-year Jupiter major period, the beginning of which coincided with the proliferation of sound and music in movies. *Rahu* is *swakshetra* in Aquarius in the 2nd house of Astaire's D-10, while Jupiter participates in a 1 – 12 *Parivartana* yoga with Saturn as it obtains cancellation of its debilitation and directional strength in the ascendant. Jupiter and yoga *karaka* Venus sit in *sambandha* across the 1 – 7 axis, as *Gauri* (*Phaladeepika* 6:21 and 6:25) yoga is formed by Jupiter's glance to exalted Moon in the 5th. As *lagna* lord in the 2nd house of Astaire's D-9, Jupiter's debilitation is cancelled by means of dispositor Saturn's one-way aspect from the 5th house, and the placement of Mars in the ascendant.

In Fred Astaire's birth chart, the sign of Leo is well fortified by *Jaimini* aspects from its exalted lord AK Sun, *vargottama* Mercury (lord of 11 from Leo as well as from the chart's ascendant), and PK Jupiter; notice that Fred Astaire's Jupiter serves *Jaimini Raj* yoga-creating double duty as PK and 5th lord. Exalted 12th lord Moon occupies the 10th house from Leo in the D-1, D-9, and D-10, just as the beneficial combination of Jupiter and Mercury activates Leo in all three charts. While Leo is again aspected by its lord in the D-10, the 10th house from Leo is similarly influenced by its ruler AmK Venus, as the exchange between Venus and the Moon involves the 10th and 12th houses. From their location in Capricorn, AK Sun and PK Jupiter also aspect the Moon in the 10th house from Leo.

Although brief, Fred Astaire's subsequent 2-year Cancer *Jaimini Chara dasha* served to advance his career in vaudeville and on Broadway. BK Mars tenants Cancer with exalted sign ruler Moon 11 houses away in the D-1, while AK Sun and *vargottama* Mercury are in the 10th. Secondary to the Moon's exaltation status in all three charts, Cancer's capability is enhanced by the aspect of its exalted lord. In Astaire's D-10, the exchange between Moon and Venus activates the 1st and 11th houses from Cancer as the two *grahas* also engage in mutual *Jaimini* aspect. *Jaimini Raj* yoga is formed as exalted Moon is aspected by PK/5th lord Jupiter in the D-9 and D-10, and by AK Sun in the D-10. In Mr. Astaire's D-9 and D-10, the sign of Cancer is activated by Venus and the Moon, as AmK Venus also aspects the 10th house from Cancer and occupants Saturn and Mercury in his D-9.

The strength and simultaneity of these periods, i.e., *Rahu* -- Jupiter and *Jaimini* Leo *Chara dasha*, (followed by Cancer) as seen in Fred Astaire's birth chart, D-9, and D-10, propelled Fred Astaire's career to world-wide recognition as one of the foremost film actors, and particularly as one of the greatest dancers of the modern era. In 1930, humorist and critic Robert Benchley wrote, "I don't think that I will plunge the nation into war by stating that Fred is the greatest tap dancer in the world."

Our next chart, fittingly, will be that of film actress and dancer Ginger Rogers (July 16, 1911, Independence, MO, 2:18 a.m., AA). Having won a Charleston dance contest at the age of fourteen, Ginger Rogers proceeded to sing, dance, and act on the vaudeville circuit until her appearance in the 1930 George Gershwin Broadway musical *Girl Crazy* made her an overnight success; soon thereafter she moved to Hollywood and began a long and successful film career. Although she appeared in more than 70 films, Ginger Rogers is best known for her dance partnership with Fred Astaire in 10 musical films, 9 of which were made in the 1930s. The dance routines of Ginger Rogers and Fred Astaire are known for their beauty, sophistication, and intricacy; the pair is acknowledged to be the premier dance team in all of film history. Ginger Rogers was to also gain acclaim for her skill as an actress, winning the Academy Award for Best Actress in 1941 for her performance in the film *Kitty Foyle*, and as a recipient of the annual Kennedy Center Honors in 1992. Ginger Rogers is ranked 14th in the American Film Institute's list of the top 25 female film stars in the history of classic cinema.

Creativity in the Vedic Astrology Chart

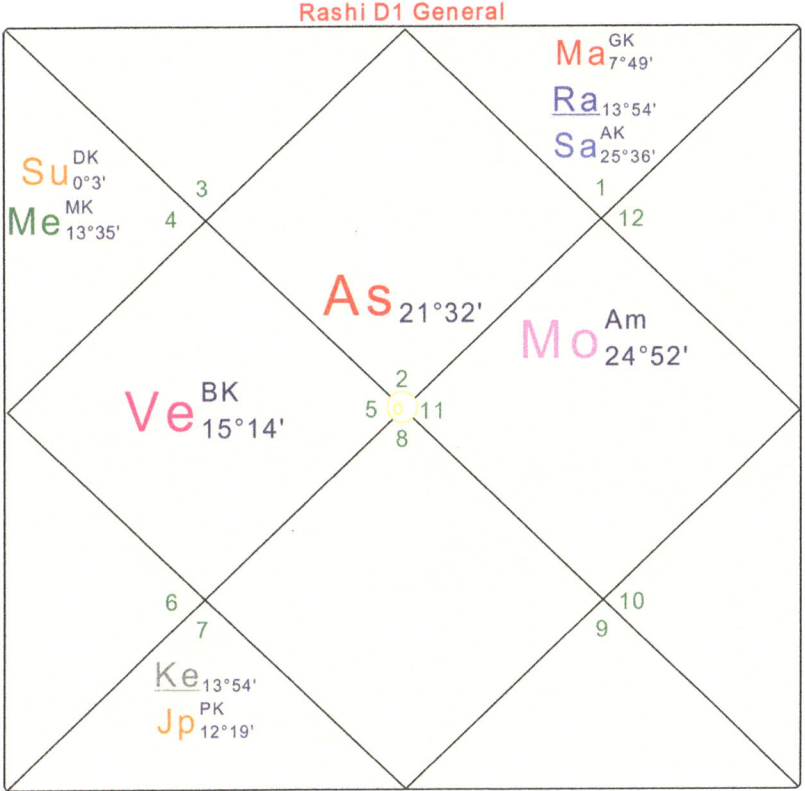

Rashi D1 General

	Ma GK 7°49' Ra 13°54' Sa AK 25°36'		As 21°32'
Mo Am 24°52'			Su DK 0°3' Me MK 13°35'
	Ginger Rogers Sun. 7/16/1911 2:18:00 Independence, MO		Ve BK 15°14'
		Ke 13°54' Jp PK 12°19'	

The Taurus ascendant chart of Ginger Rogers has *Rohini* rising with *vargottama* ascendant lord Venus obtaining directional strength in the 4th house in *Purva Phalguni nakshatra*. From the 4th house Venus aspects the 10th and resident 3rd lord Moon. The configuration of Venus, Jupiter, and the Moon, with bright Moon in aspect with doubly strong Venus, and in reception of Jupiter's 5th glance, constitutes a *Raj* yoga, especially capable of conferring artistic expression and a high degree of success and public recognition. (See BPHS chapter 37 verses 2 – 4 as well as *Phaladeepika* 7:23.) The Moon's strength is enhanced by its exaltation status in the D-9, where it rules the ascendant and occupies the 11th. Ms. Rogers' Moon is placed in *Purva Bhadrapada nakshatra*; recall that *Purva Bhadrapada* can grant skill in the realm of visual expression. BPHS *Kahala* yoga forms secondary to the mutual *kendra* placement of Jupiter and 4th lord

Sun, qualified by Venus' directional strength and *vargottama* status. The potential of an acting career for Ms. Rogers is confirmed by the placement of yoga *karaka* 9th and 10th lord Saturn in the 12th house of visual artistry with *swakshetra* 12th lord Mars. The most influential planet in the chart, however, is Jupiter, as lord of the 11th house of dance. We notice Jupiter's aspect to 10th house and 3rd lord Moon, as well as Jupiter's *sambandha* relationship with 10th and 12th lords Saturn and Mars, respectively. Jupiter's status as 11th lord is reinforced by its rulership of the 11th house from the Moon. Ginger Rogers' *Swati* Jupiter lies within a 2-degree orb of the Jupiter of dance partner Fred Astaire, ruler of the 11th house from the Moon in his chart. Having now seen *Swati nakshatra* occur in more than a few of our charts, it is worth recalling *Swati*'s symbolic connection to the celestial musicians and dancers known as *Gandharvas*.

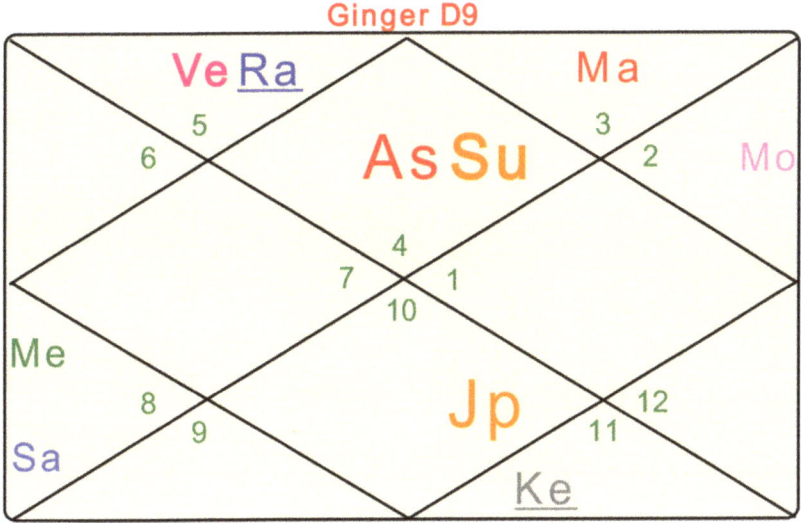

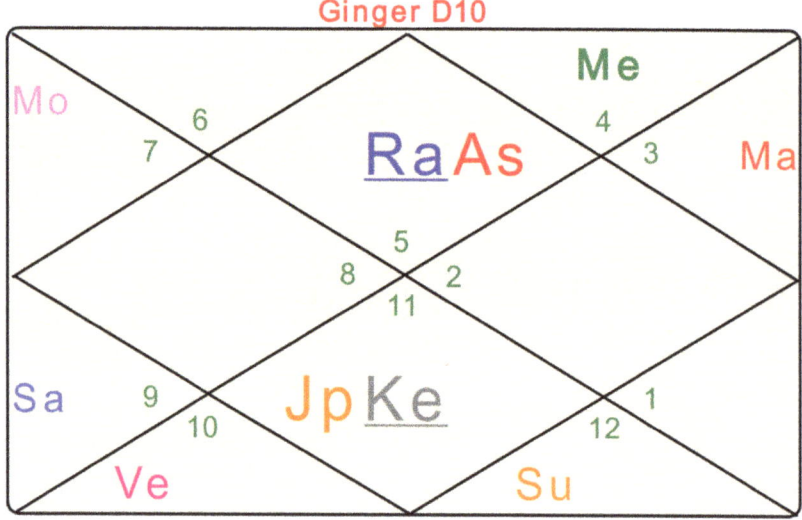

Ginger D10

Su			Ma
Ke Jp			Me
Ve			As Ra
	Sa	Mo	

As was the case with Fred Astaire, Ginger Rogers benefited from the advent of the use of sound in film, and saw her career ascend to film stardom soon after her Broadway success in 1930. At that time, Ginger Rogers was in the middle of her 19-year Saturn major period, in the sub-period of ascendant lord Venus. Saturn is yoga *karaka* and 10th house ruler in her birth chart, while Venus as ascendant lord in the 5th house from Saturn participates in the earlier cited *Raj* yoga with Moon across the 4 – 10 axis. Saturn's debilitation in the birth chart will be cancelled by its association with *swakshetra* dispositor Mars in the 12th house, as well as the *kendra* placements of Venus from the ascendant and Moon. As the *vargottama* 11th lord in the 10th house from Saturn in her D-9, Venus is the 10th lord in her D-10. Venus in the 6th house of her D-10 gets a one-way aspect from 9th lord Mars and sits in 2-way *sambandha* with 11th lord Mercury in the chart.

The strength in Ginger Rogers' chart is equally evident from the *Jaimini* system perspective. A powerful *Jaimini Raj* yoga is formed by the aspects of seven *grahas* (all except Venus) to the Moon. These include aspects from the (*Jaimini*) yoga-making planets PK Jupiter, DK Sun, AK Saturn, and natal 5th lord Mercury to the Moon in the

Moon's role as AmK. The chart's Scorpio KL is strongly activated as well, as it benefits from glances from the Sun, Mercury, Saturn, *Rahu*, and *swakshetra* ruler Mars. The placement of BK Venus in the 10th house from the KL, where it is aspected by Jupiter, Saturn, Mars, and *Rahu/Ketu* is instrumental in its contribution to Ginger Rogers' success in an artistic career. On her 20th birthday in 1931, Ginger Rogers began a 10-year *Jaimini Chara dasha* of the sign which holds AmK Moon, Aquarius; the potential for sustained success during the Aquarius period can also be seen in Ginger Rogers' D-10, where PK Jupiter and AK Saturn engage in a 1 – 11 *Parivartana* yoga. In her D-9, AK Saturn and 5th lord Mercury inhabit the 10th house from Aquarius and are aspected by PK Jupiter and DK Sun. For ten months in the heart of her *Vimshottari* Saturn -- Moon period, beginning March of 1933, Ginger Rogers ran the *Jaimini* Aquarius -- Taurus period, which features multiply aspected AmK Moon in the 10th house (from Taurus). 1933 was a breakout year for Ginger Rogers, as she received critical acclaim for her roles in several films, including *42nd Street* and *Gold Diggers of 1933*. More notably, 1933 saw the first of the ten films in which she was to dance with Fred Astaire, *Flying Down to Rio*.

GR: Vimshottari

Start Date	Age	Dashas	
9/ 9/ 1924	13.2	Sa	Me
5/ 21/ 1927	15.8	Sa	Ke
6/ 28/ 1928	17.0	Sa	Ve
8/ 29/ 1931	20.1	Sa	Su
8/ 10/ 1932	21.1	Sa	Mo
3/ 11/ 1934	22.7	Sa	Ma
4/ 20/ 1935	23.8	Sa	Ra
2/ 24/ 1938	26.6	Sa	Jp
9/ 6/ 1940	**29.1**	**Me**	**Me**
2/ 3/ 1943	31.6	Me	Ke
1/ 31/ 1944	32.5	Me	Ve
12/ 1/ 1946	35.4	Me	Su
10/ 8/ 1947	36.2	Me	Mo
3/ 8/ 1949	37.6	Me	Ma
3/ 5/ 1950	38.6	Me	Ra
9/ 22/ 1952	41.2	Me	Jp
12/ 29/ 1954	43.5	Me	Sa
9/ 7/ 1957	**46.1**	Ke	Ke
2/ 3/ 1958	46.6	Ke	Ve
4/ 5/ 1959	47.7	Ke	Su
8/ 11/ 1959	48.1	Ke	Mo
3/ 11/ 1960	48.7	Ke	Ma
8/ 7/ 1960	49.1	Ke	Ra
8/ 26/ 1961	50.1	Ke	Jp
8/ 2/ 1962	51.0	Ke	Sa
9/ 10/ 1963	52.2	Ke	Me

GR: Chara

Start Date	Age	Dashas	
6/ 15/ 1929	17.9	Pis	Sco
11/ 14/ 1929	18.3	Pis	Sag
4/ 15/ 1930	18.8	Pis	Cap
9/ 14/ 1930	19.2	Pis	Aqu
2/ 14/ 1931	19.6	Pis	Pis
7/ 16/ 1931	20.0	Aqu	Pis
5/ 15/ 1932	20.8	Aqu	Ari
3/ 15/ 1933	21.7	Aqu	Tau
1/ 14/ 1934	22.5	Aqu	Gem
11/ 14/ 1934	23.3	Aqu	Can
9/ 15/ 1935	24.2	Aqu	Leo
7/ 15/ 1936	25.0	Aqu	Virg
5/ 15/ 1937	25.8	Aqu	Libr
3/ 16/ 1938	26.7	Aqu	Sco
1/ 14/ 1939	27.5	Aqu	Sag
11/ 15/ 1939	28.3	Aqu	Cap
9/ 14/ 1940	29.2	Aqu	Aqu
7/ 15/ 1941	30.0	Cap	Sag
4/ 15/ 1942	30.8	Cap	Sco
1/ 14/ 1943	31.5	Cap	Libr
10/ 15/ 1943	32.2	Cap	Virg
7/ 15/ 1944	33.0	Cap	Leo
4/ 15/ 1945	33.8	Cap	Can
1/ 14/ 1946	34.5	Cap	Gem
10/ 15/ 1946	35.2	Cap	Tau
7/ 16/ 1947	36.0	Cap	Ari

In Ms. Rogers' D-9, Taurus is the sign on the 11th house of dance, and that which holds her D-9 exalted ascendant lord/AmK Moon. The Moon in the 11th is activated by PK Jupiter and DK Sun. In Ginger Rogers' Leo rising D-10, Taurus is aspected by its owner BK Venus, AmK Moon and natal 5th lord Mercury. In the 10th house from Taurus PK Jupiter enjoys mutual aspect with the Moon and Mercury. Ginger

Rogers' Aquarius -- Taurus period was instrumental in propelling her to the high degree of fame and fortune which she was to achieve in her life. In 1941, while running her Aquarius -- Aquarius *Chara dasha*, Ginger Rogers won her first and only best actress Oscar, for her performance in the film *Kitty Foyle*.

Also notable across Miss Rogers' D-1, D-9, and D-10 charts is the relationship, and the consistency of the relationship, between AmK Moon and PK Jupiter. In all three charts, the two *grahas* are found in mutual aspect. This connection persists from a *Parashara* perspective as well: Moon receives Jupiter's glance in each of the three charts. In addition to Jupiter's 11th house lordship in her D-1, Jupiter rules the 9th house in her D-9 and the 5th house in her D-10. From its position in the 7th house in both D-9 and D-10 divisional charts, Jupiter aspects the ascendant, as well as the 11th house of dance (*Parashara* aspects). Although it does not meet strict criteria for *Gauri* yoga, Jupiter's aspect to exalted D-9 ascendant ruler Moon in the 11th house can be regarded as "*Gauri*-like" and contributes to Ginger Rogers' expertise as a dancer.

Our next chart will be that of renowned Italian ballet dancer Roberto Bolle (March 26th, 1975, Casale Monferrato, Italy, 2:50 p.m., AA). Roberto Bolle began the study of dance at the age of seven and at twelve he was accepted at La Scala Ballet School in Milan. At the age of fifteen, Roberto Bolle caught the attention of Rudolf Nureyev and was selected by Nureyev to perform the role of Tadzio in the Benjamin Britten opera *Death in Venice*. Following Bolle's performance at age twenty in a La Scala production of *Romeo and Juliet*, he was promoted to principal dancer. As a freelance artist, Roberto Bolle has performed with virtually every prestigious ballet company in the world, including the Royal Ballet, Mariinsky Ballet, Paris Opera, Stuttgart Ballet, and the Bolshoi. In 2007 Roberto Bolle danced for the first time with the American Ballet Theatre, at the farewell performance of Italian ballerina Alessandra Ferri. In January 2009, Roberto Bolle became American Ballet's principal dancer, a position he held for 10 years.

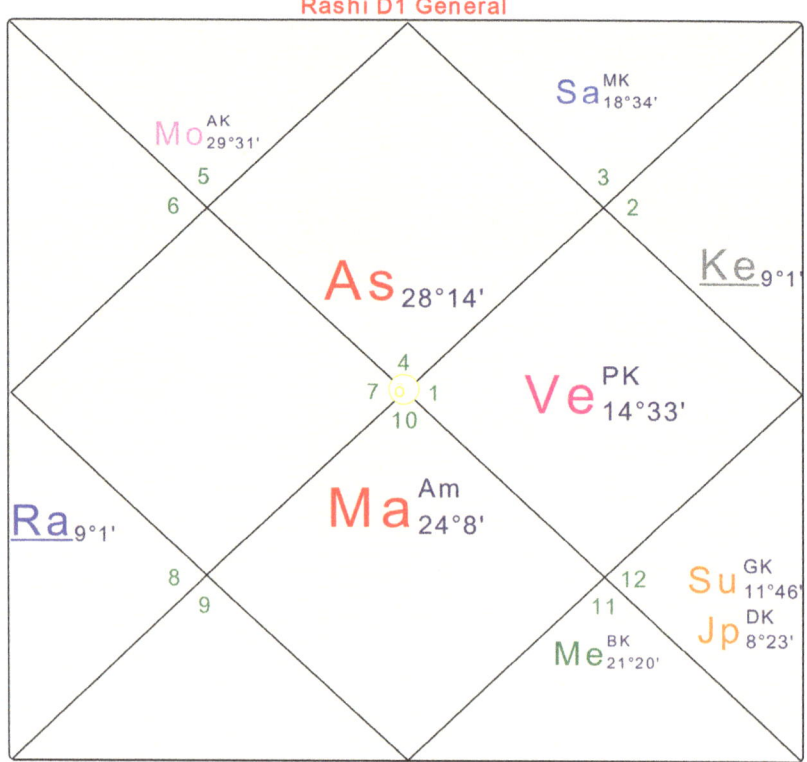

Rashi D1 General

```
+----------------+----------------+----------------+----------------+
| Jp  DK 8°23'   | Ve  PK 14°33'  | Ke  9°1'       |                |
| Su  GK 11°46'  |                |                | Sa  MK 18°34'  |
+----------------+----------------+----------------+----------------+
| Me  BK 21°20'  |                                 |                |
+----------------+                                 | As  28°14'     |
| Ma  Am 24°8'   |    Roberto Bolle                |                |
|                |    Wed. 3/26/1975 14:50:00      | Mo  AK 29°31'  |
+----------------+    Casale Monferrato, IT        +----------------+
|                |                                 |                |
|                +----------------+----------------+                |
|                |       Ra 9°1'  |                |                |
+----------------+----------------+----------------+----------------+
```

The chart of Roberto Bolle has 11th lord Venus in the 10th house in *Bharani nakshatra* where it is aspected one-way by its exalted dispositor Mars. As yoga *karaka* lord of houses 5 and 10 for Cancer ascendant, Mars forms *Ruchaka* yoga in the 7th house and at 24 degrees is approaching its highest point of exaltation. From its location in the 7th house, Mars aspects both the ascendant and lord Moon in the 2nd house; Mars' strong influence is consistent with Roberto Bolle's reputation for athleticism and physicality as a ballet dancer. From ascendant ruler Moon, Mercury rules the 11th house and has *sambandha* with the Moon across the 2 – 8 axis. Mercury and Saturn form an 8 – 12 *Parivartana* yoga which places Saturn in the 11th house from the Moon. Bolle's 2nd lord Sun is flanked by benefics in a *Shubha Ubhayachari* yoga, made more favorable by the Sun's association with *swakshetra* Jupiter in Pisces. Notice that an *Adhi*-like yoga is formed opposite the 3rd house of artistic expression. In Roberto Bolle's D-9, 11th lord Saturn prominently occupies the chart's ascendant, forming *sambandha* with *lagna* and 10th lord Jupiter and activated by an aspect from 9th lord Mars.

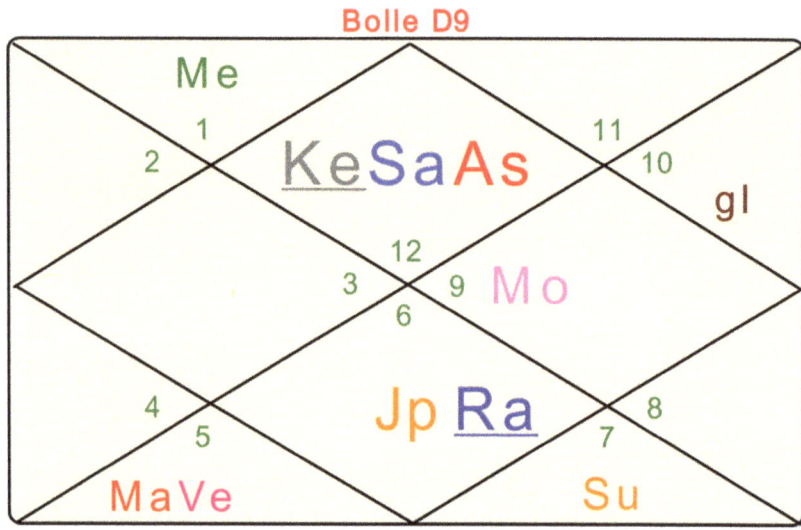

Creativity in the Vedic Astrology Chart

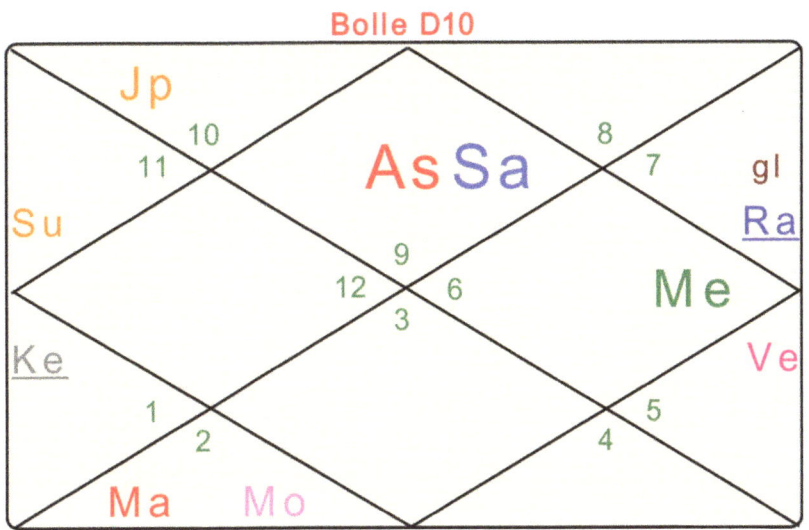

Bolle: Vimshottari

Start Date			Age	Dashas	
3/	13/	1984	9.0	Mo	Sa
10/	13/	1985	10.6	Mo	Me
3/	14/	1987	12.0	Mo	Ke
10/	13/	1987	12.6	Mo	Ve
6/	13/	1989	14.2	Mo	Su
12/	**13/**	**1989**	**14.7**	**Ma**	**Ma**
5/	11/	1990	15.1	Ma	Ra
5/	29/	1991	16.2	Ma	Jp
5/	4/	1992	17.1	Ma	Sa
6/	13/	1993	18.2	Ma	Me
6/	10/	1994	19.2	Ma	Ke
11/	6/	1994	19.6	Ma	Ve
1/	6/	1996	20.8	Ma	Su
5/	13/	1996	21.1	Ma	Mo
12/	**12/**	**1996**	**21.7**	**Ra**	**Ra**
8/	26/	1999	24.4	Ra	Jp
1/	18/	2002	26.8	Ra	Sa
11/	24/	2004	29.7	Ra	Me
6/	14/	2007	32.2	Ra	Ke
7/	1/	2008	33.3	Ra	Ve
7/	2/	2011	36.3	Ra	Su
5/	26/	2012	37.2	Ra	Mo
11/	24/	2013	38.7	Ra	Ma
12/	**13/**	**2014**	**39.7**	**Jp**	**Jp**
1/	30/	2017	41.9	Jp	Sa
8/	14/	2019	44.4	Jp	Me

Bolle: Chara

Start Date	Age	Dashas	
7/ 26/ 1989	14.3	Gem	Sag
3/ 26/ 1990	15.0	Gem	Sco
11/ 24/ 1990	15.7	Gem	Libr
7/ 26/ 1991	16.3	Gem	Virg
3/ 25/ 1992	17.0	Gem	Leo
11/ 24/ 1992	17.7	Gem	Can
7/ 26/ 1993	18.3	Gem	Gem
3/ 26/ 1994	19.0	Tau	Ari
2/ 24/ 1995	19.9	Tau	Pis
1/ 25/ 1996	20.8	Tau	Aqu
12/ 24/ 1996	21.8	Tau	Cap
11/ 24/ 1997	22.7	Tau	Sag
10/ 25/ 1998	23.6	Tau	Sco
9/ 25/ 1999	24.5	Tau	Libr
8/ 25/ 2000	25.4	Tau	Virg
7/ 26/ 2001	26.3	Tau	Leo
6/ 25/ 2002	27.2	Tau	Can
5/ 26/ 2003	28.2	Tau	Gem
4/ 25/ 2004	29.1	Tau	Tau
3/ 26/ 2005	30.0	Ari	Tau
12/ 25/ 2005	30.8	Ari	Gem
9/ 25/ 2006	31.5	Ari	Can
6/ 26/ 2007	32.2	Ari	Leo
3/ 26/ 2008	33.0	Ari	Virg
12/ 25/ 2008	33.8	Ari	Libr
9/ 25/ 2009	34.5	Ari	Sco

Roberto Bolle became principal dancer with La Scala during his *Vimshottari* Mars – Venus period; Venus replicates its 11th house lordship in Bolle's D-10 where it is again activated by 5th house ruler Mars. Venus and Mars enjoy a strong *sambandha* relationship as the result of Mars' placement in Taurus and 4th glance to Venus. Bolle's 18-year *Rahu* major period followed soon after and brought him international fame in the realm of professional ballet. *Rahu* in the 5th house of the birth chart is disposited by exalted Mars and aspected by *swakshetra* 9th lord Jupiter. In his D-9 *Rahu* and chart ruler Jupiter in the 7th are aspected by 11th lord Saturn from the ascendant. *Rahu* in the 11th house of dance in the D-10 chart is disposited by 9th house resident Venus.

At age nineteen, Roberto Bolle began his 11-year *Jaimini Chara dasha* of the sign of Taurus, the 11th house of the chart. Taurus contains *Ketu* in *Krittika nakshatra*; the physically energizing capability of *Krittika* is amplified by the *Jaimini* aspect from exalted 5th lord/AmK Mars. PK Venus has mutual aspect with AK Moon and BK Mercury as Venus aspects the 10th house from Taurus and occupant Mercury. The Sun and *swakshetra* DK Jupiter occupy the 11th house from Taurus and are aspected by Saturn from the 2nd house. Roberto Bolle's success in the Taurus period is ensured by the placement of natal/local 5th lord AmK Mars and exalted AK Moon in Taurus in his D-10, forming a strong *Jaimini Raj* yoga. Mars and Moon receive the aspect of DK Jupiter as the Sun obtains directional strength in the 10th house. Taurus owner PK Venus gets directional strength and is aspected by Jupiter as well as by *Rahu* and *Ketu*. Roberto Bolle's fame and success were to increase in his subsequent 9-year *Jaimini* Aries *Chara dasha*; this was the period during which he became principal dancer with the American Ballet Theater. The sign of Aries holds PK Venus in *Jaimini sambandha* with the Moon as Aries ruler AmK Mars sits in exaltation in the 10th house. The location of Venus in the 5th house from Bolle's Sagittarius KL and in aspect to the Moon is the *Raj* yoga cited in BPHS 39:11. In the D-9, the sign of Aries and tenant BK Mercury benefit from the aspects of sign ruler AmK Mars and PK Venus; Venus and Mars aspect the 10th house as well. Venus and the Sun aspect Aries in the D-10 as the 10th house contains DK Jupiter in reception of aspects from Venus, Mars, and exalted AK Moon.

Creativity in the Vedic Astrology Chart

The next chart in the dance section is that of ballerina Heather Watts (September 27, 1953, Long Beach, CA, 2:06 a.m., AA). Heather Watts began the study of dance at age ten and at age seventeen joined the New York City Ballet. At age twenty-six in 1979, Ms. Watts was promoted by NYCB founder George Balanchine to the role of principal dancer and was awarded leading roles in many of the company's productions. In the 1970s and 1980s, Heather Watts regularly appeared in the television series *Dance in America*, often as the dance partner of Mikhail Baryshnikov. In addition to dance, Heather Watts has cultivated a multiplicity of careers, as a dance teacher and mentor for children, college lecturer, choreographer, writer and editor, and costume designer.

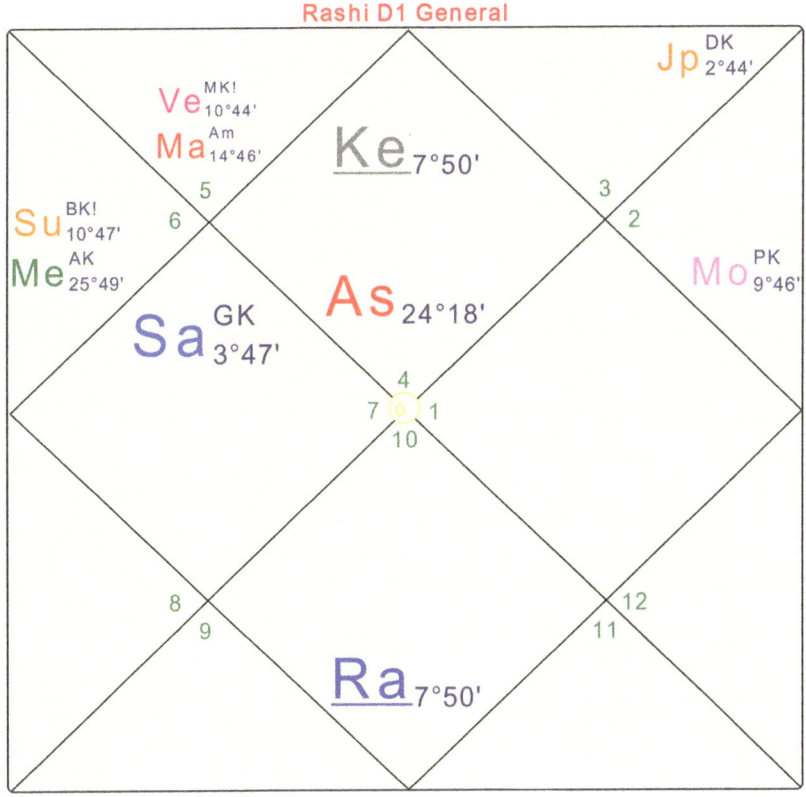

Rashi D1 General

		Mo PK 9°46'	Jp DK 2°44'
	Heather Watts Sun. 9/27/1953 2:06:00 Long Beach, CA		Ke 7°50' As 24°18' Ve MK! 10°44' Ma Am 14°46'
Ra 7°50'			Me AK 25°49'
		Sa GK 3°47'	Su BK! 10°47'

The ascendant of Heather Watts' Cancer rising chart is flanked by natural benefics Jupiter and Venus, forming *Shubha* yoga, while exalted ascendant lord Moon occupies the 11th house in the *nakshatra* of *Krittika*. The chart meets criteria for *Maha Bhagya* yoga as narrated in *Phaladeepika* chapter 6, verses 14 & 15. Lord of 10th house of career Mars joins 11th lord Venus in the 2nd house of the chart, with Mars in the Venus-ruled *nakshatra* of *Purva Phalguni*. From the 2nd, both planets aspect the 10th house from ascendant ruler Moon. As lord of the 11th house from the Moon, Jupiter also aspects the 10th house from the Moon and casts its 5th glance to exalted 10th house ruler (from Moon) Saturn. The 11th house from the Moon is activated by the Sun, *swakshetra* Mercury, and Mars.

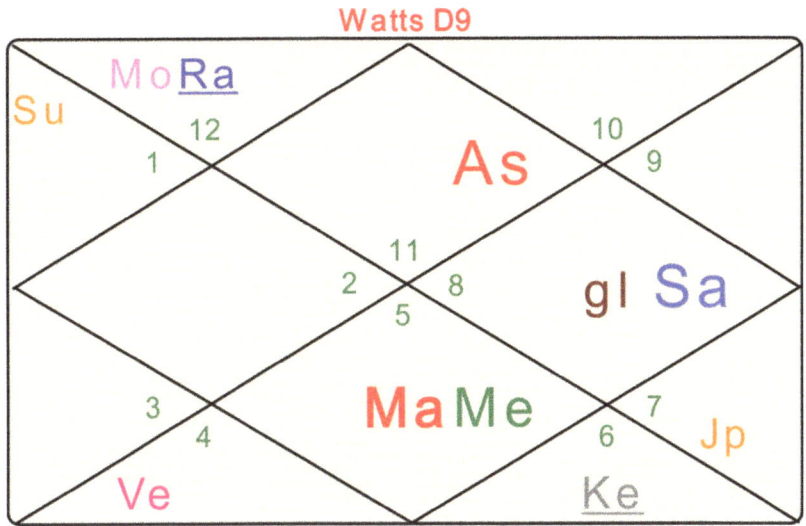

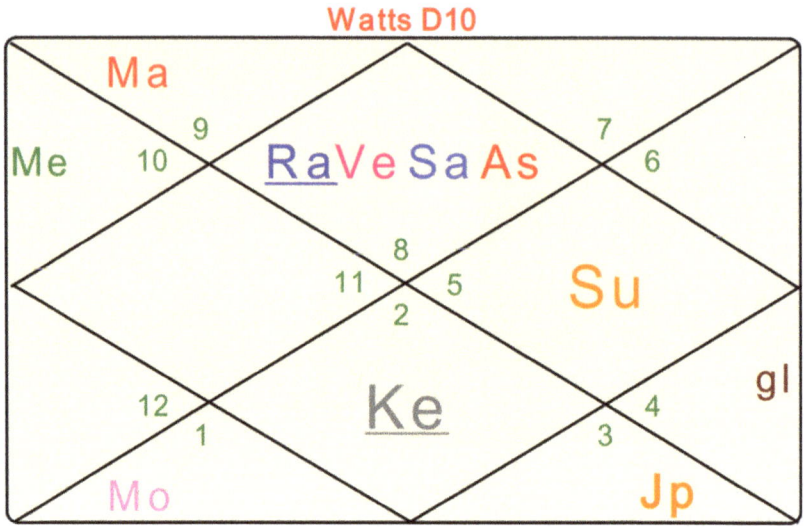

Watts: Vimshottari

Start Date			Age	Dashas	
9/	3/	1961	7.9	Mo	Ve
5/	5/	1963	9.6	Mo	Su
11/	3/	1963	10.1	Ma	Ma
3/	31/	1964	10.5	Ma	Ra
4/	19/	1965	11.6	Ma	Jp
3/	26/	1966	12.5	Ma	Sa
5/	5/	1967	13.6	Ma	Me
5/	1/	1968	14.6	Ma	Ke
9/	27/	1968	15.0	Ma	Ve
11/	27/	1969	16.2	Ma	Su
4/	4/	1970	16.5	Ma	Mo
11/	3/	1970	17.1	Ra	Ra
7/	16/	1973	19.8	Ra	Jp
12/	10/	1975	22.2	Ra	Sa
10/	16/	1978	25.1	Ra	Me
5/	4/	1981	27.6	Ra	Ke
5/	23/	1982	28.7	Ra	Ve
5/	23/	1985	31.7	Ra	Su
4/	16/	1986	32.6	Ra	Mo
10/	16/	1987	34.1	Ra	Ma
11/	3/	1988	35.1	Jp	Jp
12/	22/	1990	37.2	Jp	Sa
7/	4/	1993	39.8	Jp	Me
10/	10/	1995	42.0	Jp	Ke
9/	15/	1996	43.0	Jp	Ve
5/	17/	1999	45.6	Jp	Su

Watts: Chara

Start Date	Age	Dashas	
12/ 27/ 1967	14.2	Pis	Can
9/ 26/ 1968	15.0	Pis	Leo
6/ 27/ 1969	15.8	Pis	Virg
3/ 28/ 1970	16.5	Pis	Libr
12/ 27/ 1970	17.2	Pis	Sco
9/ 27/ 1971	18.0	Pis	Sag
6/ 27/ 1972	18.8	Pis	Cap
3/ 28/ 1973	19.5	Pis	Aqu
12/ 27/ 1973	20.2	Pis	Pis
9/ 27/ 1974	**21.0**	**Aqu**	**Pis**
10/ 27/ 1974	21.1	Aqu	Ari
11/ 27/ 1974	21.2	Aqu	Tau
12/ 27/ 1974	21.2	Aqu	Gem
1/ 27/ 1975	21.3	Aqu	Can
2/ 26/ 1975	21.4	Aqu	Leo
3/ 29/ 1975	21.5	Aqu	Virg
4/ 28/ 1975	21.6	Aqu	Libr
5/ 29/ 1975	21.7	Aqu	Sco
6/ 28/ 1975	21.8	Aqu	Sag
7/ 28/ 1975	21.8	Aqu	Cap
8/ 28/ 1975	21.9	Aqu	Aqu
9/ 27/ 1975	**22.0**	**Cap**	**Sag**
12/ 28/ 1975	22.2	Cap	Sco
3/ 28/ 1976	22.5	Cap	Libr
6/ 27/ 1976	22.8	Cap	Virg
9/ 27/ 1976	23.0	Cap	Leo
12/ 27/ 1976	23.2	Cap	Can
3/ 28/ 1977	23.5	Cap	Gem
6/ 27/ 1977	23.8	Cap	Tau
9/ 27/ 1977	24.0	Cap	Ari
12/ 27/ 1977	24.2	Cap	Pis
3/ 28/ 1978	24.5	Cap	Aqu
6/ 28/ 1978	24.8	Cap	Cap
9/ 27/ 1978	**25.0**	**Sag**	**Sco**
3/ 29/ 1979	25.5	Sag	Libr
9/ 27/ 1979	26.0	Sag	Virg
3/ 28/ 1980	26.5	Sag	Leo
9/ 27/ 1980	27.0	Sag	Can
3/ 28/ 1981	27.5	Sag	Gem
9/ 27/ 1981	28.0	Sag	Tau
3/ 28/ 1982	28.5	Sag	Ari

Heather Watts' career ascended at age seventeen, late in the year 1970, when she was invited to join the New York City Ballet. This event corresponds closely to the onset of Ms. Watts' *Rahu* major period about a month after her 17th birthday. From its placement in the 7th house in Capricorn, *Rahu* is disposited by Saturn in *Shasha Maha Purusha* yoga in the 4th house. In Heather Watts' D-9 *Rahu* joins the Moon in the 2nd house, is aspected by 3rd and 10th lord Mars and disposited by 11th lord Jupiter. *Rahu* is joined in the ascendant of her Scorpio rising D-10 chart by Venus and 3rd house ruler Saturn.

At age twelve, Heather Watts began a 9-year Pisces *Chara dasha*. In her D-1, the sign of Pisces and the *kendra* houses therefrom are strengthened by activation from their respective sign rulers in addition to that of BK Sun. From Pisces, Ms. Watts' 11th house is aspected by AmK/natal 5th lord Mars as well as by Venus and exalted PK Moon; notice also Saturn's exalted status as owner of the sign of Capricorn. In Ms. Watts' D-10, the sign of Pisces is again aspected by its lord as well by AmK Mars who gains directional strength in the 10th house. The 11th house from Pisces contains AK Mercury and is activated by five additional *grahas*, including sign ruler Saturn, Venus and *swakshetra* BK Sun. In Heather Watts' D-9 the sign of Capricorn is similarly aspected by its lord as well as by AK Mercury and *vargottama* AmK Mars. The potential inherent in the *dasha* of the sign of Pisces is realized during the Scorpio sub-period, when Ms. Watts was seventeen and was invited to join the NYCB. Exalted AK Mercury and BK Sun occupy the 11th house from Scorpio in the D-1, while receiving an aspect from DK Jupiter. Scorpio sign ruler AmK Mars gains directional strength in the 10th house in the sign of Leo, which also serves as Ms. Watts' KL. Mars is joined in Leo by Venus as the 2 planets are aspected by exalted Saturn.

As has been observed with some consistency, periods or sub-periods of a strong KL, or the sign 4th from the KL (placing the KL in the 10th), can yield significant career gains. The placement of AmK Mars and Venus in Heather Watts' Leo KL, with exalted PK Moon in the 10th house, creates a powerful contribution to the chart's potential for artistic achievement and the success she first realized at seventeen. In her D-9, AK Mercury and *vargottama* AmK/natal 5th lord Mars form *Raj* yoga in the 10th house from Scorpio. A 1 – 9 *Parivartana* yoga involving Mars and Sun occurs, as sign ruler Sun is exalted in the 9th and aspects back to Leo, which is also influenced by DK Jupiter. Sub-period sign Scorpio is the ascendant of the D-10, and holds Venus, Saturn, and *Rahu*. *Swakshetra* and directional strength BK Sun in the 10th house is aspected by AK Mercury and PK Moon, both of whom aspect Scorpio as well. The 11th house from the Scorpio D-10 ascendant is aspected by *vargottama* (in the D-10) DK Jupiter and D-10 chart ruler AmK Mars.

The following chart is that of prominent French dancer and choreographer Benjamin Millepied (June 10, 1977, Bordeaux, France, 1:30 p.m., AA). Benjamin Millepied began his ballet training at the age of eight and joined the New York City Ballet at the age of eighteen, in 1995. Seven years later Millepied was made principal dancer with the company. In 2011 Benjamin Millepied left NYCB to initiate and lead the LA Dance Project, and in 2014 he became Director of Dance for the Paris Opera Ballet. Benjamin Millepied has choreographed for the New York City Ballet, American Ballet Theatre, the School of American Ballet, the Metropolitan Opera, and the Paris Opera Ballet. In 2009 Benjamin Millepied choreographed and danced in the film *Black Swan*. In 2010 he was awarded the high honor of *Chevalier* in the Order of Arts and Letters by the French Ministry of Culture.

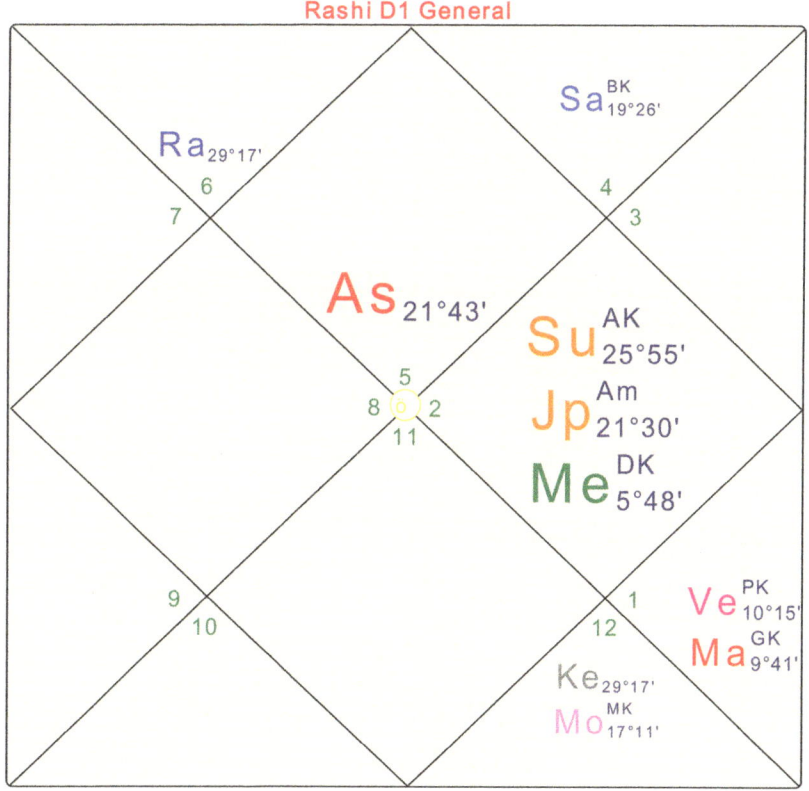

Rashi D1 General

Mo MK 17°11' Ke 29°17'	Ma GK 9°41' Ve PK 10°15'	Me DK 5°48' Jp Am 21°30' Su AK 25°55'	
			Sa BK 19°26'
	Benjamin Millepied Fri. 6/10/1977 13:30:00 Bordeaux, FR		As 21°43'
			Ra 29°17'

The Leo rising chart of Benjamin Millepied has creatively inspired *Purva Phalguni nakshatra* on the ascendant at 21 degrees 43 minutes; notice 5th lord Jupiter's placement in the 10th house in *Rohini nakshatra* within 13 minutes of the precise degree of the ascendant. Ascendant ruler Sun gains directional strength in the 10th house, which also holds 11th house ruler Mercury in *Krittika*, and once again we have activation of *Krittika nakshatra* in connection with the 11th house of dance. 10th house ruler Venus joins 9th lord Mars in *Ashwini* in the 9th house to give *Dharma Karma Adhipati Raj* yoga. *Phaladeepika Kahala* (6:36) yoga is formed as Venus, the dispositor of ascendant ruler Sun, is itself disposed by *swakshetra* Mars in the 9th house. *Kahala* yoga is said to confer prosperity, benevolence, and popularity. From the Moon the 11th house is aspected by its ruler Saturn and Moon's dispositor Jupiter. In similarity to the chart of Michael Flatley (*Ashwini* Mars aspects 12th lord Sun), *swakshetra* Mars in nimble *Ashwini nakshatra* influences the 12th house of the feet and occupant (and lord of 12 from Moon) Saturn. *Saraswati* yoga is formed by natural benefics Jupiter and Mercury in the 10th and Venus in the 9th house. *Jaimini Raj* yogas are created in the 10th house by Sun as AK, Jupiter in dual role as 5th lord and AmK, and Mercury as DK, all in (*Jaimini*) *sambandha* with BK Saturn in the 12th, and occurring in the 10th from Mr. Millepied's Leo KL, which is identical with his natal ascendant.

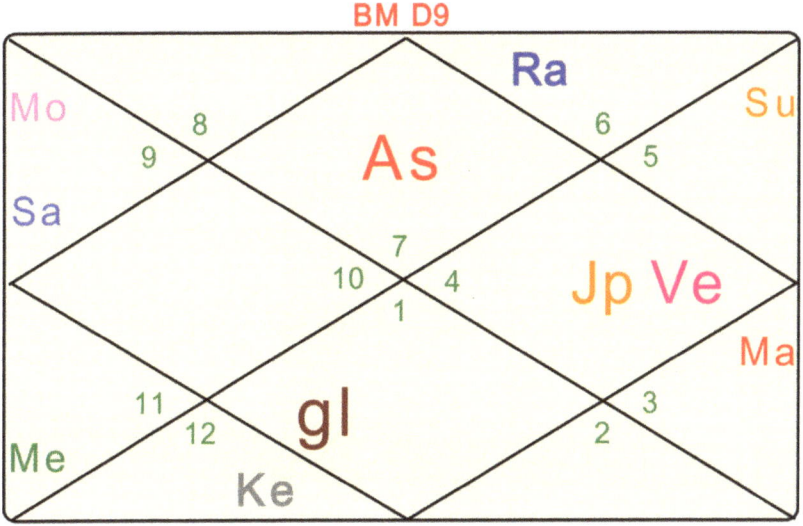

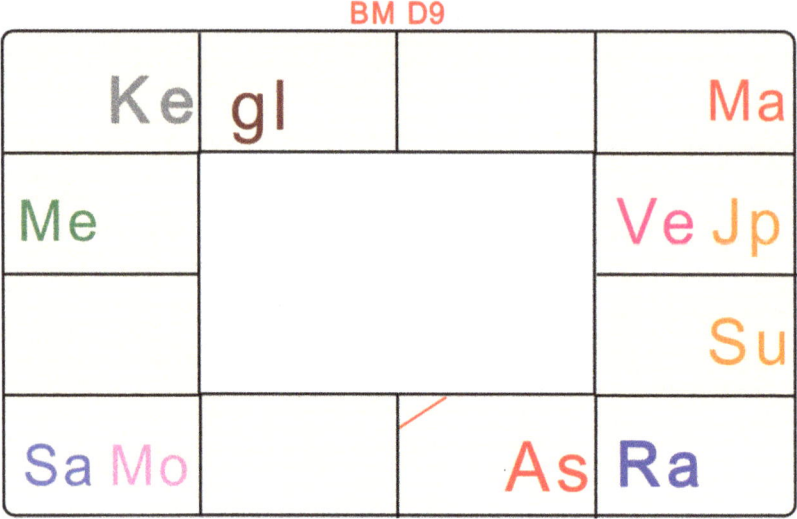
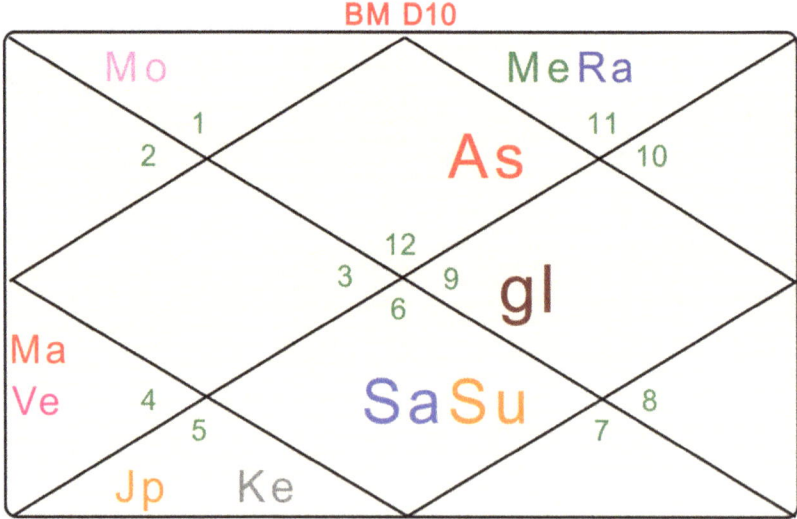

BM D10

As	Mo		
Me Ra			Ma Ve
			Jp Ke
gl			Su Sa

BM: Chara

Start Date	Age	Dashas
6/ 10/ 1977	-0.0	Leo
6/ 10/ 1980	3.0	Virg
6/ 10/ 1984	7.0	Libr
6/ 10/ 1990	13.0	Sco
6/ 10/ 1994	17.0	Sag
6/ 11/ 1999	22.0	Cap
6/ 10/ 2005	28.0	Aqu
6/ 11/ 2010	33.0	Pis
6/ 10/ 2020 n	43.0	Ari
6/ 10/ 2032	55.0	Tau
6/ 11/ 2043	66.0	Gem
6/ 11/ 2054	77.0	Can

BM: Vimshottari

Start Date			Age	Dashas	
4/	9/	1986	8.8	Me	Ra
10/	26/	1988	11.4	Me	Jp
2/	1/	1991	13.6	Me	Sa
10/	**11/**	**1993**	**16.3**	**Ke**	**Ke**
3/	10/	1994	16.7	Ke	Ve
5/	10/	1995	17.9	Ke	Su
9/	15/	1995	18.3	Ke	Mo
4/	15/	1996	18.8	Ke	Ma
9/	11/	1996	19.3	Ke	Ra
9/	29/	1997	20.3	Ke	Jp
9/	5/	1998	21.2	Ke	Sa
10/	15/	1999	22.3	Ke	Me
10/	**11/**	**2000**	**23.3**	**Ve**	**Ve**
2/	11/	2004	26.7	Ve	Su
2/	10/	2005	27.7	Ve	Mo
10/	12/	2006	29.3	Ve	Ma
12/	12/	2007	30.5	Ve	Ra
12/	12/	2010	33.5	Ve	Jp
8/	12/	2013	36.2	Ve	Sa
10/	11/	2016	39.3	Ve	Me
8/	12/	2019	42.2	Ve	Ke
10/	**11/**	**2020**	**43.3**	**Su**	**Su**
1/	29/	2021	43.6	Su	Mo
7/	31/	2021	44.1	Su	Ma
12/	5/	2021 n	44.5	Su	Ra
10/	30/	2022	45.4	Su	Jp

Benjamin Millepied joined the New York City Ballet in his *Vimshottari Ketu -- Sun* period. Both *Ketu*'s sign dispositor Jupiter and *nakshatra* dispositor Mercury are in the 10th house of the birth chart with the Sun, who gains *swakshetra* status in the 11th house in Millepied's D-9. In the D-9, *Ketu* is disposited and aspected by exalted 3rd and 6th lord Jupiter from the 10th house. In his D-10 Ketu joins 10th lord Jupiter in the 6th house as *Ketu*'s dispositor and sub-period lord Sun is accompanied by 11th lord Saturn in the 7th. M. Millepied's D-10 has two *Parivartana* yogas, with Mars and Moon exchanging between houses 2 and 5, and Saturn and Mercury between houses 7 and 12.

At age seventeen, Benjamin Millepied began a 5-year Sagittarius *Jaimini Chara dasha*. The 11th house from Sagittarius in the birth chart is influenced by *Jaimini* aspects from AK Sun and the beneficial Mercury/Jupiter combination, made more favorable by Mercury's status as DK and Jupiter's as 5th lord/AmK. In the D-9, there is a *Parivartana* yoga between houses 3 and 10 with MK Moon in the 3rd house in Sagittarius while exalted 3rd lord Jupiter goes to the 10th. The 11th house from Sagittarius is aspected by DK Mercury and *swakshetra* AK Sun. In his D-10, BK Saturn and Sun reside in the 10th house from Sagittarius while the 11th house is again activated by Mercury and Jupiter, also *Rahu* and *Ketu*.

The next chart in the section on dance, Dancer 12840 (April 12th, 1955, New York NY, 12:03 a.m., A), was taken from the research section of Astro-databank where the accompanying description states, "American dancer in a stage chorus in New York. She moved to Los Angeles, CA in 1982."

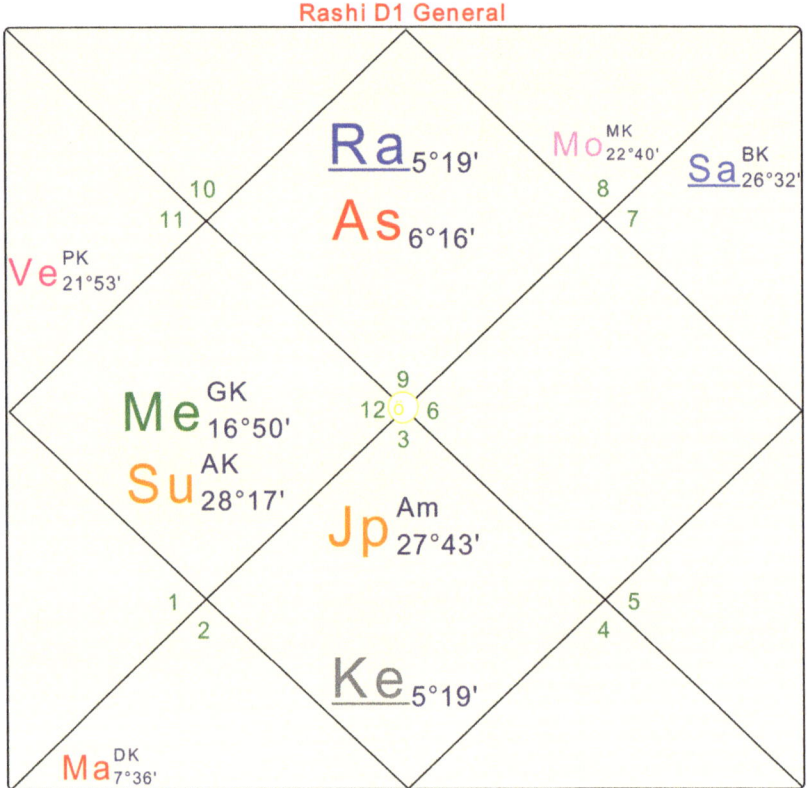

Creativity in the Vedic Astrology Chart

Rashi D1 General

Me GK 16°50' Su AK 28°17'		Ma DK 7°36'	Ke 5°19' Jp Am 27°43'
Ve PK 21°53'			
	Dancer 12840 Tue. 4/12/1955 0:03:00 New York, NY		
As 6°16' Ra 5°19'	Mo MK 22°40'	Sa BK 26°32'	

This chart features two prominent *Parivartana* yogas. There is an exchange between houses 3 and 11 with exalted 3rd lord Saturn in the 11th house and Venus placed in the 3rd house in the sign of Aquarius. Both sides of this exchange are strengthened by *vargottama* ascendant lord Jupiter's glances from the 7th house of the chart. The second exchange involves 4th lord Jupiter and 7th lord Mercury. From the 7th house Jupiter activates the ascendant, which also receives the aspect from 5th and 12th (feet) lord Mars. Mars confers a high level of energy and physicality due to its placement in the 6th house in *Krittika nakshatra*. The 11th house from the Moon is activated by the aspect from 10th lord (from Moon) Sun as well as that of its ruler Mercury. Mercury's debilitation will be cancelled by Jupiter's location in a *kendra*, as well as the placement of Venus in a *kendra* from the Moon.

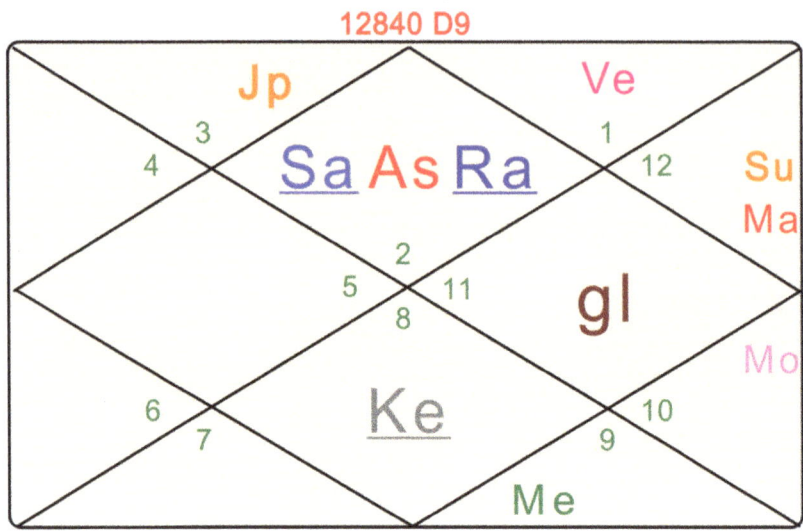

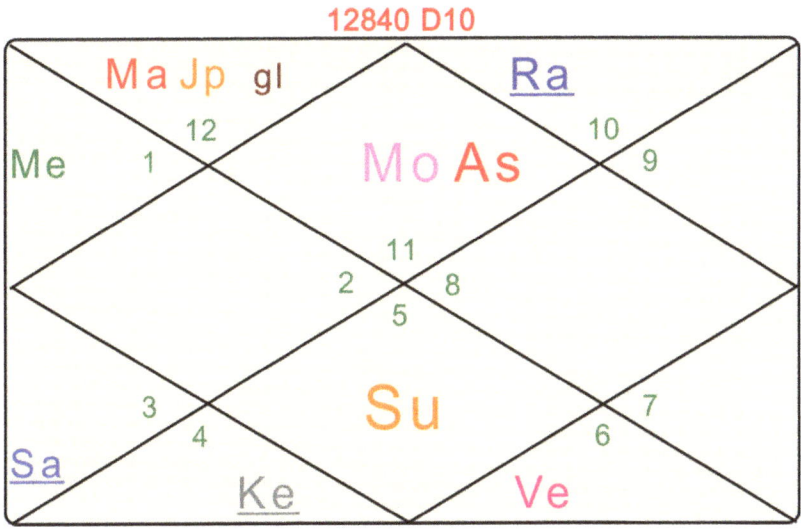

12840: Vimshottari

Start Date			Age	Dashas	
7/	15/	1966	11.3	Ke	Mo
2/	13/	1967	11.8	Ke	Ma
7/	12/	1967	12.3	Ke	Ra
7/	30/	1968	13.3	Ke	Jp
7/	6/	1969	14.2	Ke	Sa
8/	15/	1970	15.3	Ke	Me
8/	**12/**	**1971**	**16.3**	**Ve**	**Ve**
12/	11/	1974	19.7	Ve	Su
12/	12/	1975	20.7	Ve	Mo
8/	11/	1977	22.3	Ve	Ma
10/	12/	1978	23.5	Ve	Ra
10/	11/	1981	26.5	Ve	Jp
6/	11/	1984	29.2	Ve	Sa
8/	12/	1987	32.3	Ve	Me
6/	12/	1990	35.2	Ve	Ke
8/	**12/**	**1991**	**36.3**	**Su**	**Su**
11/	30/	1991	36.6	Su	Mo
5/	30/	1992	37.1	Su	Ma
10/	5/	1992	37.5	Su	Ra
8/	30/	1993	38.4	Su	Jp
6/	18/	1994	39.2	Su	Sa
5/	31/	1995	40.1	Su	Me
4/	5/	1996	41.0	Su	Ke
8/	11/	1996	41.3	Su	Ve
8/	**12/**	**1997**	**42.3**	**Mo**	**Mo**
6/	12/	1998	43.2	Mo	Ma

Chara		
Start Date	Age	Dashas
4/ 12/ 1955	-0.0	Sag
4/ 11/ 1961	6.0	Sco
4/ 11/ 1968	13.0	Libr
4/ 11/ 1972	17.0	Virg
4/ 11/ 1978	23.0	Leo
4/ 12/ 1983	28.0	Can
4/ 12/ 1991	36.0	Gem
4/ 11/ 2000	45.0	Tau
4/ 11/ 2009	54.0	Ari
4/ 12/ 2010	55.0	Pis
4/ 12/ 2019 n	64.0	Aqu
4/ 12/ 2023	68.0	Cap

In Dancer 12840's D-9 and D-10 charts, 11th lord Jupiter aspects the 10th house of career from its location in the 2nd. In the D-9, the Jupiter -- Mercury *Parivartana* yoga is replicated across the 2 -- 8 axis. In her D-10 Jupiter gains strength in the sign of Pisces, where it is joined by 10th lord Mars, as both planets are aspected by 9th lord Venus from the 8th house as well as by *lagna* lord Saturn from the 5th.

Although no detail is provided, it seems likely that Dancer 12840's career ascended during her *Vimshottari* 11th lord Venus period, which ran from ages 16 to 36. Simultaneously, she began her Virgo *Jaimini Chara dasha* at age seventeen. AmK Jupiter is found in the 10th house from Virgo while *vargottama* AK Sun inhabits the 7th with Virgo sign ruler Mercury. Notice that the 11th house from Virgo is activated by aspects from sign owner Moon, PK Venus, and DK Mars. In Dancer 12840's D-9 chart, *vargottama* Jupiter again sits in the 10th house from Virgo as the *dwishwabhava* signs are also activated by Mercury, the Sun, and Mars. In her D-10, PK Venus in Virgo is aspected by Saturn, Mars and *swakshetra* Jupiter. The following period of Leo finds Mars in the 10th house in *Krittika*, while the 11th house and sign of Gemini is strongly activated in all 3 charts, as narrated above. In the D-1 and

D-9 of Dancer 12840, the *dwishwabhava* signs are each aspected by their ruling planets. AK Sun achieves *swakshetra* status in the 7th house of Dancer 12840's D-10 chart.

Creativity in the Vedic Astrology Chart

The next chart for our consideration is that of Alvin Ailey (January 5th, 1931, Rogers (Bell County), TX, 5:30 a.m., B). Alvin Ailey was the esteemed dancer and choreographer who founded and directed the Alvin Ailey American Dance Theater. Alvin Ailey became fascinated with dance in his teens and took up the serious pursuit of dance at age eighteen, when he began to study with dancer and choreographer Lester Horton. Ailey joined Lester Horton's company in 1953, and when Horton died suddenly later that year, Ailey assumed the role of choreographer and artistic director for the company. Five years later Alvin Ailey founded the Alvin Ailey American Dance Theater, which is still thriving. Alvin Ailey was honored by the Kennedy Center in 1988 and was posthumously awarded the Presidential Medal of Freedom in 2014.

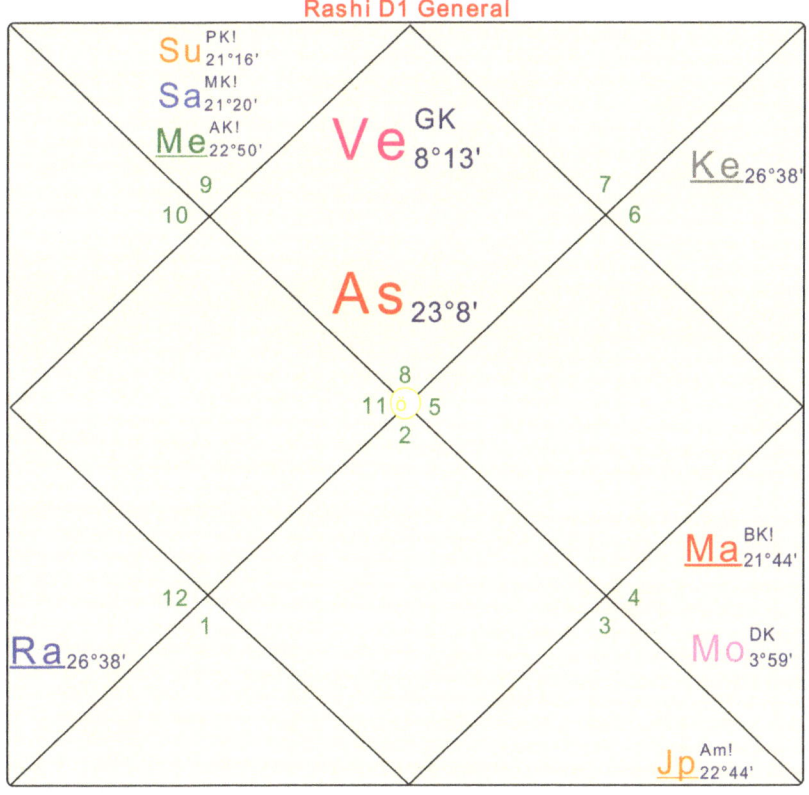

Rashi D1 General

			Am!
Ra 26°38'			Jp 22°44'
			DK Mo 3°59' BK! Ma 21°44'
	ö **Alvin Ailey** Mon. 1/5/1931 5:30:00 Rogers, Bell, TX		
Me AK! 22°50' Sa MK! 21°20' Su PK! 21°16'	As 23°8' Ve GK 8°13'		Ke 26°38'

Alvin Ailey's Scorpio rising chart features the extremely tight conjunction of 10th lord (career) Sun, 11th lord (dance) Mercury and 3rd lord (artistic expression) Saturn in the 2nd house in the Venus-owned *nakshatra* of *Purva Ashadha*. Although both Saturn and Mercury are combust and adverse for certain *jiva* (living) significations as represented in the chart, the close placement of these three *grahas* constitutes the foundation of Alvin Ailey's successful career in the realm of dance. Notice as well the *Parivartana* yoga and strong *sambandha* which occurs across the 2 – 8 axis between Mercury and Jupiter. As lord of the 5th house of creativity, Jupiter aspects the collection of planets in the 2nd house; Jupiter's degree is quite close to that of Sun and Saturn, but even closer, within six minutes, to that of Mercury. To accentuate the theme of dance, the planet Venus aspects its own house of Taurus, which serves as the 11th house from Moon and ascendant lord Mars. The chart is enhanced by the presence of *Parvata* yoga, as ascendant ruler Mars is disposited by *swakshetra* Moon in the 9th house. The association of Mars and Moon in Cancer will cancel Mars' debilitation. Mars achieves exaltation in the D-9 ascendant and meets criteria for *Neecha Bhanga Raj* yoga.

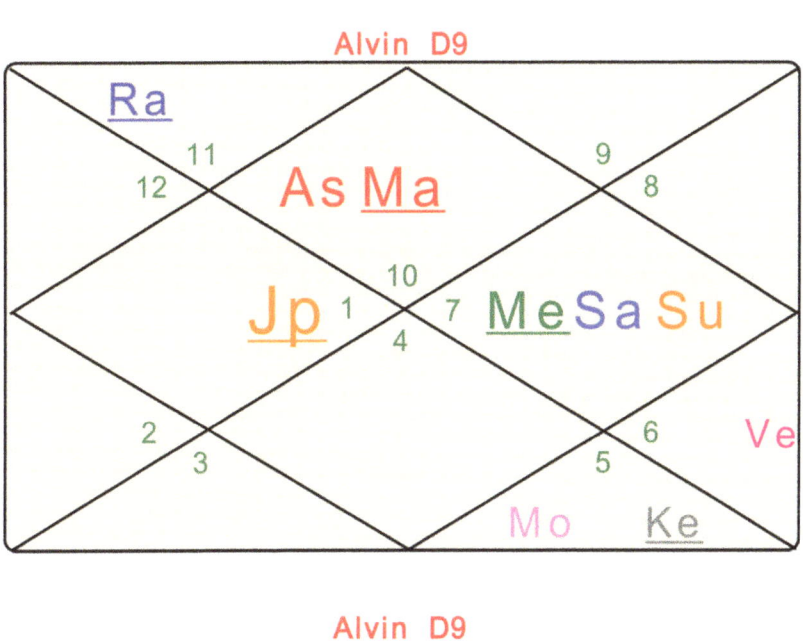

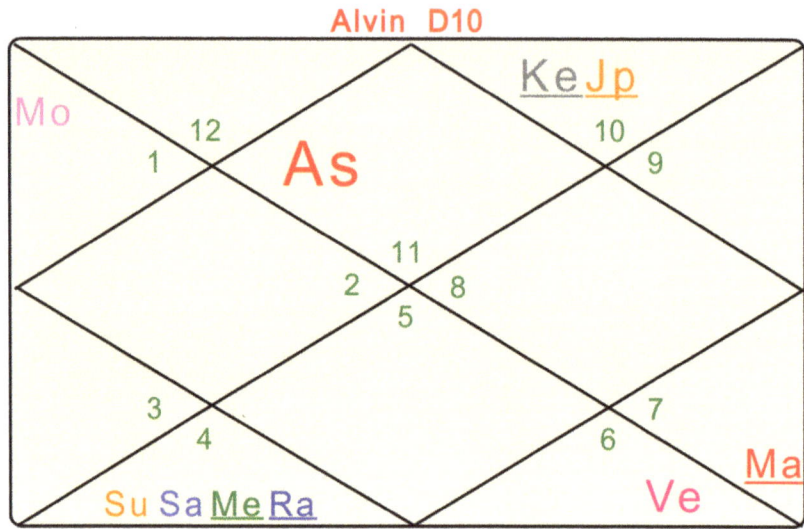

Alvin: Vimshottari

Start Date			Age	Dashas	
7/	13/	1946	15.5	Sa	Jp
1/	23/	1949	18.1	Me	Me
6/	22/	1951	20.5	Me	Ke
6/	18/	1952	21.5	Me	Ve
4/	19/	1955	24.3	Me	Su
2/	24/	1956	25.1	Me	Mo
7/	25/	1957	26.6	Me	Ma
7/	22/	1958	27.5	Me	Ra
2/	8/	1961	30.1	Me	Jp
5/	17/	1963	32.4	Me	Sa
1/	24/	1966	35.1	Ke	Ke
6/	22/	1966	35.5	Ke	Ve
8/	22/	1967	36.6	Ke	Su
12/	28/	1967	37.0	Ke	Mo
7/	28/	1968	37.6	Ke	Ma
12/	24/	1968	38.0	Ke	Ra
1/	12/	1970	39.0	Ke	Jp
12/	18/	1970	40.0	Ke	Sa
1/	27/	1972	41.1	Ke	Me
1/	23/	1973	42.1	Ve	Ve
5/	25/	1976	45.4	Ve	Su
5/	25/	1977	46.4	Ve	Mo
1/	24/	1979	48.1	Ve	Ma
3/	25/	1980	49.2	Ve	Ra
3/	26/	1983	52.2	Ve	Jp
11/	24/	1985	54.9	Ve	Sa

Start Date	Age	Dashas
1/ 5/ 1931	-0.0	Sco
1/ 5/ 1939	8.0	Libr
1/ 5/ 1940	9.0	Virg
1/ 4/ 1949	18.0	Leo
1/ 4/ 1957	26.0	Can
1/ 4/ 1969	38.0	Gem
1/ 5/ 1975	44.0	Tau
1/ 5/ 1981	50.0	Ari
1/ 5/ 1984	53.0	Pis
1/ 5/ 1993	62.0	Aqu
1/ 5/ 1995	64.0	Cap
1/ 5/ 1996	65.0	Sag

AA: Chara

Less than a month after he turned eighteen, Alvin Ailey began his 17-year Mercury period. With the onset of Mercury, Alvin Ailey made the decision to pursue dance as a career, and by the time his Mercury *dasha* had concluded in early 1966 the Alvin Ailey American Dance Theater had been become one of the world's leading dance companies. In his D-9, 11th lord Mars is exalted in the ascendant while Mercury engages in a 9 – 10 *Parivartana* yoga with Venus, joining exalted Saturn and debilitated Sun in the 10th house. The Sun achieves *Neecha Bhanga Raj* yoga secondary to its *kendra* placement, its association with exalted Saturn, and Mars' *kendra* location in the D-9 ascendant. In his D-10, 5th lord Mercury joins Sun, *lagna* lord Saturn and *Rahu* in the 6th house, and maintains its *sambandha* status with Jupiter, which is the 11th lord of the chart. Jupiter's debilitation in the D-10 will be cancelled by its *sambandha* with dispositor Saturn.

Alvin Ailey's 8-year Leo *Jaimini Chara dasha* had begun a few weeks earlier, on his 18th birthday; Leo is the 11th sign from Alvin Ailey's Libra KL. The presence of the AK and PK in the 5th house from Leo forms *Jaimini Raj* yoga; this yoga is amplified by the powerful *sambandha*, including the exchange, between AmK Jupiter and AK Mercury, across the 5/11 axis. Natal 5th lord Jupiter duplicates its status as 5th house ruler from the sign of Leo and tenants the 11th house in Gemini, where it is aspected by AK Mercury, PK Sun and Saturn. In the birth chart, the 10th house from Leo is aspected by *swakshetra* DK Moon and BK Mars. In the D-9, Leo is occupied by DK Moon (and *Ketu*) and is energized by the activation of all the *Jaimini Raj* yoga forming planets, including AK Mercury, PK Sun, and AmK/natal 5th lord Jupiter, as well as exalted BK Mars and exalted Saturn. With the exception of Jupiter, this group of planets also aspects the 10th house from Leo. The sign of Leo is similarly activated in Ailey's D-10, by aspects from the Moon, Jupiter, and Mars, while the 10th house from Leo, the sign of Taurus, receives the aspects of seven *grahas* in total, with Venus and Moon as the only exceptions.

Next we will consider another chart from the Research section of Astro-databank, Dancer 35925 (August 9, 1953, Los Angeles, CA, 10:30 a.m., AA). The narrative states, "Female American dancer, modern dance and choreography."

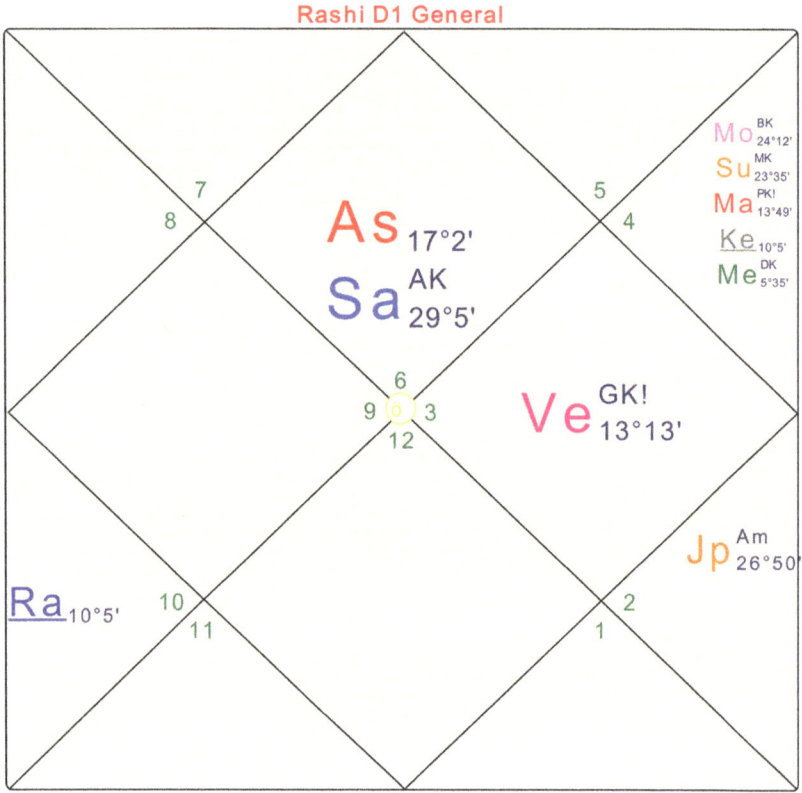

Creativity in the Vedic Astrology Chart

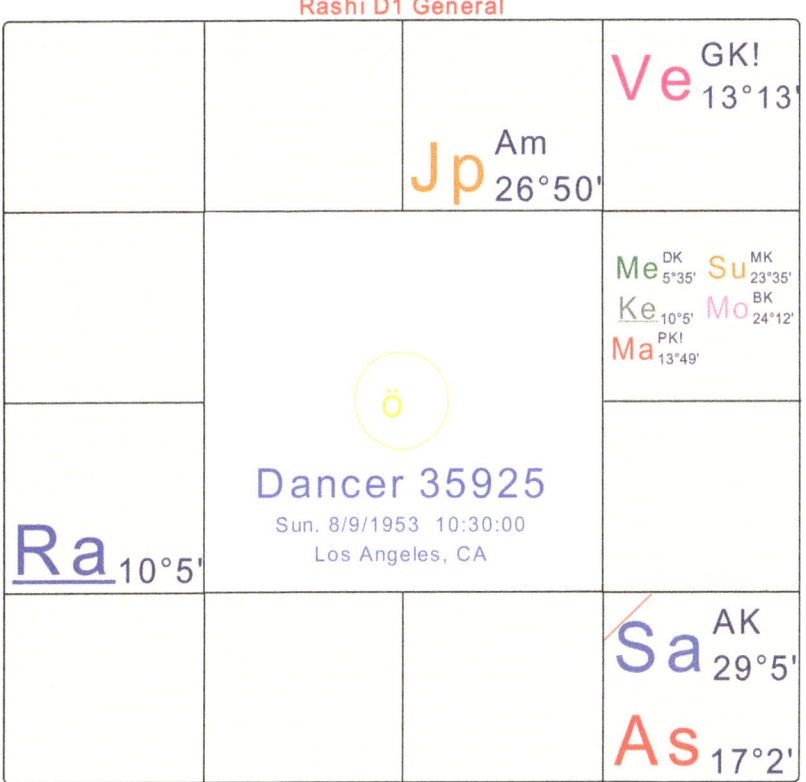

The theme of dance should be obvious, as the 11th house of the chart holds five *grahas*, including 11th lord Moon and ascendant and 10th lord Mercury. They are joined by 12th lord (feet) Sun, debilitated 3rd lord (artistic expression) Mars, and *Ketu*, as the 11th house from the Moon contains Jupiter in the sign of Taurus. The debilitation of Mars is cancelled as the result of its association with *swakshetra* Moon, Saturn's position in the ascendant, and Mars' *swakshetra* status in the D-9. 5th house ruler Saturn in *Chitra nakshatra* aspects Venus (lord of 11th from Moon) in the 10th house, and benefits from Jupiter's one-way aspect. This dancer ran her Venus major period from ages 14 to 34 and it is assumed that she was active in the realm of dance during this time. Notice the prominence of Venus in the D-10 of Dancer 35925, as it forms *Malavya* yoga in the ascendant and is joined by 11th lord Sun, whose debilitation is cancelled. In her D-9 *swakshetra* 11th lord Mars aspects the ascendant from the 6th house as well as 9th house occupants Moon and 3rd lord Sun.

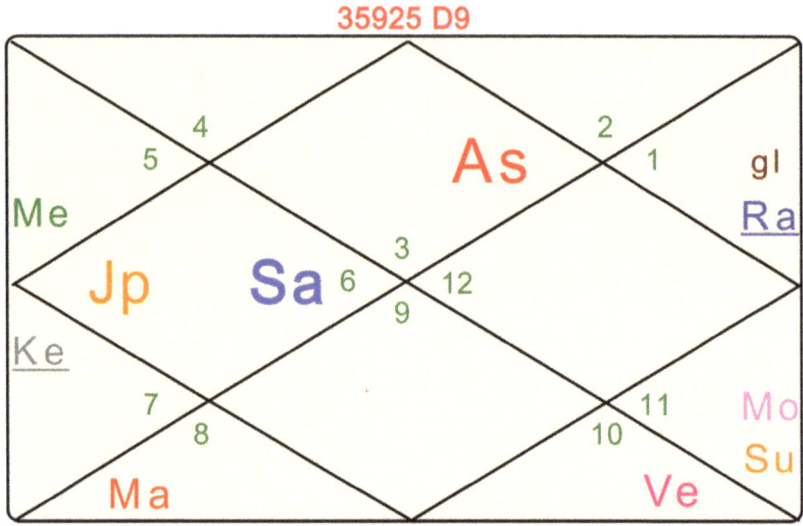

Creativity in the Vedic Astrology Chart

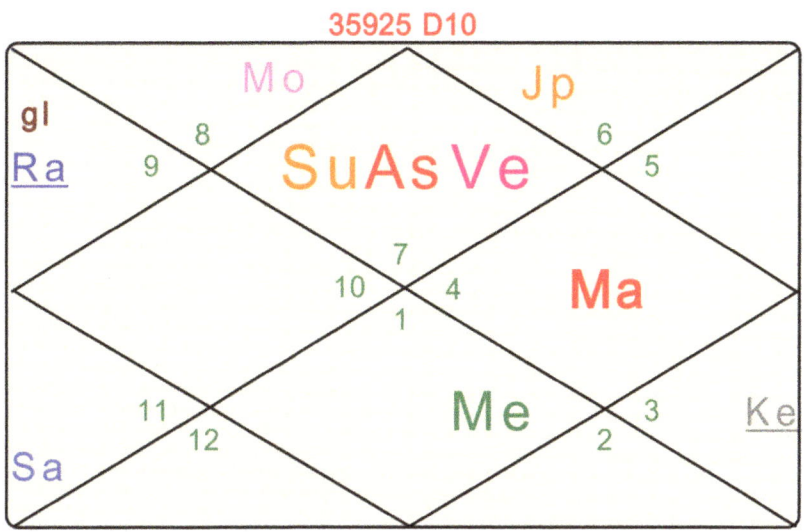

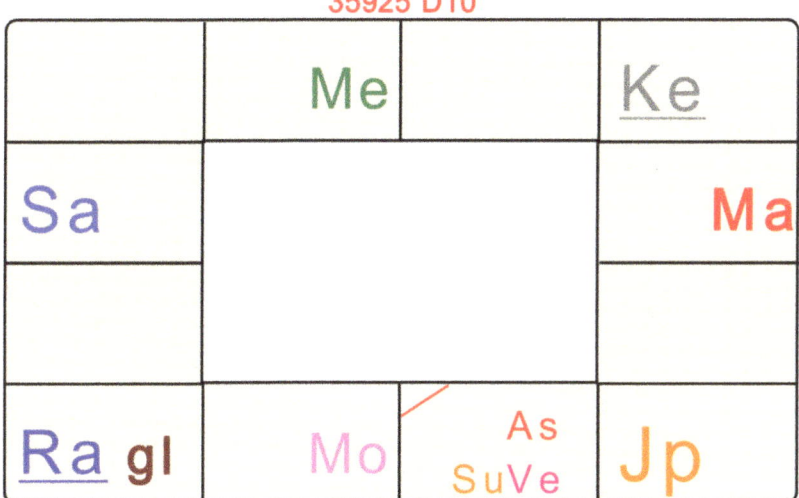

35925: Vimshottari

Start Date			Age	Dashas	
12/	12/	1964	11.3	Ke	Jp
11/	18/	1965	12.3	Ke	Sa
12/	27/	1966	13.4	Ke	Me
12/	**25/**	**1967**	**14.4**	**Ve**	**Ve**
4/	25/	1971	17.7	Ve	Su
4/	24/	1972	18.7	Ve	Mo
12/	24/	1973	20.4	Ve	Ma
2/	23/	1975	21.5	Ve	Ra
2/	23/	1978	24.5	Ve	Jp
10/	24/	1980	27.2	Ve	Sa
12/	25/	1983	30.4	Ve	Me
10/	25/	1986	33.2	Ve	Ke
12/	**25/**	**1987**	**34.4**	**Su**	**Su**
4/	12/	1988	34.7	Su	Mo
10/	12/	1988	35.2	Su	Ma
2/	17/	1989	35.5	Su	Ra
1/	11/	1990	36.4	Su	Jp
10/	31/	1990	37.2	Su	Sa
10/	13/	1991	38.2	Su	Me
8/	18/	1992	39.0	Su	Ke
12/	24/	1992	39.4	Su	Ve
12/	**24/**	**1993**	**40.4**	**Mo**	**Mo**
10/	25/	1994	41.2	Mo	Ma
5/	26/	1995	41.8	Mo	Ra
11/	24/	1996	43.3	Mo	Jp
3/	26/	1998	44.6	Mo	Sa

Chara

Start Date	Age	Dashas
8/ 9/ 1955	2.0	Libr
8/ 10/ 1963	10.0	Sco
8/ 10/ 1971	18.0	Sag
8/ 9/ 1976	23.0	Cap
8/ 9/ 1980	27.0	Aqu
8/ 9/ 1985	32.0	Pis
8/ 10/ 1995	42.0	Ari
8/ 9/ 1998	45.0	Tau
8/ 10/ 1999	46.0	Gem
8/ 9/ 2000	47.0	Can
8/ 9/ 2012	59.0	Leo
8/ 9/ 2013	60.0	Virg

Dancer 35925 ran her 5-year *Jaimini Chara dasha* of Sagittarius beginning at the age of eighteen; *vargottama* AK Saturn in the chart's KL in the 10th house from Sagittarius is aspected by 11th lord Venus. This configuration is duplicated in the D-9 where Saturn is joined in Virgo by AmK Jupiter. The subsequent *dasha* of Capricorn was operative from ages 23 to 27 and from Capricorn the 11th house, the sign of Scorpio, is aspected by the 5 *grahas* in Cancer, as well as by *Rahu*. The sign of Capricorn and the 10th house from Capricorn are aspected by AmK Jupiter. Venus in Capricorn in her D-9 sits in mutual aspect with *swakshetra* 11th lord (from Capricorn as well as D-9 ascendant) PK Mars. The 10th house from Capricorn is aspected by the Sun, Moon, and DK Mercury. *Swakshetra* Venus and Sun occupy the 10th house from Capricorn in the D-10 and are aspected there by *swakshetra* AK and natal/local 5th lord Saturn. From the sign of Capricorn in Dancer 35925's D-10, Moon and Mars form a 7 – 11 *Parivartana* yoga, cancelling the debilitation of both *grahas* as the 11th house is occupied by Moon and activated by aspects from Mars and Mercury.

The following chart, and the final chart for this section, is identified as Dancer 4224. This is a private chart, so no birth data or *dasha* timing are provided. The owner of this chart is devoted to the art of dance, and has studied and performed as an active dancer, teacher, and choreographer.

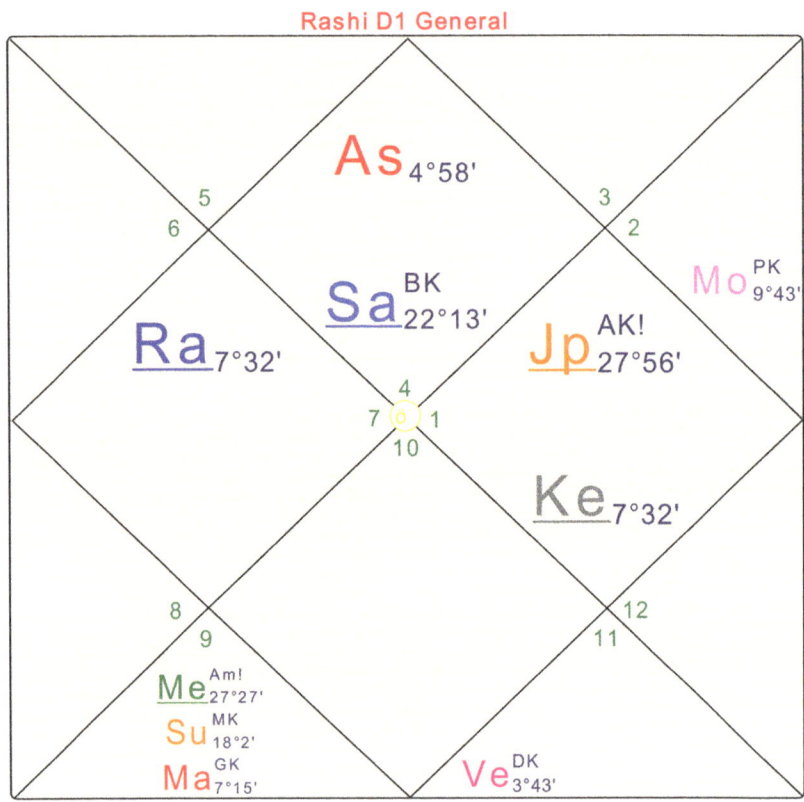

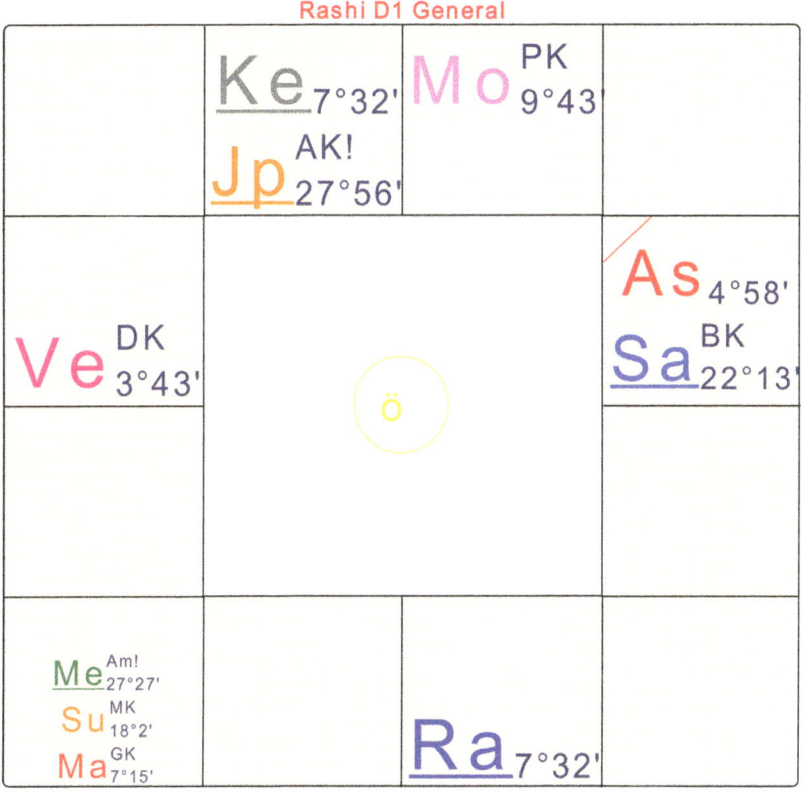

At first glance, the chart bears some resemblance to that of Heather Watts, as both charts feature Cancer rising with exalted ascendant lord Moon in the 11th house in *Krittika nakshatra*. In the chart of Dancer 4224, Jupiter rules the 11th house from the Moon and resides in the Aries portion of *Krittika* in the 10th house from the ascendant. There is a 6 -- 10 *Parivartana* yoga in the chart, with 6th lord Jupiter in the 10th while 10th lord Mars in the 6th is graced by Jupiter's 9th glance. Seen earlier in the chart of Fred Astaire, strong 6th house influence will tend to confer assiduous rehearsal habits, and is the case in the life of Dancer 4224. 5th lord Mars' 8th aspect to the ascendant (and 3rd from the Moon) grants creativity, movement, and physical strength to the chart's owner; notice also the aspect of Mars to the 11th house from the Moon. In the D-9 of Dancer 4224, the 11th house is strongly activated as 11th lord Mercury joins 5th lord

Jupiter in the 5th house while yoga *karaka* Mars is found in the 11th. In the D-10, ascendant lord Mars in the 11th is flanked by benefics and is disposited by doubly strong Saturn in the 7th house, forming *Parvata* yoga.

Dancer 4224's Sagittarius KL is occupied by the Sun, 5th lord Mars, and AmK Mercury. Recall, as seen in the chart of singer Eva Cassidy, that strong Mercury (*vargottama* in this chart) in the KL can confer artistic skill. The 11th house from the KL is favorably aspected by owner DK Venus and PK Moon. The chart's Cancer ascendant and occupant BK Saturn enjoy similar activation by Venus and exalted *lagna* lord Moon. As a dancer, 4224 enjoyed an especially active Aquarius *Chara dasha*, with Venus in Aquarius aspected by dispositor BK Saturn and AK Jupiter; notice that both Saturn and Jupiter gain *swakshetra* status in the D-9. In the birth chart, the KL and its occupants fall in the 11th house from Aquarius, while in the D-9, *vargottama* AmK Mercury, AK Jupiter and *Rahu* occupy Sagittarius and are in *sambandha* with the Sun, PK Moon, natal 5th lord Mars, and *Ketu*. 4th and 9th lord DK Venus forms *Raj* yoga in the 10th house from Aquarius and is aspected by *swakshetra* sign ruler Saturn. In the D-10, the sign of Aquarius is the 11th house of the chart and is occupied by Mars. Aquarius is aspected by its exalted ruler BK Saturn, and by PK Moon. The sign of Sagittarius has *Rahu* in aspect with the Sun and *Ketu*, but more notably, with two exalted *grahas*, AmK Mercury and DK Venus.

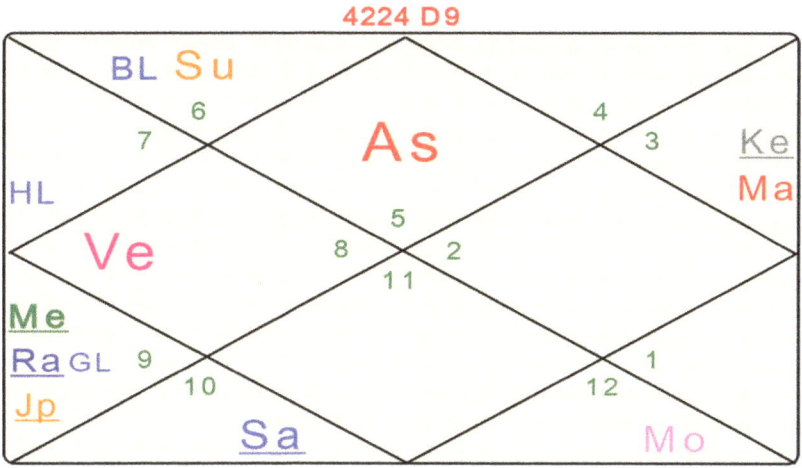

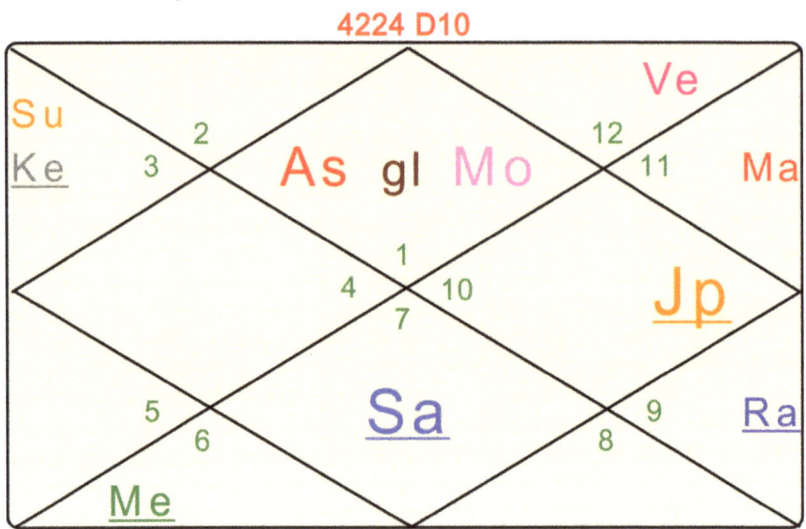

In this section on dance, we have seen a variety of ways in which activation of the 11th house occurs in each chart. In the charts of Martha Graham, Michael Ryan Flatley, Heather Watts, Dancer 35925 and Dancer 4224, the ascendant lord occupies the 11th house. In the charts of Fred Astaire, Ginger Rogers, Alessandra Ferri, Roberto Bolle, Benjamin Millepied and Alvin Ailey, there is a connection between houses 10 and 11, either by aspect, occupation, or association of the lords of the two houses. In the chart of Dancer 12840, there is an exchange between houses 3 and 11 while both sides of the exchange are aspected by ascendant lord Jupiter.

We conclude this section with an inspiring quote from Martha Graham (as told to choreographer Agnes de Mille): "*There is a vitality, a life force, a quickening that is translated through you into action, and there is only one of you in all time, this expression is unique, and if you block it, it will never exist through any other medium; and be lost. The world will not have it. It is not your business to determine how good it is, nor how it compares with other expression. It is your business to keep it yours clearly and directly, to keep the channel open. You do not even have to believe in yourself or your work. You have to keep open and aware directly to the urges that motivate you. Keep the channel open. No artist is pleased. There is no satisfaction whatever at any time. There is only a queer, divine dissatisfaction, a blessed unrest that keeps us marching and makes us more alive than the others.*"

Chapter 4

Theater, Film, & Photography

For our final section, we will analyze twelve charts of those involved in the creative process which specifically involves the realm of film/photography and theatrical production. This section will serve to highlight the importance of the 12th house of sleep and dreams as it influences the artistic sensibilities of the owner of the chart.

The first chart for our consideration in this final section is that of the influential and prolific wilderness photographer Ansel Adams (February 20, 1902, San Francisco, CA, 3:00 a.m., B).

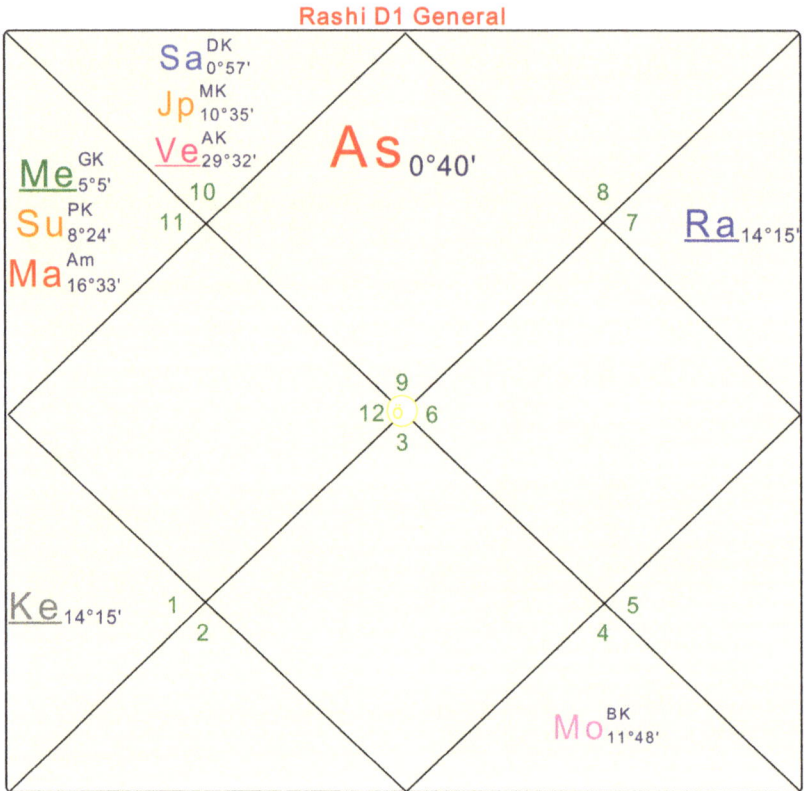

Rashi D1 General

	Ke 14°15'		
Ma Am 16°33' Su PK 8°24' Me GK 5°5'			Mo BK 11°48'
Ve AK 29°32' Jp MK 10°35' Sa DK 0°57'	**Ansel Adams** Thu. 2/20/1902 3:00:00 San Francisco, CA		
As 0°40'		Ra 14°15'	

As a child, Ansel Adams and his father shared an interest in astronomy. At the age of fourteen, during a family visit to Yosemite National Park, Ansel Adams was given his first camera, an Eastman-Kodak "Brownie" box camera. Adams later recalled "the splendor of Yosemite," being struck by the presence of "light everywhere," and described the occasion as the beginning of a "new era" in his life. Ansel Adams returned to Yosemite the following year, with more sophisticated cameras and a tripod, and over several following winters he learned film development and darkroom technique while working part-time for a San Francisco photographic finishing company. Ansel Adams contracted influenza during the Spanish flu pandemic of 1918 – 1919, and returned to Yosemite, where he was cured. Photographs by Ansel Adams were first published in 1921 and prints of his Yosemite photos were offered for sale the following year. In his twenties, Ansel Adams continued to study and refine his photographic technique and published his first portfolio in 1927. In 1931 a set of 60 of Adams' photographs taken in the High Sierra and Canadian Rockies were featured in a Smithsonian exhibition, to positive reviews. Two years later, Ansel Adams opened his own gallery in San Francisco and in 1935 published his first book, entitled *Making a Photograph*. As a founder and lifelong member of the Sierra Club, Ansel Adams' life and photographic work reflected his commitment to the protection of wilderness lands. Ansel Adams was the recipient of three prestigious Guggenheim Museum fellowships in his life, the first of which, granted in 1946, afforded Adams the opportunity to photograph all but one of the 28 U.S. National Parks. Certain of Ansel Adams' photographs, such as *The Tetons and the Snake River*, *Long's Peak*, *El Capitan*, and *Moonrise, Hernandez, New Mexico*, are considered iconic. Ansel Adams is often acknowledged as the most innovative and accomplished photographer of the 20th century. (Ansel Adams' gallery and biography can be found at www.anseladams.com.)

The Sagittarius rising chart of Ansel Adams finds ascendant ruler Jupiter in the 2nd house in its sign of debilitation, but that debilitation is cancelled several times over. Jupiter is accompanied by its sign dispositor, 2nd and 3rd lord Saturn, as the two *grahas* (joined by Venus) occupy an angle from the Moon, who is Jupiter's exaltation lord. Jupiter, the Moon, and Venus constitute a *Gaja Kesari* yoga across the 2 – 8 axis. Despite its 8th house location, the Moon is benefic and strong secondary to its *swakshetra*, bright and waxing status. The potential for artistry is seen by Jupiter's association with Venus and 3rd lord Saturn, while a *Raj* yoga (*Phaladeepika* 7:7) is formed by the bright Moon's *sambandha* relationship with *swakshetra* Saturn. By its aspect to the 10th house, *lagna* lord Jupiter confers the possibility of a self-made career. 12th house influence on the career is more clearly seen by *vargottama* 12th (and 5th) lord Mars' 8th aspect to the 10th house as well as Mars' association with 10th house ruler Mercury in the 3rd. The Sun, Mercury, and Mars in the 3rd house form 9 – 10, 5 – 9 and 5 – 10 *Raj* yogas. From *Chandra lagna* Mercury rules the 12th house, while Mars owns the 10th.

Ansel Adams' 9th lord Sun and 5th and 12th lord Mars inhabit the sharply observant *nakshatra* of *Shatabhisha*. As we recall that *Shatabhisha*'s deity is omniscient *Varuna*, lord of the all-encompassing firmament, it is interesting to note the preponderance of the sky in much of Ansel Adams' catalog, including some of his most dramatic images. In photographs such as *Yosemite Valley 1934*, *Autumn Storm 1958*, *The Golden Gate Before the Bridge 1932*, *Moon and Half Dome 1960*, and *Moonrise 1941*, the sky claims one-half or more of the frame, and dominates the image. *Shatabhisha nakshatra* can also be linked to Ansel Adams' early interest in astronomy. Notice as well that Ansel Adams' 9th and 10th lords occupy the *pakshi* (bird) *drekkana* of the first 10 degrees of Aquarius. At 14 degrees of Libra, *Rahu* also tenants a bird *drekkana*. Throughout his life, Adams was known for his willingness to climb to remote and lofty sites to capture scenes which reflected his artistic vision.

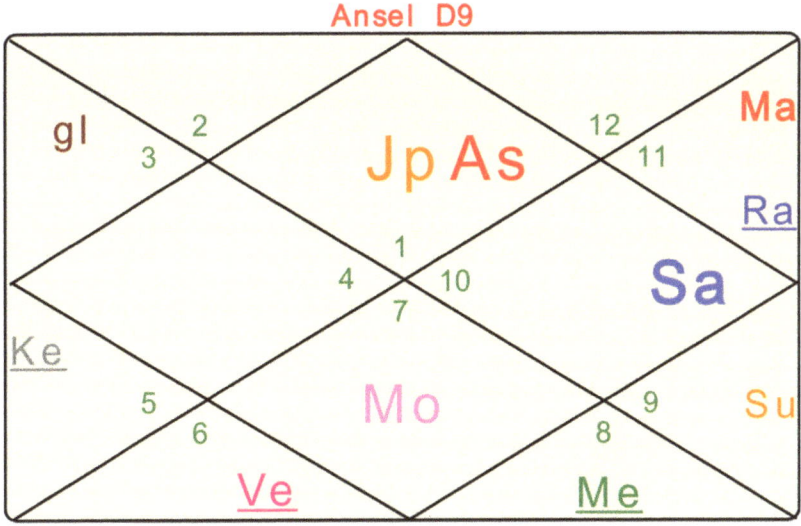

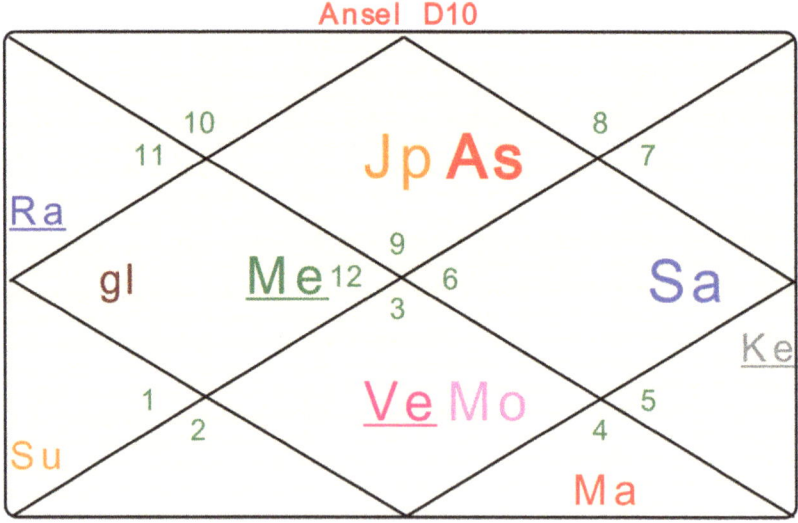

Ansel D10

gl Me	Su		Ve Mo
Ra			Ma
			Ke
Jp As			Sa

Ansel: Vimshottari

Start Date			Age	Dashas	
4/	14/	1915	13.1	Me	Su
2/	19/	1916	14.0	Me	Mo
7/	20/	1917	15.4	Me	Ma
7/	17/	1918	16.4	Me	Ra
2/	3/	1921	19.0	Me	Jp
5/	12/	1923	21.2	Me	Sa
1/	**19/**	**1926**	**23.9**	**Ke**	**Ke**
6/	17/	1926	24.3	Ke	Ve
8/	17/	1927	25.5	Ke	Su
12/	23/	1927	25.8	Ke	Mo
7/	23/	1928	26.4	Ke	Ma
12/	19/	1928	26.8	Ke	Ra
1/	7/	1930	27.9	Ke	Jp
12/	14/	1930	28.8	Ke	Sa
1/	22/	1932	29.9	Ke	Me
1/	**19/**	**1933**	**30.9**	**Ve**	**Ve**
5/	20/	1936	34.2	Ve	Su
5/	20/	1937	35.2	Ve	Mo
1/	19/	1939	36.9	Ve	Ma
3/	20/	1940	38.1	Ve	Ra
3/	21/	1943	41.1	Ve	Jp
11/	19/	1945	43.7	Ve	Sa
1/	19/	1949	46.9	Ve	Me
11/	20/	1951	49.7	Ve	Ke
1/	**19/**	**1953**	**50.9**	**Su**	**Su**
5/	8/	1953	51.2	Su	Mo

AA: Chara

Start Date	Age	Dashas	
7/ 22/ 1915	13.4	Virg	Virg
2/ 20/ 1916	14.0	Leo	Virg
8/ 21/ 1916	14.5	Leo	Libr
2/ 19/ 1917	15.0	Leo	Sco
8/ 21/ 1917	15.5	Leo	Sag
2/ 20/ 1918	16.0	Leo	Cap
8/ 21/ 1918	16.5	Leo	Aqu
2/ 20/ 1919	17.0	Leo	Pis
8/ 22/ 1919	17.5	Leo	Ari
2/ 20/ 1920	18.0	Leo	Tau
8/ 21/ 1920	18.5	Leo	Gem
2/ 19/ 1921	19.0	Leo	Can

AA: Chara

Start Date	Age	Dashas
2/ 20/ 1906	4.0	Libr
2/ 19/ 1909	7.0	Virg
2/ 20/ 1916	14.0	Leo
2/ 20/ 1922	20.0	Can
2/ 20/ 1934	32.0	Gem
2/ 20/ 1942	40.0	Tau
2/ 20/ 1950	48.0	Ari
2/ 20/ 1960	58.0	Pis
2/ 20/ 1962	60.0	Aqu
2/ 20/ 1963	61.0	Cap
2/ 20/ 1975	73.0	Sag
2/ 21/ 1976	74.0	Sco

Ansel Adams' passion for photography was ignited at the age of fourteen, during a family visit to Yosemite National Park. Having started his Mercury *Maha dasha* just before turning seven, Ansel Adams began the sub-period of Moon on the eve of his 14th birthday in 1916. *Maha dasha* and 10th lord Mercury's placement in the 3rd house is capable of steering the chart in the direction of a skill-based career; 12th house themes are activated as Mercury is joined in the 3rd house by 5th and 12th lord Mars (along with 9th lord Sun), and notice that Mercury rules the 12th house from the Moon. Mercury is strengthened by the *swakshetra* and *vargottama* status of its dispositor Saturn. Sub-period lord Moon participates in several distinctive *Raj* yogas, including *Gaja Kesari*. In Ansel Adams' D-9, the Moon is placed in the 7th house in Venus-owned Libra, in the 12th house from Mercury and in *sambandha* and *Kesari* yoga with 12th lord Jupiter, who obtains directional strength in the D-9 ascendant. The Moon and Jupiter, joined by Venus, repeat their *Gaja Kesari* formation across the 1 – 7 axis in Ansel Adams' D-10 chart, where Jupiter again achieves directional strength as well as the formation of *Hamsa* yoga in the sign of Sagittarius. Adams' following sub-periods, of Mars and then *Rahu*, contributed to his growing interest in photography through his teenage years; as 12th lord of his *vargottama* D-10 chart, Mars aspects *swakshetra Rahu* in Aquarius in the 3rd house. Ascendant ruler Mars and *swakshetra Rahu* occupy the 11th house in Ansel Adams' D-9.

The 6-year Leo *Jaimini Chara dasha*, occurring between ages fourteen and twenty, was equally influential at a formative time in the life of Ansel Adams. From the sign of Leo, the 9th house of the chart, a strong BK (skills) Moon owns and occupies the 12th house of visual expression, where the Moon is activated by aspects from (*Jaimini*) yoga-forming *grahas* PK Sun and *vargottama* natal 5th lord/AmK Mars, as well as Mercury. In Adams' D-9, the Moon, Jupiter, and Saturn aspect the sign of Leo and occupant *Ketu*, as BK Moon and DK Saturn also aspect the 10th house from Leo, the sign of Taurus. From Leo, 12th lord Moon in the 3rd house in Libra is nicely flanked by benefics, and is aspected there by AmK Mars, also by *Rahu* and *Ketu*.

As he turned fourteen, Ansel Adams' first sub-period was the sign of Virgo, which happens to be his KL. From Virgo in the birth chart, AK Venus, DK Saturn, and D-1 ascendant lord Jupiter lie in the 5th house of creative inspiration and aspect the 3rd, 9th, and 12th houses, the signs of Scorpio, Taurus, and Leo, respectively. The placement of Venus associated with Jupiter in the 5th house from Adams' KL constitutes the *Jaimini Raj* yoga mentioned in BPHS 39:11. BK Moon and *Rahu* join in the collective activation of the 9th house from Virgo as Moon and *Ketu* aspect the 3rd; *Rahu* and *Ketu* join Saturn, Venus, and Jupiter in the activation of the 12th house from Virgo. In his D-9, Virgo holds AK Venus while PK Sun also aspects the *dwishwabhava* signs from its placement in the sign of Sagittarius. The 12th house from Virgo, with *Ketu*, receives aspects from Jupiter, BK Moon, and DK Saturn, as 12th house lord (from Virgo) Sun aspects the 10th house and sign of Gemini. In Ansel Adams' D-10, the 12th house from Virgo is aspected by its exalted lord. Virgo holds DK Saturn in aspect with Jupiter, Mercury, Venus, and the Moon.

The high degree of success and recognition which Ansel Adams achieved during his 8-year Gemini period, from ages thirty-two to forty, is reflected in his D-10, as AK Venus and BK Moon reside in the sign of Gemini and re-create the birth chart's *Gaja Kesari* yoga across the 1 – 7 axis of the chart, with doubly strong Jupiter in the ascendant. Mercury's debilitation is cancelled secondary to its location in an angle and the *kendra* placements of Jupiter and Venus. The *dwishwabhava* signs in Adams' D-10 benefit from activation by their lords as well as the cumulative effect of all the natural benefics.

Moving on, our next chart in this section is that of Greta Garbo (September 18, 1905, Stockholm, Sweden, 7:30 p.m., AA), one of the world's foremost film actresses. Greta Garbo's career began in the silent era of the 1920s and made a successful transition into the era of sound, but was cut short when she abruptly retired at the age of thirty-six.

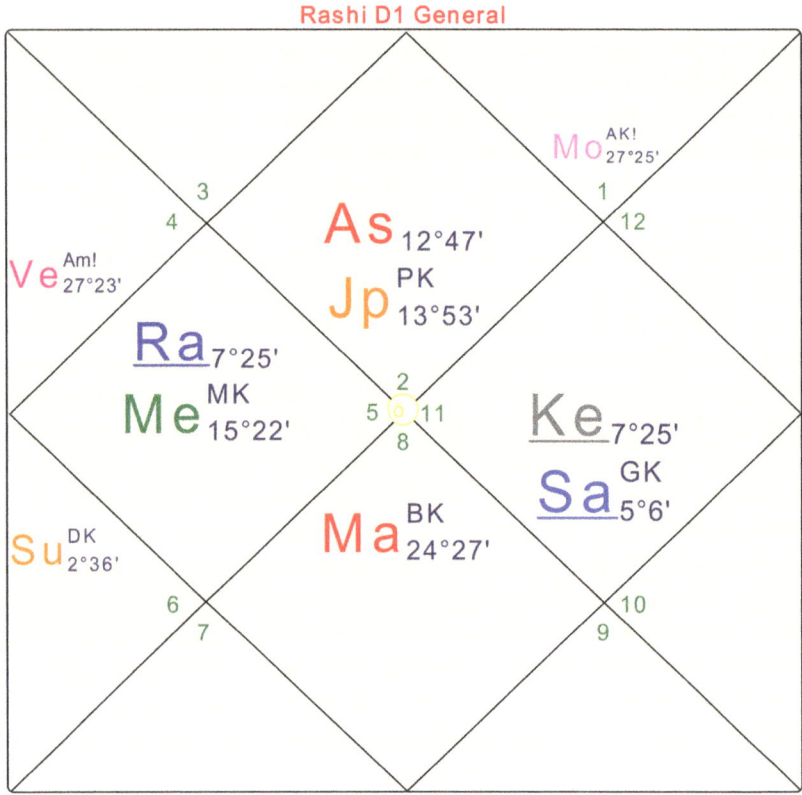

Creativity in the Vedic Astrology Chart

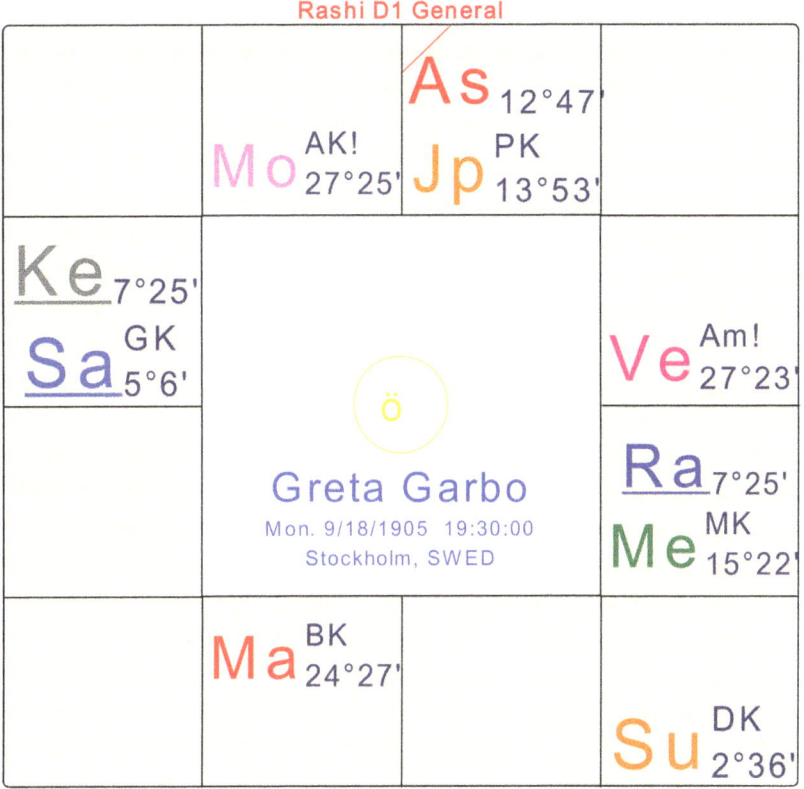

Greta Garbo studied acting at the Royal Dramatic Training Academy in Stockholm between 1922 and 1924 and appeared in her first film later the same year. She travelled to the U.S., and ultimately to Hollywood, in 1925. Signed to MGM, she acted for the studio in her first Hollywood film, *Torrent*, in 1926. Greta Garbo received strongly positive reviews for her next several films, and by 1929, with the advent of sound in movies, she had become one of the leading film stars of her era. In the 1930s, Greta Garbo had leading roles in a set of successful films, including *Anna Christie* (1930), *Grand Hotel* (1932), *Queen Christina* (1933), *Anna Karenina* (1935), *Camille* (1936), and (her first comedy role), *Ninotchka* (1939). Following her appearance in *Two-Faced Woman* (1941), Greta Garbo retired and did not appear in another film. Although Ms. Garbo never won a

Best Actress Oscar (she received three nominations), she was given an Academy Honorary Award in 1954 for "luminous and unforgettable screen performances." Despite the relative brevity of her acting career, Greta Garbo continues to be critically honored as one of the most naturally expressive actresses in the history of film. Clarence Brown, who directed Ms. Garbo in seven films, stated, "Garbo has something behind the eyes that you couldn't see until you photographed it in close-up. You could see thought. If she had to look at one person with jealousy, and another with love, she didn't have to change her expression. You could see it in her eyes as she looked from one to the other. And nobody else has been able to do that on screen." (Stevenson Swanson, *Chicago Tribune,* October 27, 2005). The American Film Institute places Greta Garbo 5th on its list of greatest film actresses. (https://www.afi.com/afis-100-years-100-stars/).

Greta Garbo's Taurus rising chart has *Rohini nakshatra* on the ascendant degree, closely joined by Jupiter. Ascendant ruler Venus is placed in the 3rd house of artistic expression in the hypnotic *nakshatra* of *Ashlesha*, while 3rd house ruler Moon goes to the 12th in *Krittika nakshatra*. *Kahala* yoga is formed secondary to the chain of disposition of ascendant ruler Venus concluded by Mars in *Ruchaka* yoga in the 7th house. The chart features several compelling *sambandha* relationships, as the result of a yoga known as *Chatussagara*, which is said to obtain when all four *kendra* houses are occupied. (B.V. Raman, *300 Important Combinations*). The planets Mars and Saturn each form *Maha Purusha* yogas as both inhabit their own signs in angular houses, Saturn in Aquarius in the 10th house and Mars in Scorpio in the 7th. Mutual *sambandha* is obtained due to Mars' 4th aspect and Saturn's 10th. Mars' strength and influence contribute significantly to Greta Garbo's success in the realm of film; see that Mars as lord of the 12th house (and sign of Aries, its *mooltrikona* sign) of visual expression aspects the 10th house and lord as well as the chart's ascendant, while Saturn as 10th lord reciprocates that influence as it glances back at Mars as well as to the 12th house and occupant 3rd lord

Moon. In fact, it was during her *Vimshottari* Mars -- Saturn period when Greta Garbo completed her studies at the Royal Academy in Stockholm and appeared in her first film. The *sambandha* formed by 11th lord Jupiter and 12th lord Mars confers mass appeal (11th) through the media of film (12th) but notice also Jupiter's lordship of 12th house from the Moon, creating *sambandha* of the two different 12th house-ruling *grahas*.

Employing the Moon as ascendant, we find 12th lord Jupiter in the abundantly creative *nakshatra* of *Rohini* aspecting the 10th house. The Moon and Venus, on the same degree and within two minutes of each other, form a precise *kendra sambandha* as Venus sits in the 4th house from the Moon and aspects the 10th. Greta Garbo's chart contains two *Chaya Graha Raj* yogas, as *Rahu* and *Ketu* each accompany *trikona* lords, Mercury and Saturn, respectively, in *kendra* houses. As the subtlest and most imperceptible *graha*, *Ketu* joins 9th and 10th lord Saturn in the 10th house and contributes to the refined naturalism of Greta Garbo's screen presence. The gracefulness of Greta Garbo's visual presentation is reinforced by *Ketu*'s placement in the *nakshatra* of *Shatabhisha*. Fifth house ruler Mercury participates in a *Parivartana* yoga with 4th lord Sun. Mercury's 4th house location gives it a mutually aspecting *sambandha* relationship with 9th and 10th lord Saturn as the two *grahas* form 5 -- 9 and 5 -- 10 *Raj* yogas across the 4 – 10 axis of the chart. Mercury's creative potential as 5th lord is enhanced due to its placement in *Purva Phalguni nakshatra* as well as Mercury's role in a nodal *Raj* yoga. As her *Rahu* major period unfolded, Greta Garbo achieved world-wide recognition for her enigmatic beauty, grace, and powerfully understated skills as an actress.

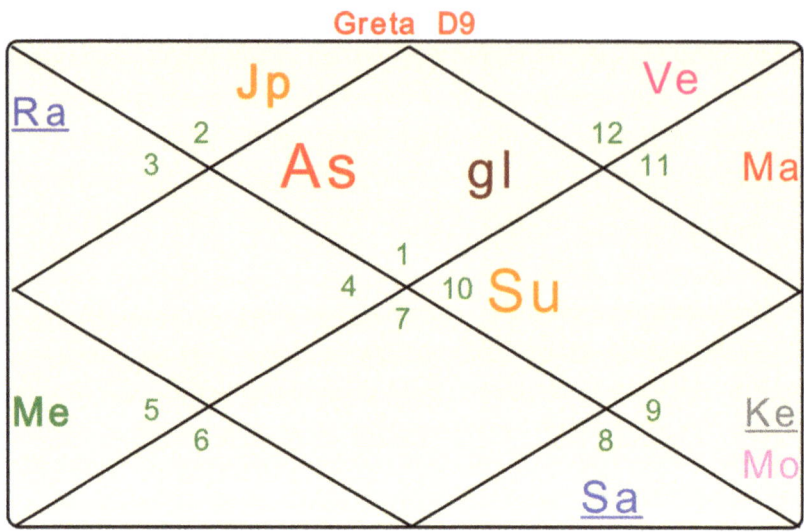

Creativity in the Vedic Astrology Chart

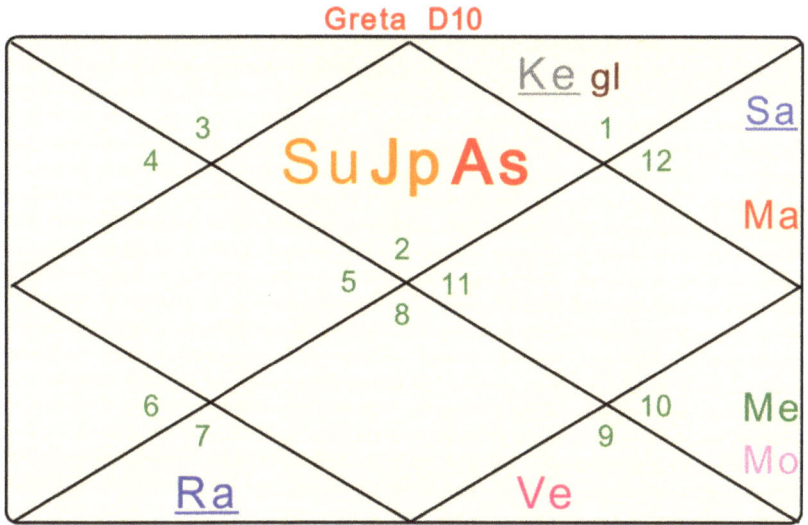

Greta: Vimshottari

Start Date			Age	Dashas	
3/	16/	1919	13.5	Mo	Ve
11/	14/	1920	15.2	Mo	Su
5/	**15/**	**1921**	**15.7**	**Ma**	**Ma**
10/	12/	1921	16.1	Ma	Ra
10/	30/	1922	17.1	Ma	Jp
10/	6/	1923	18.0	Ma	Sa
11/	14/	1924	19.2	Ma	Me
11/	11/	1925	20.1	Ma	Ke
4/	9/	1926	20.6	Ma	Ve
6/	9/	1927	21.7	Ma	Su
10/	15/	1927	22.1	Ma	Mo
5/	**15/**	**1928**	**22.7**	**Ra**	**Ra**
1/	26/	1931	25.4	Ra	Jp
6/	21/	1933	27.8	Ra	Sa
4/	27/	1936	30.6	Ra	Me
11/	14/	1938	33.2	Ra	Ke
12/	3/	1939	34.2	Ra	Ve
12/	3/	1942	37.2	Ra	Su
10/	27/	1943	38.1	Ra	Mo
4/	27/	1945	39.6	Ra	Ma
5/	**16/**	**1946**	**40.7**	**Jp**	**Jp**
7/	3/	1948	42.8	Jp	Sa
1/	14/	1951	45.3	Jp	Me
4/	21/	1953	47.6	Jp	Ke
3/	28/	1954	48.5	Jp	Ve
11/	26/	1956	51.2	Jp	Su

Creativity in the Vedic Astrology Chart

GG: Chara

Start Date	Age	Dashas	
9/ 18/ 1924	19.0	Aqu	Pis
3/ 20/ 1925	19.5	Aqu	Ari
9/ 18/ 1925	20.0	Aqu	Tau
3/ 20/ 1926	20.5	Aqu	Gem
9/ 19/ 1926	21.0	Aqu	Can
3/ 20/ 1927	21.5	Aqu	Leo
9/ 19/ 1927	22.0	Aqu	Virg
3/ 20/ 1928	22.5	Aqu	Libr
9/ 18/ 1928	23.0	Aqu	Sco
3/ 20/ 1929	23.5	Aqu	Sag
9/ 18/ 1929	24.0	Aqu	Cap
3/ 20/ 1930	24.5	Aqu	Aqu
9/ 19/ 1930	25.0	Cap	Sag
8/ 20/ 1931	25.9	Cap	Sco
7/ 19/ 1932	26.8	Cap	Libr
6/ 19/ 1933	27.8	Cap	Virg
5/ 20/ 1934	28.7	Cap	Leo
4/ 20/ 1935	29.6	Cap	Can
3/ 20/ 1936	30.5	Cap	Gem
2/ 17/ 1937	31.4	Cap	Tau
1/ 18/ 1938	32.3	Cap	Ari
12/ 19/ 1938	33.2	Cap	Pis
11/ 19/ 1939	34.2	Cap	Aqu
10/ 19/ 1940	35.1	Cap	Cap
9/ 19/ 1941	36.0	Sag	Sco
2/ 18/ 1942	36.4	Sag	Libr

12th house emphasis persists in Greta Garbo's D-9 and D-10 charts. Ms. Garbo's Aries rising D-9 features two *Parivartana* yogas. Exalted Venus in the 12th exchanges with *vargottama* Jupiter, as 12th lord Jupiter aspects the 10th house and has *sambandha* with 10th lord Saturn. Saturn and D-9 chart ruler Mars also exchange between the 8th house and the 11th. From the 11th, Mars activates 12th lord Jupiter with its 4th glance. The D-9 ascendant is flanked by benefics. In her Taurus rising D-10, 12th lord Mars joins 10th lord Saturn in the 11th house. Jupiter and Venus again exchange signs, with Jupiter in the ascendant and Venus in Sagittarius in the 8th house. It turned out that Greta Garbo's career did not survive her *Rahu* major period, as she retired during *Rahu* -- Venus; Venus' 8th house placement in her D-10 will be at least partially responsible for her retirement during its sub-period.

Greta Garbo appeared in her first film in 1924, precisely at the outset of her 6-year *Jaimini* Aquarius *Chara dasha*. Aquarius is the 10th house of her birth chart and contains *swakshetra* Saturn. The 10th house from Aquarius is favorably activated by the presence of *swakshetra* BK (skills) Mars and the *Jaimini* yoga-forming aspects from the AmK Venus/AK Moon combination, who also aspect the sign of Aquarius itself and occupant Saturn. The 12th house is activated by artistic/creatively oriented BK Mars, 5th lord Mercury, and PK Jupiter. In the D-9 of Greta Garbo, Mars and Saturn form a 1 – 10 *Parivartana* between Aquarius and Scorpio, while the 12th house from Aquarius is strongly activated by the presence of DK Sun and aspects to the sign of Capricorn from *vargottama* planets (natal) 5th lord Mercury and PK Jupiter, as well as sign ruler Saturn. In fact, Greta Garbo's subsequent 11-year Capricorn period saw her greatest success as an actress. In her D-1, Saturn, Jupiter, and Mercury (as well as *Rahu* and *Ketu*) all cast aspects to the 10th house from Capricorn while AmK Venus and AK Moon occupy *kendra* houses. In Ms. Garbo's Taurus rising D-10, Capricorn holds AK Moon and natal/local 5th lord Mercury, as DK Sun and (again in D-10), *vargottama* PK Jupiter aspect Capricorn and the sign of Libra and occupant *Rahu*.

Since Greta Garbo's retirement from film in 1941 occurred at the conclusion of her Capricorn *Chara dasha*, it is worth exploring why her following Sagittarius *dasha* did not sustain her career. (We have already noted the impact of *Vimshottari* sub-period lord Venus' location in the 8th house of Greta Garbo's D-10, corresponding to the timing of her retirement.) In Garbo's D-1, the sign of Sagittarius is the 8th house of the chart. DK Sun does reside in Virgo in the 10th

house from Sagittarius, but there is no further activation of the 10th or the other angular houses from Sagittarius, while Sagittarius' ruler Jupiter sits six houses away in the sign of Taurus. Because Jupiter attains *vargottama* status in her D-9 and D-10, this pattern (Jupiter in the 6th) persists in both divisional charts. We notice as well that from Sagittarius in the D-1 AmK (career) Venus is placed in the 8th house of transformation in the sign of Cancer.

In Ms. Garbo's D-9, AK Moon occupies the chart's 9th house in Sagittarius with *Ketu*, as exalted AmK Venus locates four houses away in the 12th. The Moon and Venus in *kendras* from Sagittarius will confer *Jaimini Raj* yoga, but the influence of *Rahu* and *Ketu* on those same angular houses is adverse. Also not insignificant is the location (from Sagittarius) of 10th lord Mercury in the 9th house in the sign of Leo; this configuration repeats from the D-1, while in the D-9 Mercury is additionally influenced by 9th lord Sun. Although the 9th is naturally a beneficial house, it is however the house of retirement and/or potential negation of career, as it is 12th from the 10th. Despite the presence of AmK Venus in the sign of Sagittarius in Garbo's D-10, this placement occurs in the 8th house of the chart and is afflicted by two natural malefics, Saturn and Mars, from the sign of Pisces. The adverse 6th house from Sagittarius, the sign of Taurus, is activated by the exchange between Venus and Jupiter and the occupation of the sign of Taurus by Jupiter and the Sun, as well as aspects to Taurus from Mercury, the Moon, and *Rahu*. The placement of Saturn and Mars in the 4th house (contentment, permanence) from Sagittarius in the D-10 implies the manifestation of a sense of dissatisfaction with her career. Recalling this time in her life, Greta Garbo told her biographer Sven Broman, "I was tired of Hollywood. I did not like my work. There were many days when I had to force myself to go to the studio … I really wanted to live another life." (Sven Broman, *Conversations with Greta Garbo*, 1990). Greta Garbo was to refer to her final film, *Two-Faced Woman* (1941) as "my grave." (John Bainbridge, *Life* magazine, January 24th, 1955).

The following chart is that of actor, film director, and producer Ron Howard (March 1, 1954, Duncan, OK, 9:03 a.m., AA).

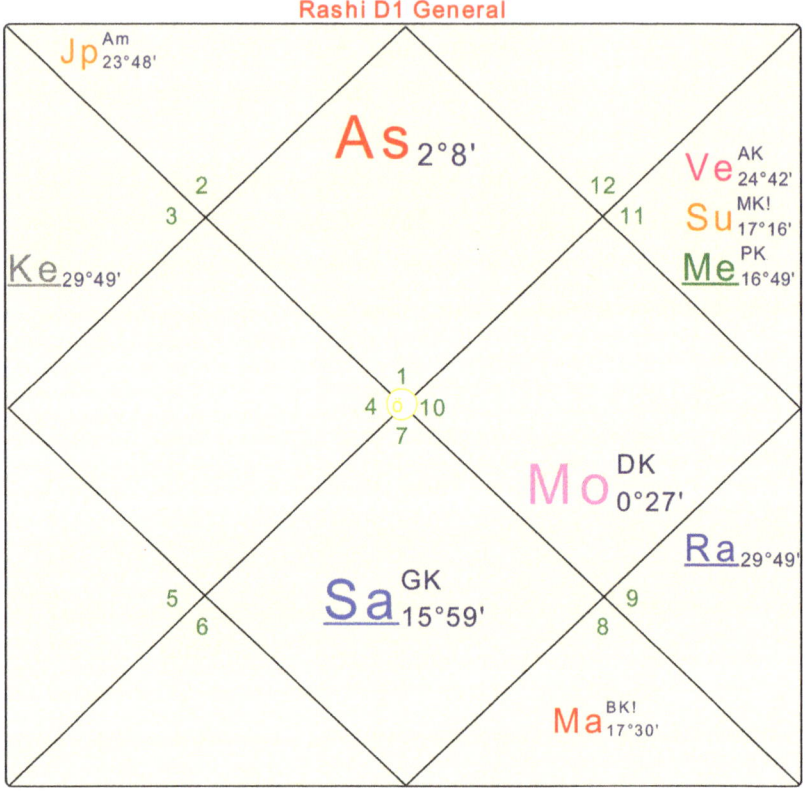

Creativity in the Vedic Astrology Chart

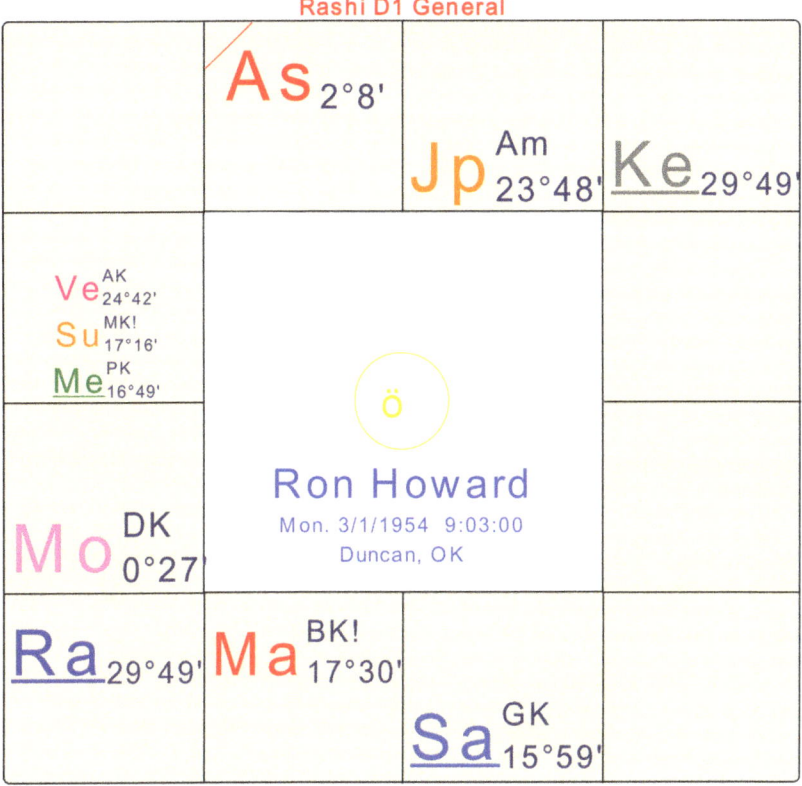

Ron Howard has enjoyed an exceptionally long and successful career, which began at the age of five, with his appearance in a film called *The Journey* (1959). This debut was soon followed by roles in a variety of TV shows, including episodes of *The Twilight Zone*, *Dennis the Menace* and *The Many Loves of Dobie Gillis*. In late 1959, Ron Howard was cast as Opie Taylor, a prominent role as the son of Sheriff Andy Taylor (played by Andy Griffith) in *The Andy Griffith Show*. Ron Howard maintained this role for the entire eight seasons of *The Andy Griffith Show*, during which time he also acted in several films, notably *The Music Man* (1962) and *The Courtship of Eddie's Father* (1963). Ron Howard continued to act in television and films through the 1970s, including his 1973 appearance in the George Lucas film *American Graffiti* and a role in John Wayne's last film *The*

Shootist (1976). In 1974, Ron Howard was cast in a leading role in the long-running series *Happy Days*. While still appearing in *Happy Days*, Ron Howard directed his first film, *Grand Theft Auto* (1977). Between 1978 and 1982, he directed several television movies for NBC including *Skyward* (1980), starring Bette Davis. Ron Howard directed his second Hollywood film, *Night Shift*, in 1982, and has continued as an influential Hollywood film director ever since, with 27 films to his credit. These include *Splash* (1984), *Cocoon* (1985), *Parenthood* (1989), *Apollo 13* (1995), and *The Da Vinci Code* (2006). For his 2001 film, *A Beautiful Mind*, Ron Howard won the Best Director Oscar while the film was named Best Picture. In 1998, Mr. Howard served as a co-producer of the Primetime Emmy award-winning HBO mini-series *From the Earth to the Moon*. In 2003 Ron Howard was awarded a Congressional National Medal of the Arts.

Ron Howard's Aries rising chart locates ascendant lord Mars *swakshetra* in Scorpio in the 8th house of the chart in *Jyeshtha* (self-driven) *nakshatra*, and in *sambandha* opposition with 9th and 12th lord Jupiter. 4th lord *vargottama* Moon in the 10th house receives Jupiter's 9th glance. The Moon's dispositor, 10th lord Saturn, is doubly strong in exaltation in the 7th house, where it gains directional strength. As lord of the 11th house of popular entertainment, Saturn participates in a *Parivartana* yoga with 7th lord Venus as it aspects the ascendant. Consistent with the theme of the 12th as the house of film and photography, Jupiter rules the 12th house from the Moon as well as from the ascendant, and aspects the 10th house of career and occupant Moon. Both 10th (Saturn) and 12th (Jupiter) lords of the chart reside in Venus-owned signs; Venus itself gains strength through its *swakshetra* status in both the D-9 (Taurus) and D-10 (Libra). The 11th house of the birth chart holds a creatively inspired *Budha Aditya* yoga; 3rd lord Mercury and 5th lord Sun are joined by influential 2nd and 7th lord Venus. From the Capricorn Moon, Venus has yoga *karaka* status as 5th and 10th lord. The collection of three *grahas* in the 11th is activated by a one-way aspect from ascendant lord Mars; notice that Mars by degree enjoys an almost exact angular relationship with the Sun and Mercury. The 5th house of the chart, although uninhabited, is aspected by the three planets in the 11th as the theme of creativity and, just as significantly, creative authority, is emphasized by Mars' precise aspect to 5th lord Sun. Mars contributes to the theme of intelligence and visionary direction by its aspect to 5th lord (from Moon) Venus in the 11th as well as to the 5th house from the Moon and tenant Jupiter. In another chart, a similar abundance of 5th house (royalty) activation might create a political leader or business executive; due primarily however, to a strong and influential planet Venus in the chart, Ron Howard's executive abilities will be expressed through the arts, specifically film.

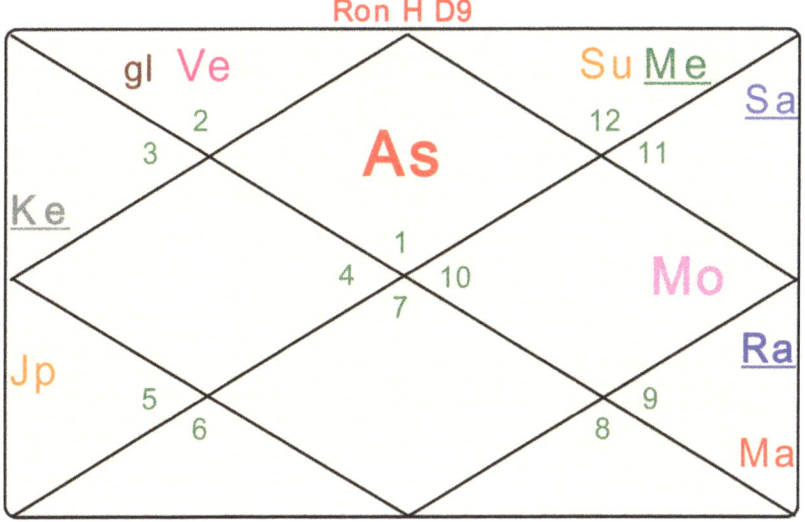

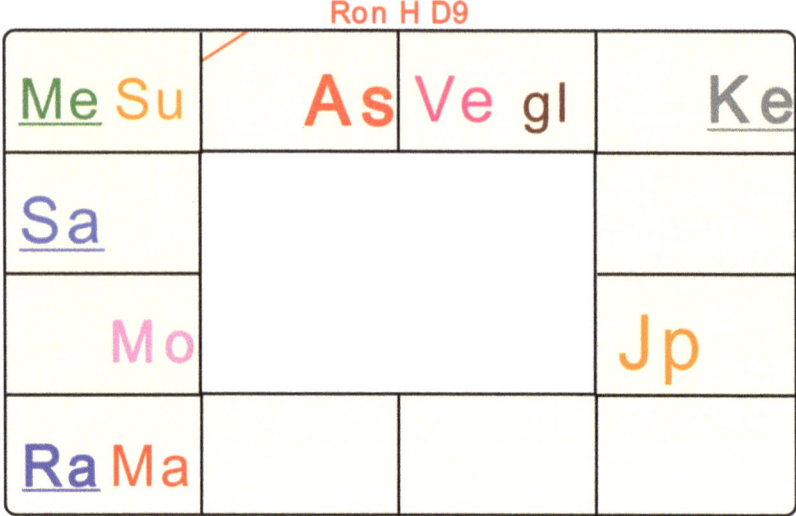

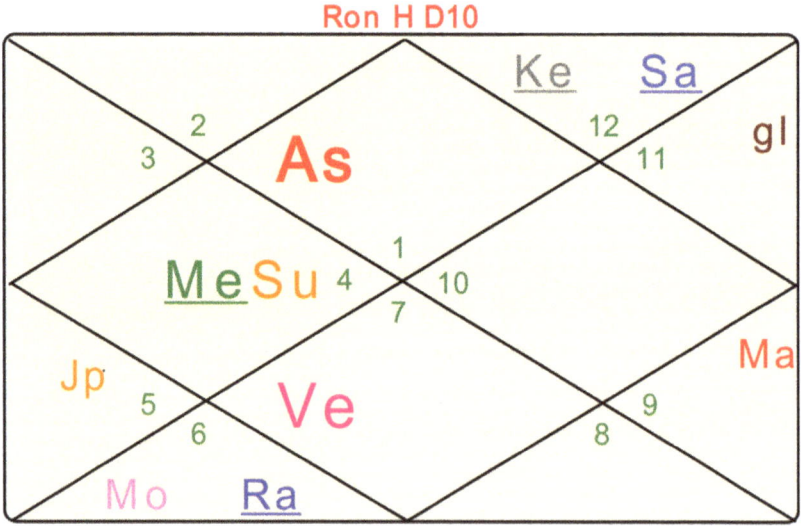

Creativity in the Vedic Astrology Chart

Ron H D10

Sa Ke	As		
gl			Me Su
			Jp
Ma		Ve	Ra Mo

Ron H: Vimshottari

Start Date			Age	Dashas	
6/	15/	1957	3.3	Su	Ve
6/	16/	1958	4.3	Mo	Mo
4/	16/	1959	5.1	Mo	Ma
11/	15/	1959	5.7	Mo	Ra
5/	16/	1961	7.2	Mo	Jp
9/	15/	1962	8.5	Mo	Sa
4/	15/	1964	10.1	Mo	Me
9/	15/	1965	11.5	Mo	Ke
4/	16/	1966	12.1	Mo	Ve
12/	16/	1967	13.8	Mo	Su
6/	15/	1968	14.3	Ma	Ma
11/	11/	1968	14.7	Ma	Ra
11/	30/	1969	15.8	Ma	Jp
11/	6/	1970	16.7	Ma	Sa
12/	16/	1971	17.8	Ma	Me
12/	12/	1972	18.8	Ma	Ke
5/	10/	1973	19.2	Ma	Ve
7/	10/	1974	20.4	Ma	Su
11/	15/	1974	20.7	Ma	Mo
6/	16/	1975	21.3	Ra	Ra
2/	26/	1978	24.0	Ra	Jp
7/	22/	1980	26.4	Ra	Sa
5/	29/	1983	29.2	Ra	Me
12/	15/	1985	31.8	Ra	Ke
1/	3/	1987	32.8	Ra	Ve
1/	2/	1990	35.8	Ra	Su
11/	27/	1990	36.7	Ra	Mo
5/	28/	1992	38.2	Ra	Ma
6/	16/	1993	39.3	Jp	Jp
8/	4/	1995	41.4	Jp	Sa
2/	14/	1998	44.0	Jp	Me
5/	22/	2000	46.2	Jp	Ke
4/	28/	2001	47.2	Jp	Ve
12/	28/	2003	49.8	Jp	Su
10/	15/	2004	50.6	Jp	Mo
2/	14/	2006	52.0	Jp	Ma
1/	21/	2007	52.9	Jp	Ra
6/	16/	2009	55.3	Sa	Sa
6/	19/	2012	58.3	Sa	Me
2/	27/	2015	61.0	Sa	Ke
4/	7/	2016	62.1	Sa	Ve

Ron : Chara

Start Date	Age	Dashas
3/ 1/ 1954	-0.0	Ari
3/ 1/ 1961	7.0	Tau
3/ 1/ 1970	16.0	Gem
3/ 1/ 1978	24.0	Can
3/ 1/ 1984	30.0	Leo
3/ 1/ 1990	36.0	Virg
3/ 1/ 1997	43.0	Libr
3/ 1/ 2001	47.0	Sco
3/ 1/ 2008	54.0	Sag
3/ 1/ 2013	59.0	Cap
3/ 1/ 2016	62.0	Aqu
3/ 1/ 2018 n	64.0	Pis

Ron : Chara

Start Date	Age	Dashas	
10/ 30/ 1958	4.7	Ari	Cap
5/ 31/ 1959	5.2	Ari	Aqu
12/ 31/ 1959	5.8	Ari	Pis
7/ 31/ 1960	6.4	Ari	Ari
3/ 1/ 1961	7.0	Tau	Ari
11/ 30/ 1961	7.8	Tau	Pis
8/ 31/ 1962	8.5	Tau	Aqu
5/ 31/ 1963	9.2	Tau	Cap
2/ 29/ 1964	10.0	Tau	Sag
11/ 29/ 1964	10.8	Tau	Sco
8/ 30/ 1965	11.5	Tau	Libr
5/ 31/ 1966	12.2	Tau	Virg

Ron Howard's acting career began in 1959, soon after the onset of his 10-year Moon *dasha*. The Moon becomes *vargottama* in the 10th house of Ron Howard's D-9, where Moon's dispositor Saturn is *swakshetra* in the 11th house and enjoys *sambandha* opposition with 9th and 12th lord Jupiter. In Ron Howard's D-10, the Moon in the 6th opposes 10th lord Saturn in the 12th. In both his D-9 and D-10, ascendant ruler Mars activates the 12th house, which is occupied by 3rd and 5th lords Mercury and Sun, respectively, in the D-9, and by 10th lord Saturn in the D-10. The D-9 features an exchange between the houses of creativity (5th) and film (12th), placing 12th lord Jupiter in the 5th house and 5th lord Sun in the 12th. Ron Howard's career as a movie director began, and then flourished, during his 18-year *Vimshottari Rahu* major period. In the birth chart *Rahu* is placed in the 9th house from ascendant and in the 12th from the Moon. *Rahu*'s primary influences are dispositor Jupiter and exalted 10th lord Saturn, both of whom are themselves disposited by Venus. In his D-9, *Rahu* remains in the 9th house where it is aspected by its dispositor, 9th and 12th lord Jupiter. In Ron Howard's D-10, we find *Rahu* in the 6th house where it is aspected by 10th lord Saturn from Saturn's location in the 12th. Notably, Ron Howard's first significant career opportunity, the *Andy Griffith Show*, occurred in late 1959 in the sub-period of *Rahu* in his *Vimshottari* Moon major period.

Ron Howard's first credited appearance, in the 1959 film *The Journey*, occurred in his *Jaimini* Aries -- Capricorn *Chara dasha*. Aries is the rising sign of the chart, from where 9th and 12th lord AmK Jupiter and ascendant ruler BK Mars aspect DK Moon in Capricorn in the 10th. Aries is aspected by its own *swakshetra* lord from the 8th, along with the potent *Jaimini Raj* yoga-forming combination of AK Venus, PK Mercury, and 5th lord Sun from the 11th. Sub-period Capricorn ruler Saturn is exalted in the 10th house in *Jaimini sambandha* with the Sun and all the natural benefics, each in their role as *Jaimini Raj* yoga-creating *graha*. In Ron Howard's D-9, Capricorn holds *vargottama* DK Moon in aspect with AK Venus and AmK Jupiter. The sign of Libra becomes highly capable secondary to the aspect from its *swakshetra* ruler Venus and those of AK Jupiter and *swakshetra* Saturn. Venus achieves *Malavya* yoga in the 10th house and is aspected by 3rd and 12th lord (from Capricorn) Jupiter in Ron Howard's D-10. The following sub-period of Aquarius, holding AK Venus, 5th lord Sun and PK Mercury, was that during which Ron Howard and his family were notified that he had been selected for the role of Opie Taylor in the *Andy Griffith Show*, to begin airing in the fall of 1960. Aquarius is the sign on the 10th house from Ron Howard's Taurus KL, which is inhabited by AmK Jupiter. BPHS Chapter 33 verses 57 – 60 promises professional success and accomplishment of "great deeds" when Mercury and Venus locate in the 10th house from the KL. Their respective status as PK and AK, in accompaniment with 5th lord Sun, further elevates the chart's potential for significant achievement. BK Mars gives *Ruchaka* yoga in the 10th house from Aquarius, as the sign contains its lord in the D-9 and is aspected by natal/local 5th lord Sun, PK Mercury and *swakshetra* AK Venus in the D-10.

As will be evident in the majority of charts in this section, *Shatabhisha nakshatra* plays an important role; 5th lord Sun and 3rd and 6th lord Mercury occupy *Shatabhisha* in the 11th house. The visionary capability of *Shatabhisha*'s deity *Varuna* contributes to Ron Howard's skill as a film director. Notice as well that several of Ron Howard's films are devoted to themes of the sky and outer space; these include the 1980 made-for-TV film *Skyward*, his 1985 film *Cocoon* (alien visitation), *Apollo 13* (1995) and *Solo: A Star Wars Story* (2018). *Purva Bhadrapada nakshatra* is also capable of conferring interest and skill in the art of visual representation; Ron Howard's AK Venus in this *nakshatra* in the 10th house from his Taurus KL will contribute to his craft and the remarkable longevity of his career in the realm of television and film. The reader is referred to the recent memoir by Ron Howard and his brother Clint, entitled *The Boys* (William Morrow/Harper Collins, 2021).

The next chart in this section will be that of innovative photographer and documentary film-maker Robert Frank (November 9, 1924, Zurich, Switzerland, 2:30 a.m. AA).

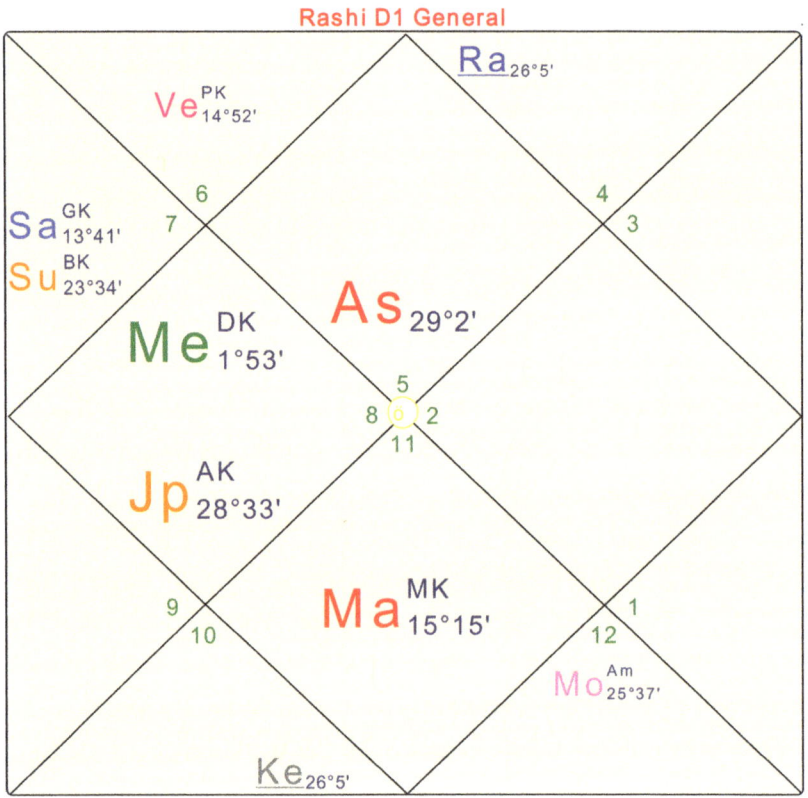

Creativity in the Vedic Astrology Chart

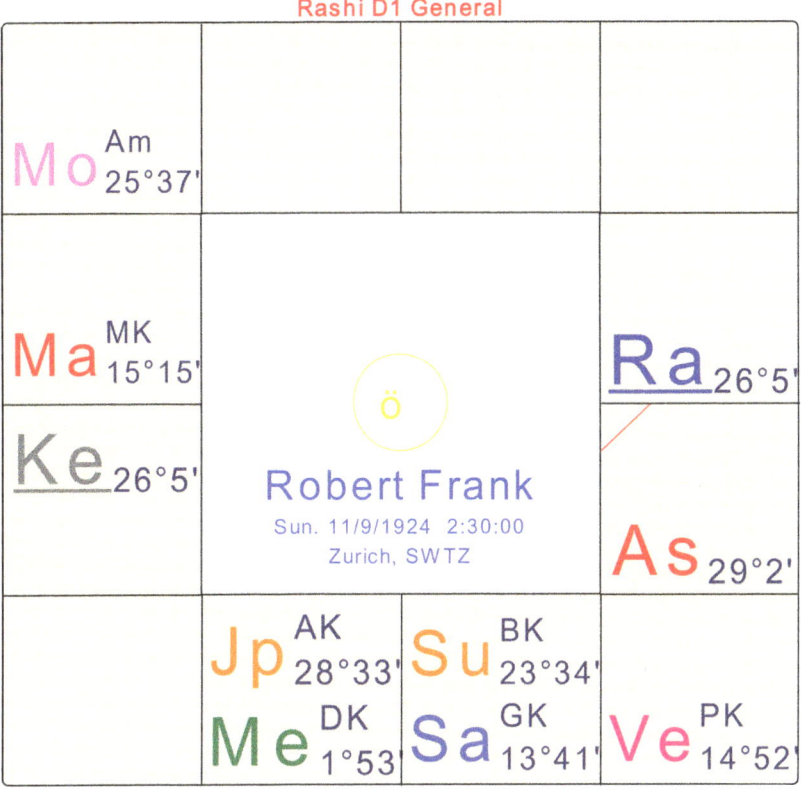

Robert Frank became enthralled with photography in his teens, during which time he studied and apprenticed with several photographers in his native Switzerland. At age twenty-two he produced a self-made folio of photographs, entitled *40 Fotos*. Having emigrated to the United States the following year, Frank obtained a position as fashion photographer for *Harper's Bazaar* magazine. In 1950, Robert Frank produced another book of photographs, taken during a voyage to South America. The same year, Frank had several of his photographs featured in an exhibition entitled *51 American Photographers* at the Museum of Modern Art in New York. In 1955, seven of Robert Frank's photographs were included in *The Family of Man*, an exhibition compiled by the Museum of Modern Art and shown around the world to an estimated to 9 million visitors. (The accompanying catalog has been continuously in print since its first publication.) Within the same year Frank was awarded a Guggenheim Foundation fellowship to travel across the United States and create a photographic record of his journey, the result of which was published in 1959 and entitled *The Americans*. With an introduction by Jack Kerouac, *The Americans* was initially received with mixed reviews, but has since become honored as a seminal contribution to the art of photography, known for its realistic subject matter and controversial photographic techniques. In 1961 an exhibition devoted exclusively to the work of Robert Frank was featured at the Art Institute of Chicago, followed by a similar show a year later at the Museum of Modern Art in New York. In 2007, a signed and numbered print of one of Frank's most memorable photographs, *Trolley-New Orleans*, sold for $623,400. By the early 1960s Robert Frank had become more interested and involved in film, as he produced and directed a series of documentary films through the 1960s and 1970s. Robert Frank's 2019 *New York Times* obituary referred to him as "one of the most influential photographers of the 20th century, whose visually raw and personally expressive style was pivotal in changing the course of documentary photography." (Philip Gefter, *New York Times*, September 10th, 2019).

The Leo rising chart of Robert Frank has ascendant ruler Sun in Libra in the 3rd house of artistic expression. The Sun's debilitation is cancelled by the placement of sign dispositor Venus in the 7th house from the Moon and that of Mars in a *kendra* from the ascendant. In addition to its position from the Moon, Venus attains *Neecha Bhanga Raj* yoga status due to the location of Jupiter and Mercury in a *kendra* and Venus' *navamsha* placement in Taurus. The birth chart contains a *Saraswati* yoga, formed by Venus in the 2nd house with Mercury and Jupiter in the 4th; notice as well that *lagna* lord Sun is flanked, creating *Shubha Ubhayachari* yoga. As this flanking is formed by all three natural benefics, it becomes especially positive. The *sambandha* opposition formed by Venus and the bright Moon establishes a strong connection between the owner of the 12th house of film and photography (Moon), and the lord of the houses of artistic expression and career (Venus). The 12th house is also activated by an aspect from exalted Saturn; creativity in the realm of visual expression is evidenced by 5th lord Jupiter's glance to the Moon and the 12th house. *Phaladeepika* 7:22 ascribes "pre-eminent" *Raj* yoga status to the bright Pisces Moon in reception of an aspect from a friendly planet. The influence of 9th lord Mars in the chart of Robert Frank is considerable, as it occupies *Shatabhisha nakshatra* in the 7th house, (12th from the Moon), from which location Mars aspects the ascendant, the 10th house, and in a very tight aspect, 10th lord Venus. Recall that *Shatabhisha*'s deity is all-seeing *Varuna*; Robert Frank's photography was notably controversial for its depiction of American life across all socio-economic levels, including the elderly, impoverished, and socially marginalized. From the Moon, exalted 12th lord Saturn aspects the 10th house of career as the Moon is aspected by its dispositor, 10th lord Jupiter.

12th house themes persist in the D-9 and D-10 charts of Robert Frank, as in both charts Mars rules the 12th house and aspects the 10th from its position in the 3rd. In the D-9, the 12th house is activated by aspects from three *swakshetra* planets, *lagna* lord Jupiter, 3rd house ruler Saturn and 11th lord Venus. *Rahu* also attains *swakshetra* status in the 3rd house of the D-9. In the D-10, 12th lord Mars joins *swakshetra* 3rd lord Moon and aspects the 10th house and lord Saturn, as the 12th is occupied by 11th lord Jupiter and aspected there by 10th lord Saturn.

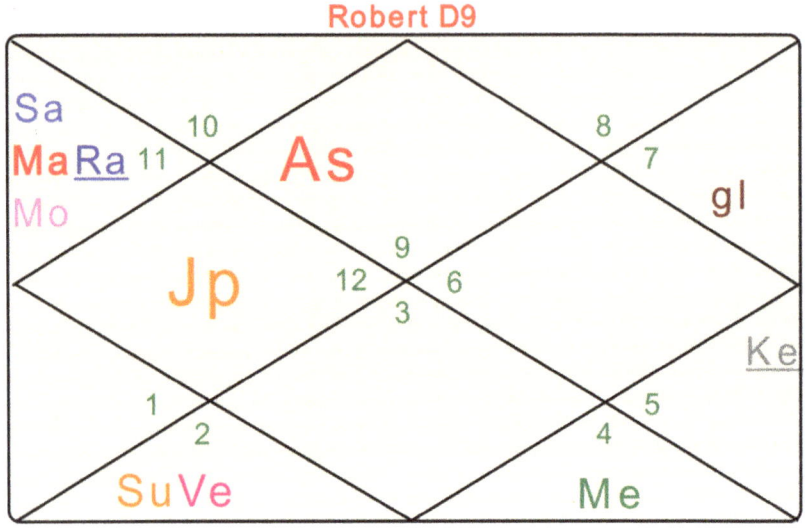

Creativity in the Vedic Astrology Chart

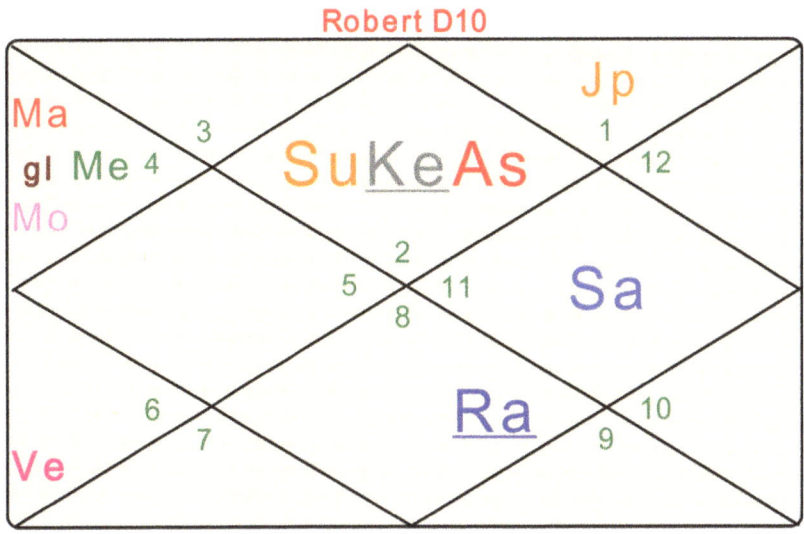

RF: Vimshottari

Start Date	Age	Dashas	
10/ 8/ 1940	15.9	Ve	Su
10/ 8/ 1941	16.9	Ve	Mo
6/ 9/ 1943	18.6	Ve	Ma
8/ 8/ 1944	19.7	Ve	Ra
8/ 9/ 1947	22.7	Ve	Jp
4/ 9/ 1950	25.4	Ve	Sa
6/ 8/ 1953	28.6	Ve	Me
4/ 8/ 1956	31.4	Ve	Ke
6/ 8/ 1957	**32.6**	**Su**	**Su**
9/ 26/ 1957	32.9	Su	Mo
3/ 28/ 1958	33.4	Su	Ma
8/ 2/ 1958	33.7	Su	Ra
6/ 27/ 1959	34.6	Su	Jp
4/ 14/ 1960	35.4	Su	Sa
3/ 27/ 1961	36.4	Su	Me
2/ 1/ 1962	37.2	Su	Ke
6/ 9/ 1962	37.6	Su	Ve
6/ 9/ 1963	**38.6**	**Mo**	**Mo**
4/ 8/ 1964	39.4	Mo	Ma
11/ 7/ 1964	40.0	Mo	Ra
5/ 9/ 1966	41.5	Mo	Jp
9/ 8/ 1967	42.8	Mo	Sa
4/ 9/ 1969	44.4	Mo	Me
9/ 8/ 1970	45.8	Mo	Ke
4/ 9/ 1971	46.4	Mo	Ve
12/ 8/ 1972	48.1	Mo	Su

RF: Chara		
Start Date	Age	Dashas
11/ 9/ 1934	10.0	Virg
11/ 9/ 1944	20.0	Libr
11/ 10/ 1955	31.0	Sco
11/ 9/ 1957	33.0	Sag
11/ 9/ 1968	44.0	Cap
11/ 10/ 1971	47.0	Aqu
11/ 10/ 1975	51.0	Pis
11/ 10/ 1979	55.0	Ari
11/ 9/ 1989	65.0	Tau
11/ 9/ 1993	69.0	Gem
11/ 10/ 1998	74.0	Can
11/ 10/ 2002	78.0	Leo

At age twelve, Robert Frank began his 20-year Venus major period. In addition to Venus' *sambandha* with 12th lord Moon in the D-1, *swakshetra* Venus receives the one-way aspect of 5th and 12th lord Mars in the D-9. As ascendant lord, Venus occupies the 5th house of creativity in Frank's D-10. During Venus – *Rahu*, Robert Frank self-published his first folio of *40 Fotos*. In the D-1, *Rahu* is found in the 12th house, where it is disposited by the Moon and is aspected by Saturn and Jupiter. In his D-9, *Rahu* gains *swakshetra* status in the 3rd house where it is joined by the Moon, 3rd lord Saturn and 12th lord Mars, as sub-period ruler *Rahu* sits in the 10th from *Maha dasha* lord Venus. *Rahu* in the 7th house in Robert Frank's D-10 is aspected by the Sun and *swakshetra* 10th lord Saturn, and is disposited by 12th house ruler Mars. Frank's subsequent major period of ascendant ruler Sun, beginning in 1957, brought him continued success, as 9th lord Sun joins *swakshetra* Venus in the 6th house of the D-9 and is located in the ascendant in Taurus in the D-10 chart.

Between ages 20 and 31, Robert Frank ran an 11-year *Jaimini Chara dasha* of the sign of Libra. The 12th house from Libra holds sign ruler PK Venus in *sambandha* with AmK Moon, while the 10th house is aspected by the yoga-forming DK Mercury -- AK/5th lord

Jupiter combination as well as by *vargottama* Mars. The strength and potential of Libra is reinforced in both the D-9 and D-10 charts; in his D-9, the sign of Libra is energized by aspects from its *swakshetra* lord Venus, *swakshetra* yoga *karaka* Saturn, Mars, AmK Moon, BK Sun, *swakshetra Rahu* and *Ketu*. Except for *Ketu*, the same group of planets aspects the 10th house from Libra and DK Mercury as ruler of the 12th in the 10th. In his D-10, PK Venus is found again in the 12th house while the 10th is occupied by *swakshetra* AmK Moon, Mars and Mercury. The collective aspects of the Sun, Saturn, *Rahu*, and *Ketu* on the sign of Cancer contribute to a total of seven *grahas* either in or aspecting the 10th house from the sign of Libra. Finally, AK Jupiter's placement in the angular 7th house provides support for an independently driven career, which proved true for Robert Frank, as his career ascended during this time in his life.

Creativity in the Vedic Astrology Chart

Our next chart will be that of accomplished actress Beverly D'Angelo (November 15th, 1951, Columbus, OH, 12:48 a.m., AA).

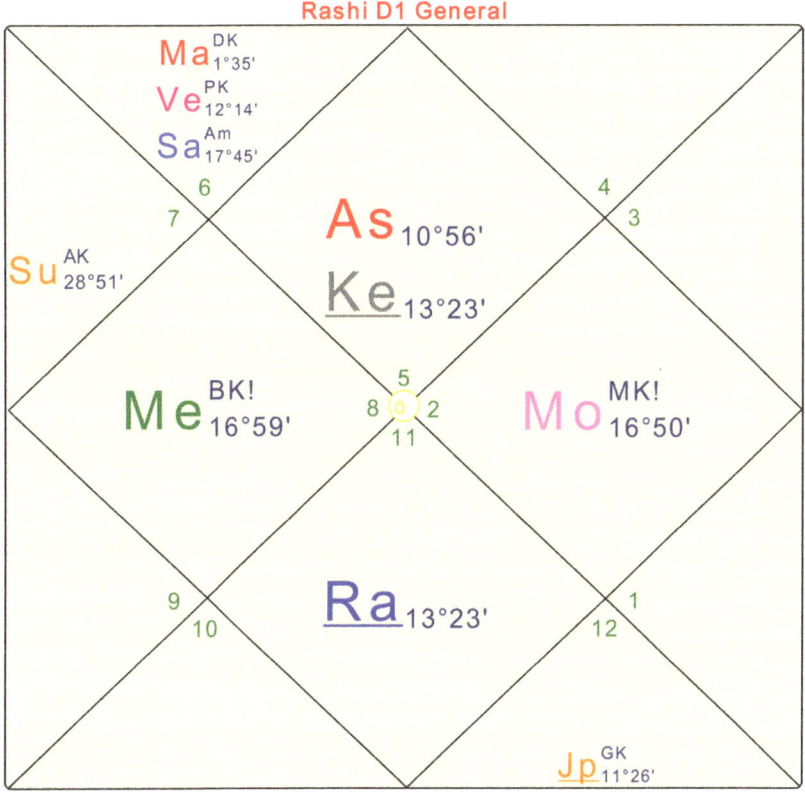

Rashi D1 General

Jp GK 11°26'		Mo MK! 16°50'	
Ra 13°23'	ö Beverly D'Angelo Thu. 11/15/1951 0:48:00 Columbus, OH		As 10°56' Ke 13°23'
	Me BK! 16°59'	Su AK 28°51'	Sa Am 17°45' Ve PK 12°14' Ma DK 1°35'

Beverly D'Angelo has had a long and successful career as a film and television actress. She first appeared on Broadway, then in three episodes of a TV mini-series in 1976. The following year Ms. D'Angelo had a small role in the Woody Allen film *Annie Hall*. Since then, Beverly D'Angelo has appeared in more than 60 films and 15 made-for-TV films, as well as numerous television shows. Ms. D'Angelo received a Golden Globe nomination for her portrayal of singer Patsy Cline in the 1980 film *Coal Miner's Daughter*, and an Emmy Award nomination for her role as Stella Kowalski in a 1984 television movie production of *A Streetcar Named Desire*. Beverly D'Angelo is also known for her role as Ellen Griswold in the series of four *National Lampoon Vacation* films. Referring to Beverly D'Angelo's performance in *Coal Miner's Daughter*, *New York Times* reviewer Janet Maslin wrote that

Ms. D'Angelo "cut such an extravagant figure that she very nearly stole the movie." (Janet Maslin, *New York Times*, October 2nd, 1985). A 1992 feature article on Ms. D'Angelo quotes an interview with *New Yorker* magazine film critic Pauline Kael: "How could an actress so beautiful and talented not get cast in better films?" (Allen Barra, *New York Times*, July 12th, 1992).

Ms. Beverly D'Angelo's Leo rising chart has exalted 12th lord Moon in the 10th house in *Rohini nakshatra*. In the 10th, the Moon finds itself in very tight *sambandha* opposition, within 9 minutes of 2nd (voice, face, appearance) and 11th (entertainment) lord Mercury. In fact, although Beverly D'Angelo was to establish a career in film, she is also an excellent singer and chose certain film roles which enabled her to display her vocal talent. Debilitated ascendant ruler Sun is placed in the 3rd house of artistic expression and benefits from *Ubhayachari* yoga. The Sun's debilitation is cancelled by the mutual *kendra* placement of Mars and Venus. (*Phaladeepika* 7:27). The Sun's dispositor Venus is also debilitated but achieves cancellation by way of Mercury's placement in *kendra* houses from the Moon and ascendant. As lord of the 5th house of creativity, *swakshetra* Jupiter's influence falls upon the 9 – 10 and 4 – 10 *Raj* yogas formed in the 2nd house by Mars and Venus, and creates 4 – 5, 5 – 9 and 5 – 10 *Raj* yogas, with Mars, Mars, and Venus, respectively. From the 8th, Jupiter aspects the 12th house of visual art as well as both sides of Ms. D'Angelo's 2 – 4 *Parivartana* yoga, formed by Mercury and Mars.

From the Moon, *sambandha* is formed across the 5 – 11 axis between *Chandra lagna* lord Venus, 9th and 10th lord Saturn, 11th lord Jupiter, and 12th lord Mars; the 12th house from the Moon is aspected by its ruler Mars, along with the Sun's 7th glance. The chart's *Parivartana* yoga becomes an exchange between the 5th house and the 7th as the Moon is aspected by 5th (and 2nd) lord Mercury.

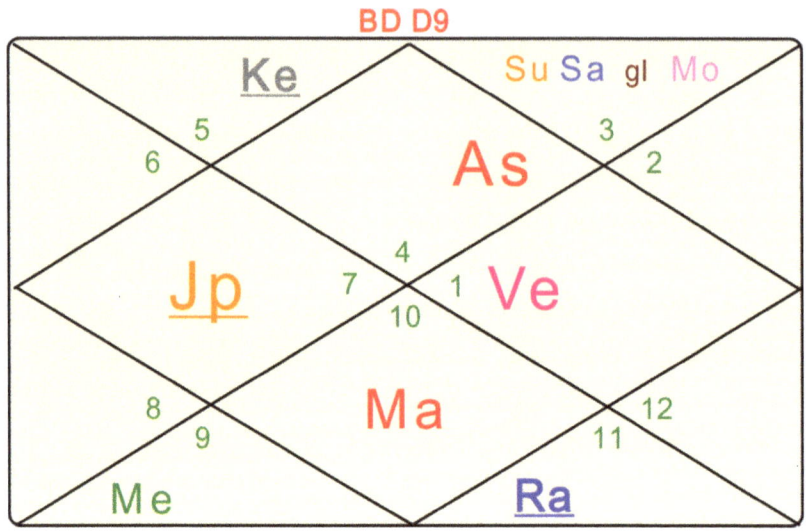

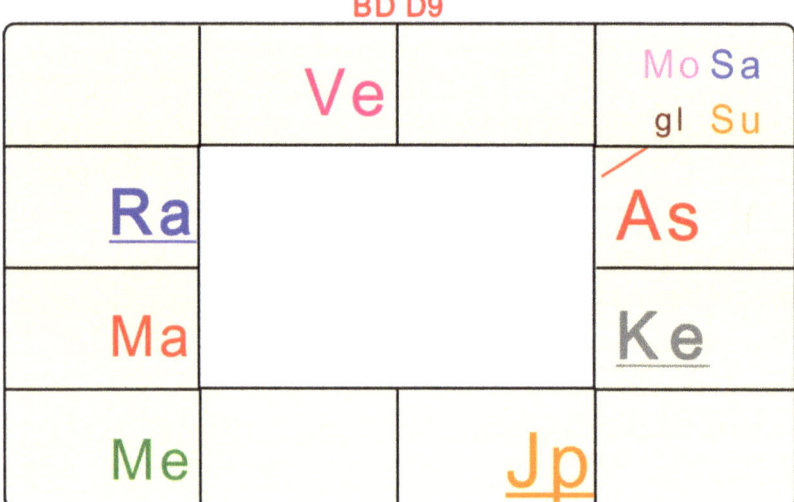

Creativity in the Vedic Astrology Chart

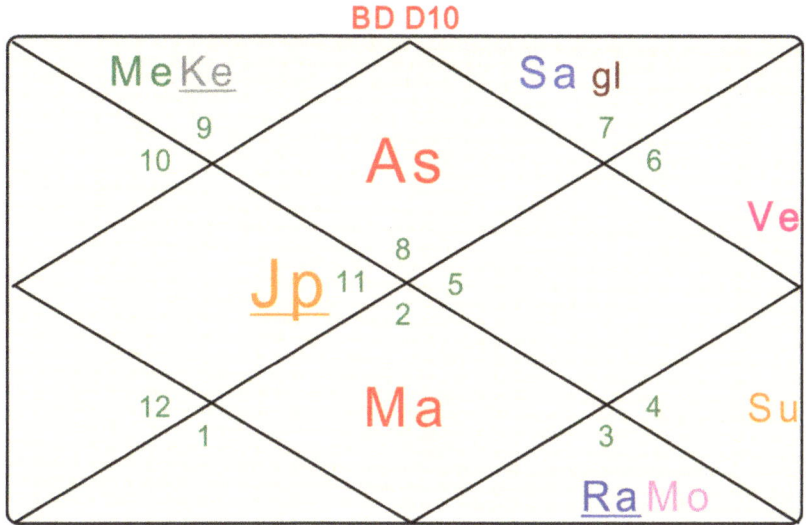

BD: Vimshottari

Start Date			Age	Dashas	
6/	12/	1966	14.6	Ra	Jp
11/	5/	1968	17.0	Ra	Sa
9/	12/	1971	19.8	Ra	Me
3/	31/	1974	22.4	Ra	Ke
4/	19/	1975	23.4	Ra	Ve
4/	18/	1978	26.4	Ra	Su
3/	13/	1979	27.3	Ra	Mo
9/	11/	1980	28.8	Ra	Ma
9/	**29/**	**1981**	**29.9**	**Jp**	**Jp**
11/	18/	1983	32.0	Jp	Sa
5/	31/	1986	34.5	Jp	Me
9/	5/	1988	36.8	Jp	Ke
8/	12/	1989	37.7	Jp	Ve
4/	12/	1992	40.4	Jp	Su
1/	29/	1993	41.2	Jp	Mo
5/	31/	1994	42.5	Jp	Ma
5/	7/	1995	43.5	Jp	Ra
9/	**30/**	**1997**	**45.9**	**Sa**	**Sa**
10/	2/	2000	48.9	Sa	Me
6/	13/	2003	51.6	Sa	Ke
7/	21/	2004	52.7	Sa	Ve
9/	21/	2007	55.8	Sa	Su
9/	2/	2008	56.8	Sa	Mo
4/	3/	2010	58.4	Sa	Ma
5/	13/	2011	59.5	Sa	Ra
3/	19/	2014	62.3	Sa	Jp

BD: Chara			
Start Date		Age	Dashas
11/ 15/ 1951		-0.0	Leo
11/ 14/ 1961		10.0	Virg
11/ 15/ 1971		20.0	Libr
11/ 14/ 1982		31.0	Sco
11/ 14/ 1992		41.0	Sag
11/ 15/ 1995		44.0	Cap
11/ 15/ 1999		48.0	Aqu
11/ 14/ 2004		53.0	Pis
11/ 14/ 2016		65.0	Ari
11/ 14/ 2021 n		70.0	Tau
11/ 15/ 2025		74.0	Gem
11/ 15/ 2030		79.0	Can

In Ms. D'Angelo's D-9, ascendant lord Moon joins Sun and Saturn in the 12th house, and is aspected by 12th lord Mercury from the 6th. 3rd lord Saturn is exalted in the 12th house of her D-10, where it receives 5th lord Jupiter's 9th glance. From its 12th house location, Saturn aspects 11th lord Mercury and 10th lord Sun. Beverly D'Angelo's first appearance on Broadway, and soon after in films, occurred during her *Rahu* – Venus period. Major period ruler *Rahu* is placed in the 10th house from the Moon in her D-1, in *Rahu*'s acutely visual *nakshatra* of *Shatabhisha*. *Rahu* achieves *vargottama* and *swakshetra* status in the 8th house of the D-9, where it is disposited by 12th house occupant Saturn. *Rahu* again locates in the 8th house of the D-10, and in both divisional charts *Rahu* is graced by Jupiter's 5th aspect from the 4th house. Sub-period lord Venus rules the 10th house of her D-1, and rules the 11th and sits in the 10th in her D-9, where it has *sambandha* opposition with 9th lord Jupiter and is aspected by exalted dispositor Mars. As 12th lord in Ms. D'Angelo's D-10, Venus is placed in the 11th house of the chart. The general condition of Venus as 10th lord of the birth chart, i.e., debilitated and associated with malefics in the D-1 and debilitated again in the D-10, is likely responsible for Ms. D'Angelo's reputation as a skilled actress who none the less never earned superstar status and was sometimes cast in lesser known and/or poorly reviewed films. Although Venus and ascendant ruler Sun gain some degree of debilitation cancellation, neither planet rises to *Raj* yoga status.

From age twenty to thirty-one, Beverly D'Angelo ran her Libra *Chara dasha*. During this period, she first appeared on Broadway, then television and film, and established a career as a steadily employed and critically acclaimed actress. The sign of Libra in the D-1 contains AK Sun while the Moon aspects Libra as do *Rahu* and *Ketu*. The 10th house from Libra benefits from the aspect of its exalted lord as well as those from BK Mercury and *Rahu*. From Libra, the 12th house of film is activated by the presence of yoga forming planets AmK Saturn, PK Venus, and DK Mars, all influenced by *swakshetra* natal 5th lord (and 3rd from Libra) Jupiter. Jupiter occupies Libra in the D-9; the 12th house is activated by its ruler Mercury and by the Sun, Moon, and Saturn. Ms. D'Angelo's D-10 offers solid indication of success in the realm of film during this time, as exalted AmK Saturn lies in the 12th house of the chart, with AK Sun 10 signs away in Cancer. Both Saturn and Sun receive aspects from natal/local 5th lord Jupiter and DK Mars. As in the D-1, Libra sign ruler PK Venus goes to the 12th house; there it obtains *sambandha* with the Moon, Virgo owner BK Mercury and *Rahu* and *Ketu*. Notice also the combined influence of Moon and Venus on the *dwishwabhava* signs in Beverly D'Angelo's D-10.

Creativity in the Vedic Astrology Chart

The next chart for our consideration will be that of American cinematographer, producer, and director Haskell Wexler. (February 6, 1922, Chicago, IL, 3:00 a.m., A).

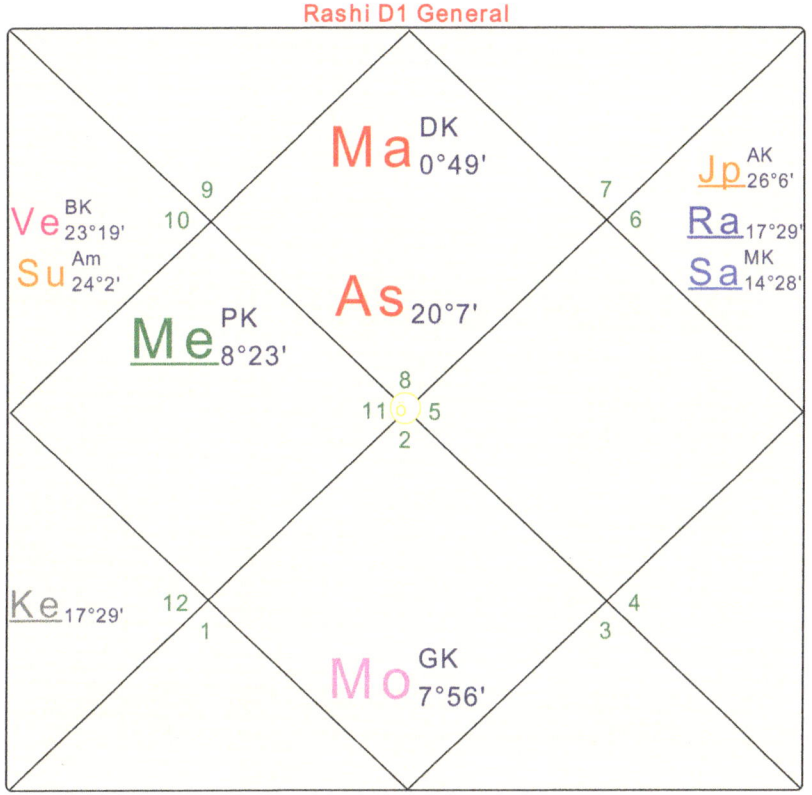

Rashi D1 General

Ke 17°29'		Mo ᴳᴷ 7°56'	
Me ᴾᴷ 8°23' Su ᴬᵐ 24°2' Ve ᴮᴷ 23°19'	ö **Haskell Wexler** Mon. 2/6/1922 3:00:00 Chicago, IL		
	As 20°7' Ma ᴰᴷ 0°49'		Jp ᴬᴷ 26°6' Ra 17°29' Sa ᴹᴷ 14°28'

Following his service in World War II, Haskell Wexler pursued a strong interest in film and began to make documentary and industrial films. Having joined the International Photographers Guild in 1947, Haskell Wexler became an assistant cameraman, then began to film and produce his own projects, including *The Living City* (1953), which was nominated for an Academy Award. In the 1960s, Haskell Wexler became one of Hollywood's most respected cinematographers, winning an Academy Award for Best Cinematography for his work on the 1966 film *Who's Afraid of Virginia Woolf*. Other films for which Haskell Wexler was credited as cinematographer include *In the Heat of the Night* (1967), *The Thomas Crown Affair* (1968), *One Flew Over the Cuckoo's Nest* (1975), and *Days of Heaven* (1978). Haskell Wexler served as photographic consultant for the film *American Graffiti*

(1973) and earned his second cinematography Academy Award for *Bound for Glory* (1976). Wexler filmed, produced, and directed the fictional film *Medium Cool* (1969), an innovative and influential film which employed real footage of the 1968 Democratic National Convention in Chicago as its setting. Haskell Wexler was given the Independent Spirit Award for Best Cinematography for his work on the 1987 film *Matewan*; he received an Academy Award nomination as well. In addition to his Hollywood studio film achievements, Haskell Wexler continued to produce and direct documentary films. His 1980 documentary *Paul Jacobs and the Nuclear Gang* earned an Emmy award; an earlier film, *Interviews with My Lai Veterans* (1970) won an Academy award. In 1993, Haskell Wexler was conferred a Lifetime Achievement Award by the American Society of Cinematographers, and in 2007 he received a similar award from the Independent Documentary Association. A year after Haskell Wexler's death in 2015, producer/director George Lucas created the Haskell Wexler Endowed Chair in Documentary at the University of Southern California School of Cinematic Arts.

The Scorpio rising chart of Haskell Wexler has Mars in the ascendant forming *Ruchaka* yoga, and in *sambandha* with exalted 9th lord Moon, creating a strong *Chandra Mangala* yoga, and a *Raj* yoga, between the 1st lord and that of the 9th. The 3rd house of creative expression is occupied by the combination of 10th lord Sun and 12th house lord of film/photography Venus as both planets are graced by 5th lord Jupiter's 5th glance from the 11th house. The theme of artistry is also evident in the combination of Jupiter and 3rd lord Saturn in the 11th house, from which placement both planets aspect back to the 5th house. The chart includes an exchange between 11th lord Mercury and 4th lord Saturn, as Mercury aspects the 10th house while 3rd and 4th lord Saturn aspects the chart's ascendant and lord Mars from the 11th. The Moon's exalted status in a *kendra*, and in reception of an aspect from Jupiter, forms the *Raj* yoga known as *Gauri* (*Phaladeepika* 6:21 & 6:25). *Gauri* yoga is said to grant benefits from royal association and praise for successes, including victory over enemies. The bright waxing Moon in *sambandha* with *swakshetra* Mars is also cited as a *Phaladeepika Raj* yoga (7:7), yielding royal status, even in instances of "questionable legitimacy." Haskell Wexler's chart also features a well-formed BPHS *Kahala* yoga, given the strength of ascendant ruler Mars and the combination of 4th lord Saturn and Jupiter in the 11th house. Applying the perspective of *Chandra lagna* to the chart, the *Parivartana* yoga between Saturn and Mercury becomes a 5 – 10 *Maha Parivartana* with 5th lord Mercury occupying the 10th house from the Moon in *Shatabhisha nakshatra*. In that 10th house from the Moon, Mercury receives a one-way aspect from Mars, who rules the 12th house from the Moon and maintains its *Ruchaka* yoga status in a *kendra* from the Moon. As 9th lord, ruler of 3rd from itself, and in *sambandha* with the chart's ascendant and lord, the Moon's location in the *nakshatra* of *Krittika* will confer innovation and particular skill in editing, essential to the film-making process.

Haskell Wexler's *Jaimini* KL is the sign of Leo. In the birth chart, exalted 12th lord (from Leo) Moon in the 10th house is aspected by AmK Sun and BK Venus, both of which also influence the KL itself from the sign of Capricorn. Exalted Moon aspects back to its sign of Cancer, which is also activated by aspects from PK Mercury and *swakshetra* DK Mars. The sign of Taurus on the 10th house from the KL is graced by aspects from its lord and that of the AmK, as well as the combined influence of Venus and the Moon. The Sun gains strength in the D-9 secondary to its *swakshetra* status in Leo where it joins AK Jupiter for a powerful AK -- AmK combination. In *Jaimini*, Saturn's location in the 10th house is considered beneficial, as the 10th and 12th houses from Leo in the D-9 are mutually activated by Saturn in the 10th and the placement of DK Mars and BK Venus in Cancer in the 12th.

Creativity in the Vedic Astrology Chart

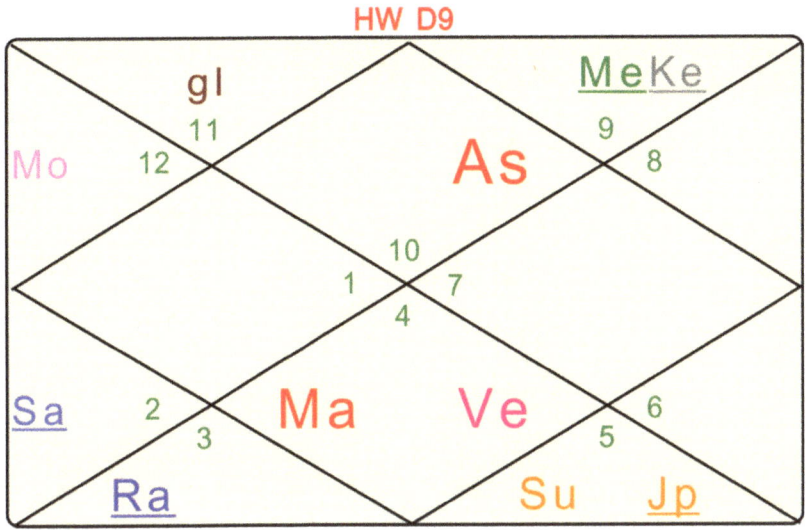

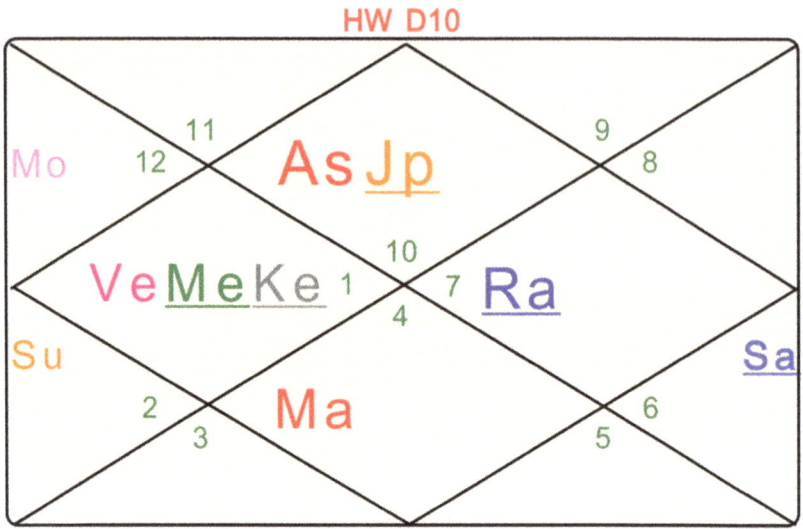

HW: Vimshottari

Start Date			Age	Dashas	
2/	15/	1945	23.0	Ra	Sa
12/	23/	1947	25.9	Ra	Me
7/	11/	1950	28.4	Ra	Ke
7/	30/	1951	29.5	Ra	Ve
7/	29/	1954	32.5	Ra	Su
6/	23/	1955	33.4	Ra	Mo
12/	22/	1956	34.9	Ra	Ma
1/	10/	1958	35.9	Jp	Jp
2/	28/	1960	38.1	Jp	Sa
9/	10/	1962	40.6	Jp	Me
12/	16/	1964	42.9	Jp	Ke
11/	22/	1965 e	43.8	Jp	Ve
7/	23/	1968	46.5	Jp	Su
5/	11/	1969	47.3	Jp	Mo
9/	10/	1970	48.6	Jp	Ma
8/	17/	1971	49.5	Jp	Ra
1/	10/	1974	51.9	Sa	Sa
1/	12/	1977 e	54.9	Sa	Me
9/	23/	1979	57.6	Sa	Ke
10/	31/	1980	58.7	Sa	Ve
1/	1/	1984	61.9	Sa	Su
12/	13/	1984	62.9	Sa	Mo
7/	14/	1986	64.4	Sa	Ma
8/	23/	1987	65.5	Sa	Ra
6/	29/	1990	68.4	Sa	Jp
1/	10/	1993	70.9	Me	Me

HW: Chara

Start Date			Age	Dashas	
3/	8/	1965	43.1	Ari	Sag
10/	7/	1965	43.7	Ari	Cap
5/	8/	1966	44.2	Ari	Aqu
12/	7/	1966 e	44.8	Ari	Pis
7/	8/	1967	45.4	Ari	Ari
2/	**6/**	**1968**	**46.0**	**Pis**	**Ari**
8/	7/	1968	46.5	Pis	Tau
2/	6/	1969	47.0	Pis	Gem
8/	7/	1969	47.5	Pis	Can
2/	6/	1970	48.0	Pis	Leo
8/	8/	1970	48.5	Pis	Virg
2/	6/	1971	49.0	Pis	Libr
8/	8/	1971	49.5	Pis	Sco
2/	6/	1972	50.0	Pis	Sag
8/	7/	1972	50.5	Pis	Cap
2/	6/	1973	51.0	Pis	Aqu
8/	7/	1973	51.5	Pis	Pis
2/	**6/**	**1974**	**52.0**	**Aqu**	**Pis**
7/	8/	1974	52.4	Aqu	Ari
12/	7/	1974	52.8	Aqu	Tau
5/	9/	1975	53.2	Aqu	Gem
10/	8/	1975	53.7	Aqu	Can
3/	8/	1976	54.1	Aqu	Leo
8/	7/	1976	54.5	Aqu	Virg
1/	6/	1977 e	54.9	Aqu	Libr
6/	8/	1977	55.3	Aqu	Sco

HW: Chara

Start Date	Age	Dashas
2/ 5/ 1929	7.0	Virg
2/ 6/ 1936	14.0	Leo
2/ 6/ 1943	21.0	Can
2/ 6/ 1945	23.0	Gem
2/ 6/ 1953	31.0	Tau
2/ 6/ 1961 e	39.0	Ari
2/ 6/ 1968	46.0	Pis
2/ 6/ 1974 e	52.0	Aqu
2/ 6/ 1979	57.0	Cap
2/ 6/ 1983	61.0	Sag
2/ 7/ 1992	70.0	Sco
2/ 7/ 1996	74.0	Libr

Haskell Wexler's 16-year *Vimshottari* Jupiter period began in 1958. This was the period during which he rose to his greatest degree of career achievement as a cinematographer, producer, and film director. As lord of the 5th house and located in the 5th house from the Moon, Jupiter occupies visually oriented *Chitra nakshatra* in the 11th house. Jupiter rules the 12th house in both Wexler's D-9 and D-10 charts. In his D-10, Jupiter achieves cancellation of its debilitated status secondary to its placement in the ascendant and *sambandha* with debilitated Mars.

Through most of the 1960s, Haskell Wexler ran his Aries *Chara dasha*. The sign of Aries is aspected by PK Mercury and Aries ruler DK Mars while the 10th house from Aries has AmK Sun and BK Venus. A *Jaimini Raj* yoga is created by exalted Moon's aspect to Venus as Mars joins in the activation of the sign of Capricorn and occupants Venus and Sun. In Haskell Wexler's D-9, the sign of Aries and the 10th house therefrom are aspected by *swakshetra* AmK Sun and AK Jupiter as Capricorn also gains the aspect of its owner Saturn. In Wexler's D-10, BK Venus and PK Mercury are found in Aries (with *Ketu*) while 12th lord Jupiter in the 10th house has mutual *Jaimini* aspect with AmK Sun.

On April 10th, 1967, Haskell Wexler was awarded the Oscar for best cinematography in a black-and-white film, *Who's Afraid of Virginia Woolf*. (Elizabeth Taylor won as best actress for her leading role in the film.) This accolade occurred during his Pisces sub-period; all the activation of the sign of Capricorn, across his D-1, D-9, and D-10 charts, as the 10th house from major period sign Aries, now also occurs as that of the 11th (honors and awards) from sub-period sign Pisces. In the D-1 the sign of Pisces benefits from an aspect by its lord Jupiter who happens to be the AK. The Moon occupies Pisces in both his D-9 and D-10, as the Sagittarius 10th house in Wexler's D-9 holds PK Mercury. In late March of 1977, Wexler was awarded his 2nd cinematography Oscar, for his work on *Bound for Glory*, the biographical film about folk singer Woody Guthrie, whom Haskell Wexler had befriended earlier in his life. Haskell Wexler was awarded this 2nd Oscar during his Aquarius -- Libra period; the 11th house from Libra, the sign of Leo, is Wexler's KL and is aspected by owner Sun and Venus in his D-1. In his D-10, Leo falls under the influence of all three natural benefics, while in his D-9 AK Jupiter in Leo is joined by *swakshetra* AmK Sun.

Creativity in the Vedic Astrology Chart

The next chart for our consideration in this section on visual art will be that of professional photographer Herb Ritts (August 13th, 1952, Santa Monica, CA, 1:04 p.m., AA).

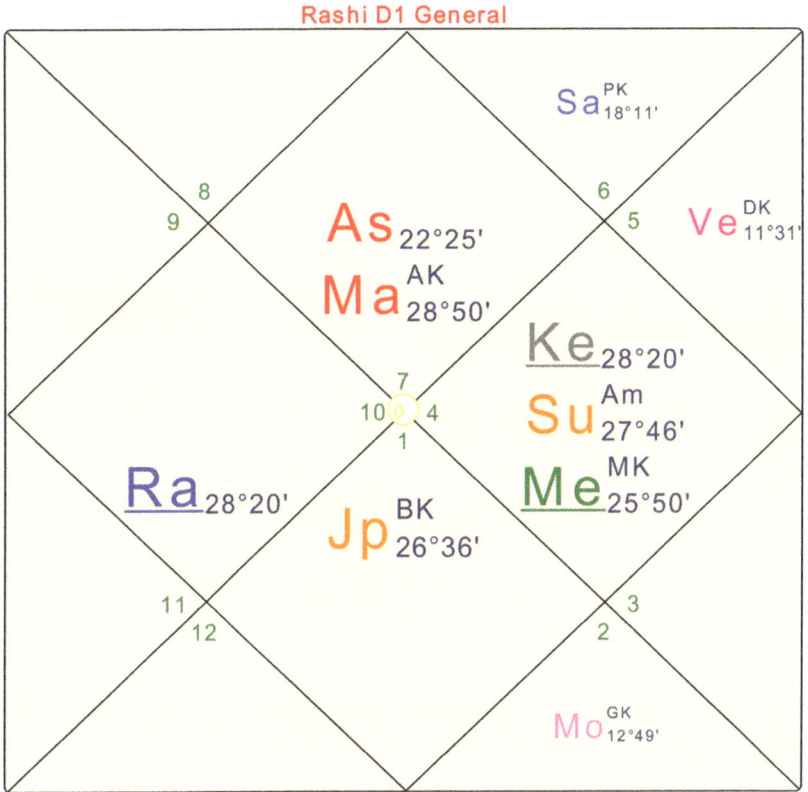

Rashi D1 General

	Jp BK 26°36'	Mo GK 12°49'	
			Me MK 25°50' Su Am 27°46' Ke 28°20'
Ra 28°20'		☉ **Herb Ritts** Wed. 8/13/1952 13:04:00 Santa Monica, CA	Ve DK 11°31'
		Ma AK 28°50' As 22°25'	Sa PK 18°11'

Primarily a fashion photographer who preferred to work in schemes of black and white, Herb Ritts became widely known in the 1980s and 1990s for his artful portraits of models, film stars, musicians, and various cultural and political celebrities. The photographs of Herb Ritts appeared in numerous magazines, including *Vanity Fair*, *Glamour*, *Vogue*, *Elle*, *GQ*, *Harper's Bazaar*, *Time*, *Newsweek*, and *Rolling Stone*. Beginning in 1988 and for the remainder of his life, Herb Ritts also produced and directed TV commercials and pop music videos; the subjects of his music videos included Madonna, Janet Jackson, Chris Isaak, Michael Jackson, Mariah Carey, Britney Spears, and Jennifer Lopez. Several books of photographs by Herb Ritts were published in the late 1980s and early 1990s. In 1996 and 1997 Herb Ritts' work was featured in an exhibition in the Boston Museum of Fine Arts and was attended by more than 250,000 viewers. The permanent Herb Ritts Gallery for Photography, subsidized by a gift from the Herb Ritts Foundation, was established at the Boston MFA in 2010. An exhibition of Herb Ritts' photographs of rock and roll musicians was displayed at the Rock and Roll Hall of Fame in Cleveland Ohio in 2015 and 2016. Following Herb Ritts' passing in 2002, Graydon Carter, the editor of *Vanity Fair* magazine, characterized the work of Ritts as "exquisite, iconic." Ritts' life-long friend, actor Richard Gere, stated of Ritts, "He had an extremely elegant aesthetic … to Herb it came effortlessly. Some photographers embalm their subjects, but he enlivened them." (Ginia Bellafante, *New York Times* obituary, December 27, 2002). In a 2012 article for the Hollywood Reporter, Richard Gere remembered Herb Ritts: "Something that I don't think everyone realizes about Herb is that he was an artist. He did fashion photography as a job but had the soul of an artist …" (Richard Gere, the *Hollywood Reporter*, March 30, 2012).

Herb Ritts' Libra rising chart locates *lagna* lord Venus in the 11th house of popular entertainment where it is aspected by 3rd lord Jupiter from the 7th. Venus' dispositor 11th lord Sun gains directional strength in the 10th house, where it is closely joined by 9th and 12th house lord Mercury in the 12th house from Venus. The combination of *Ketu* and 9th lord Mercury in the 10th forms a *Chaya Graha Raj* yoga. 5th Lord Saturn's placement in the 12th house offers creative expression in the realm of film and photography; Saturn occupies the 5th house from the Moon. Taking the Moon as ascendant, 11th lord Jupiter resides in the 12th house and is in *sambandha* with its dispositor 12th lord Mars. As lord of the 12th house from the Moon, Mars aspects the Moon with its 8th glance. The close (less than 2 degrees) angular relationship between Moon and Venus is critical to the chart, as exalted 10th lord *Rohini* Moon sits in the 10th house from ascendant ruler Venus.

In Herb Ritts' D-9, artistic expression is confirmed as 10th and 11th lord Saturn joins D-9 ascendant ruler Mars in the 3rd, while 3rd lord Mercury in the 11th house yields a 3 – 11 *Parivartana* yoga. 12th

house themes define the career as 12th house occupant/5th lord Sun receives 10th lord Saturn's one-way aspect; the Sun is also activated by 12th lord Jupiter's aspect from the 8th house. In Ritts' D-10, *vargottama* (for the D-10) exalted 3rd lord Moon in the ascendant is in *sambandha* opposition with chart lord Venus, 10th lord Saturn and 5th lord Mercury. From the 3rd house of artistry, 12th house ruler Mars aspects the 10th house of career.

In the mid-1970s, with the onset of his *Vimshottari Rahu* – Mercury period, Herb Ritts (having previously been employed in his family's furniture business) decided to take some classes in photography. In 1977, a set of Ritts' photographs of actor Richard Gere appeared in *Vogue*, *Esquire*, and *Mademoiselle* magazines, and quickly attracted attention throughout the entertainment industry. Mercury's status as ruler of the 9th (higher education) and 12th (film and photography) houses is responsible for the opportunities which propelled Herb Ritts' career; notice also that all the *grahas* in Ritts' 10th house reside in Mercury's *nakshatra* of *Ashlesha*. As major period lord, *Rahu* is sign disposited by 12th house occupant Saturn, and aspected from the 10th by Mercury and the Sun. *Rahu* in a *nakshatra* of Mars is precisely aspected by Mars from the ascendant of the chart. *Rahu*'s capability is amplified by its placement at 28 degrees of Capricorn, with four *grahas* in *kendra* houses from *Rahu*, and none exceeding an orb of 3 degrees of that of *Rahu*. In Herb Ritts' D-9, *Rahu* is aspected by 5th lord and 12th house occupant Sun, as well as by ascendant ruler Mars, and is disposited by 3rd lord Mercury who is placed in the 11th house.

Creativity in the Vedic Astrology Chart

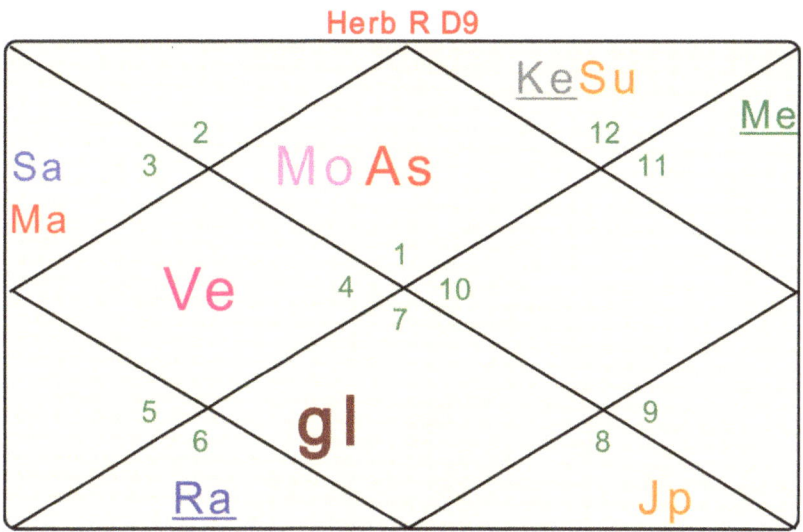

Herb R D9

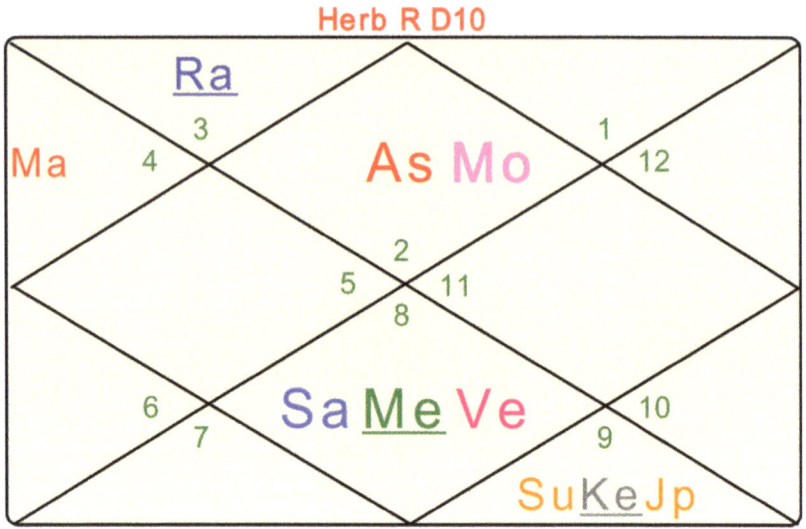

Herb : Vimshottari

Start Date			Age	Dashas	
11/	20/	1962	10.3	Ma	Sa
12/	30/	1963	11.4	Ma	Me
12/	26/	1964	12.4	Ma	Ke
5/	24/	1965	12.8	Ma	Ve
7/	24/	1966	13.9	Ma	Su
11/	29/	1966	14.3	Ma	Mo
6/	**30/**	**1967**	**14.9**	**Ra**	**Ra**
3/	12/	1970	17.6	Ra	Jp
8/	5/	1972	20.0	Ra	Sa
6/	12/	1975	22.8	Ra	Me
12/	29/	1977	25.4	Ra	Ke
1/	17/	1979	26.4	Ra	Ve
1/	17/	1982	29.4	Ra	Su
12/	11/	1982	30.3	Ra	Mo
6/	11/	1984	31.8	Ra	Ma
6/	**30/**	**1985**	**32.9**	**Jp**	**Jp**
8/	18/	1987	35.0	Jp	Sa
2/	28/	1990	37.5	Jp	Me
6/	5/	1992	39.8	Jp	Ke
5/	12/	1993	40.7	Jp	Ve
1/	11/	1996	43.4	Jp	Su
10/	29/	1996	44.2	Jp	Mo
2/	28/	1998	45.5	Jp	Ma
2/	4/	1999	46.5	Jp	Ra
6/	**30/**	**2001 e**	**48.9**	**Sa**	**Sa**
7/	3/	2004	51.9	Sa	Me

Herb: Chara			
Start Date		Age	Dashas
8/ 13/ 1952		-0.0	Libr
8/ 14/ 1962		10.0	Sco
8/ 14/ 1970		18.0	Sag
8/ 14/ 1974		22.0	Cap
8/ 14/ 1978		26.0	Aqu
8/ 14/ 1979		27.0	Pis
8/ 14/ 1990		38.0	Ari
8/ 13/ 1996		44.0	Tau
8/ 14/ 1999		47.0	Gem
8/ 13/ 2000		48.0	Can
8/ 14/ 2002		50.0	Leo
8/ 14/ 2003		51.0	Virg

The AK and AmK of Herb Ritts placed in angular houses (AK Mars in *lagna*, AmK Sun in 10th) form *Raj* yogas as described in BPHS chapter 40 verse 6. The signs of Libra and Cancer and their occupants are fortified by aspects from each of their lords. Herb Ritts pursued the study of photography and first gained success during his 4-year *Jaimini* Capricorn *Chara dasha*. From Capricorn AK Mars gains directional strength in the 10th as AmK Sun sits in the 7th house of independent career. The signs of Capricorn and Libra both benefit from the yoga-forming combined influence of Venus and the Moon. In Mr. Ritts' D-10, Capricorn is again influenced by exalted Moon and Venus as well as sign owner natal 5th lord/PK Saturn, and Mercury. From Capricorn in the D-10, artistic expression through film is highlighted by the presence of 12th (and 3rd) lord BK Jupiter in its own sign of Sagittarius with AmK Sun and *Ketu*.

Although brief, Herb Ritts' subsequent one-year Aquarius period served to multiply his career opportunities and to burnish his reputation as a gifted photographer, as well as to enable Ritts himself to be persuaded by the response to his early photographic efforts that he was now capable of making photography his profession. In Ritts' D-1, Aquarius is activated by aspects from AK Mars and AmK Sun in addition to the auspicious combination of Jupiter and Mercury, as

Jupiter, Mercury, the Sun and *Rahu* and *Ketu* aspect the 10th house from Aquarius. In the D-9, Mercury in Aquarius and Jupiter 10 signs away in Scorpio are both activated by the Venus – Moon combination. The *Parivartana* yoga involving Mercury and Saturn emphasizes the theme of creativity as it becomes a 1st house -- 5th house exchange from Aquarius, with AK Mars and PK/natal 5th lord Saturn creating *Raj* yoga in the 5th house. Aquarius is the sign on the 10th house of Ritts' D-10, as Aquarius ruler PK Saturn, Mercury and DK Venus occupy the 10th house and are aspected by Scorpio ruler AK Mars. As in his D-1, the 12th house from Aquarius gains the influence of Venus and exalted Moon, along with (in the D-10), Saturn and Mercury. Creative influence on the 12th house abounds; notice that Mercury rules the 5th house of the D-10 and the 5th from the sign of Aquarius, while Saturn serves as both PK and natal 5th house lord as it aspects its own sign of Capricorn.

The next chart in this section will be that of American stage and film actor Kevin Kline (October 24th, 1947, St. Louis, MO, 9:11 a.m., AA).

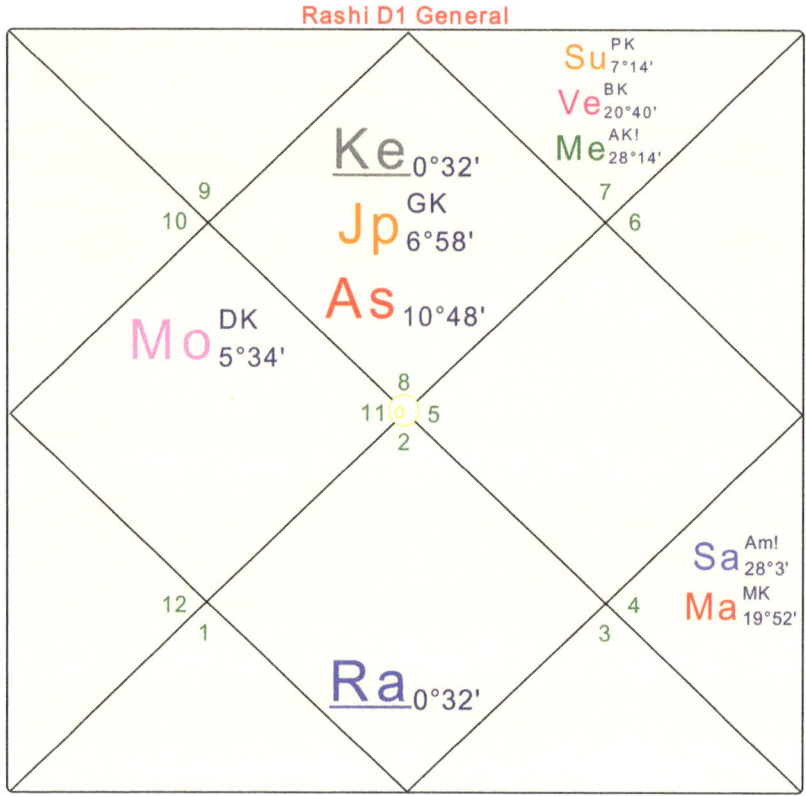

Creativity in the Vedic Astrology Chart

Kevin Kline studied theater in college at Indiana University, then attended the Julliard School of Drama, where he joined a successful repertory group, the City Center Acting Company, in 1972. Under the sponsorship and guidance of veteran actor John Houseman, the Company toured the United States, performing classical dramas, musicals, and the plays of William Shakespeare, to great acclaim. Kevin Kline ceased touring and settled in New York in 1976. Except for a brief appearance in a television soap opera that year, Kline continued to perform in Broadway plays and musicals until his first film appearance in *Sophie's Choice* in 1982. Since then, Kevin Kline has consistently maintained parallel careers as an actor in prominent theatrical productions while enjoying a successful film career. Kline earned Tony awards for Best Featured Actor in a Musical for his performances in *On the Twentieth Century* (1978), and in the New York Shakespeare Festival's 1981 Central Park production of Gilbert and Sullivan's *The Pirates of Penzance*. In 2017, Kevin Kline earned his third Tony award, for Best Actor in a Play, for his performance in the Noel Coward play *Present Laughter*. In his ongoing association with the Shakespeare Festival, Kevin Kline performed in leading roles in *Richard III* (1983), *Henry V* (1984), *Much Ado About Nothing* (1988), and two productions of *Hamlet* (1986, 1990), the latter which Kline also directed. In addition to *Sophie's Choice*, Kline's film appearances have included roles in *The Big Chill* (1983), *Cry Freedom* (1987), *Grand Canyon* (1991), *Dave* (1993), *French Kiss* (1995) and *The Ice Storm* (1997). For his performance in the 1988 comedy film *A Fish Called Wanda*, Kevin Kline was given the Academy Award for Best Supporting Actor. *New York Times* film and theater critic Frank Rich referred to Kevin Kline as "the American Olivier" (*New York Times*, 1/1/2008), while *Newsday* critic Lynn Darling had described Kline as "one of the most talented and versatile actors of his generation." (*Newsday*, 7/13/1988).

Kevin Kline's Scorpio rising chart finds 5th lord Jupiter in the ascendant in directional strength, from which location Jupiter aspects chart lord Mars in the 9th house. Mars' debilitation is cancelled by Jupiter's placement in *kendra* houses from the ascendant and Moon, and the Moon's location in a *kendra*. Given the placements of the Moon and Jupiter, and that of Mars in a *trikona*, Mars qualifies for *Neecha Bhanga Raj* yoga. Mars is joined in the 9th house by 3rd and 4th lord Saturn, as Saturn participates in a *Maha Parivartana* yoga with the Moon, linking houses 4 and 9 and enabling directionally strong 9th lord Moon to aspect the 10th house of career. The 12th house of theater and film is strongly activated, as it holds 10th house ruler Sun, its own ruling planet Venus and 11th lord Mercury. Like Mars, the Sun's debilitation is cancelled, as Sun is joined by its dispositor Venus, who is in a mutual *kendra* relationship with Mars as ruler of Aries, where the Sun is exalted. Mars' activation of the three *grahas* in the

12th house is especially notable for the very close aspect, less than one degree, between Mars and 12th lord Venus. The bright waxing Moon and Jupiter form a strong *Kesari* yoga, as both *grahas* enjoy directional strength and occupy *kendra* houses from the ascendant as well as from each other. As referenced earlier and described in BPHS 36 verses 3 – 4 and *Phaladeepika* 6 verses 14 & 16, the *Kesari* yoga confers elevated status, public recognition, courage, and forceful, "lofty" oratory. Jupiter's association with *Ketu* in the ascendant constitutes a *Chaya Graha Raj* yoga. Employing *Chandra lagna*, ascendant and 12th house ruler Saturn joins 3rd and 10th lord Mars in the 6th house, as the 12th house from the Moon is activated by aspects from its owner Saturn and 3rd and 10th lord (from Moon) Mars.

In Kevin Kline's Libra D-9, 3rd lord Jupiter occupies the 12th house and has *sambandha* with 5th lord Saturn in Jupiter's sign of Pisces in the 6th. *Swakshetra* 9th and 12th house ruler Mercury opposes 11th lord Sun and 2nd house (voice, appearance) lord Mars. A career related to 2nd house themes is suggested by the presence of 10th lord Moon in the 2nd and the aspect of 2nd (and 7th) house ruler Mars to the 10th house. In Kline's D-10, also a Libra rising chart, creativity manifested through 12th house themes becomes more pronounced as Jupiter again is placed in the 12th, this time in association with 2nd lord Mars. From the 3rd house 5th lord Saturn aspects its own 5th house as well as the 12th and occupants 3rd lord Jupiter and Mars. Saturn is joined in the 3rd by 11th lord Sun. The birth chart's *Kesari* yoga is re-created across the 6 – 12 axis in the D-10 as 10th lord Moon resides in Pisces in the 6th house. Mars' and Jupiter's dispositor 12th house ruler Mercury is located in the 10th house; as the sign on the 12th house, Virgo is Mercury's *mooltrikona* sign while Mercury's status as 9th lord in the 10th creates a *Raj* yoga in the chart. Finally, both the D-9 and D-10 charts benefit from ascendant ruler Venus' aspect back to the ascendant from the 7th house of the chart.

Kevin Kline's chart holds the *Jaimini Raj* yoga described in BPHS chapter 39 verses 6 – 7, specifically the placement of the

AK (Mercury in this chart) and PK (Sun) in the 5th house from the chart's KL of Gemini, said to confer "happiness and fame." (See also the charts of Artur Rubinstein and Wolfgang Amadeus Mozart for discussion of this yoga.) This *Raj* yoga is made stronger, and slanted in the direction of artistic expression, by the additional presence of *swakshetra* BK Venus. Venus in the 5th house from the KL in aspect to the Moon meets criteria described in BPHS 39:11 and confers elevated status. The 12th house from Kline's Gemini KL is strongly enabled by the collective *Raj* yoga-creating influence from the chart's AK, AmK, and PK, along with Mars and Taurus sign ruler *swakshetra* Venus. As earlier noted (Ginger Rogers and Niccolo Paganini), the Moon's activation by four or more planets is also ascribed *Jaimini Raj* yoga status; Kevin Kline's 4th house DK Moon is aspected by the same five *grahas*.

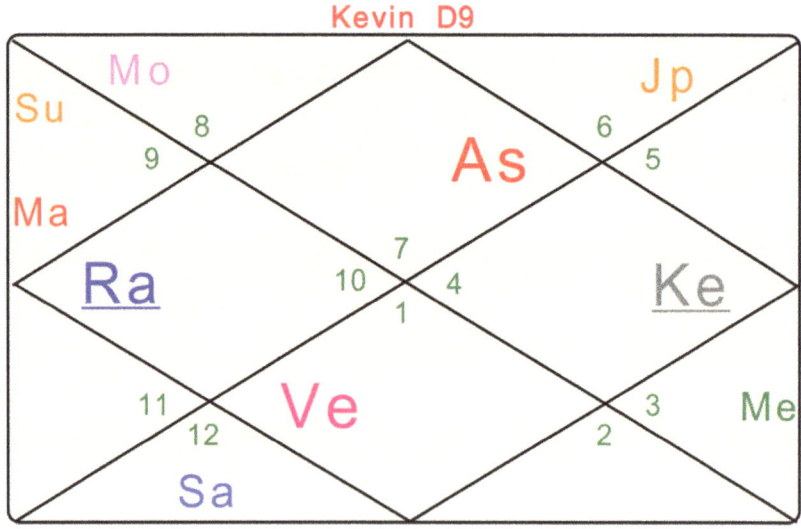

Creativity in the Vedic Astrology Chart

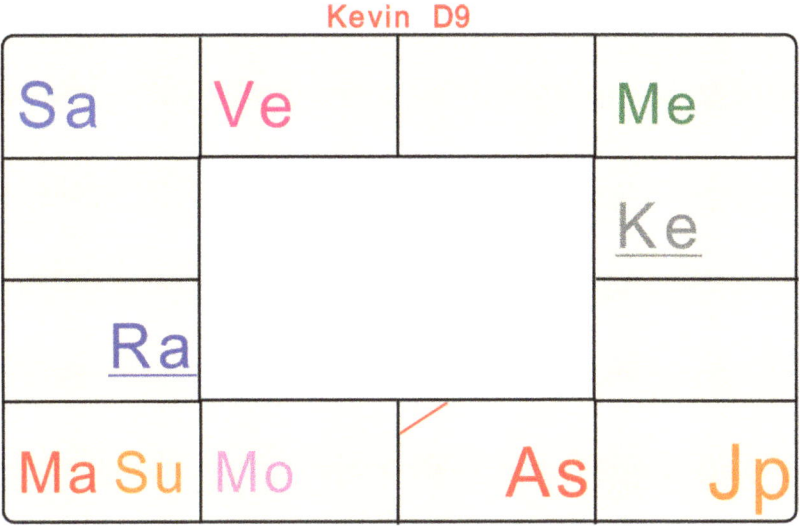

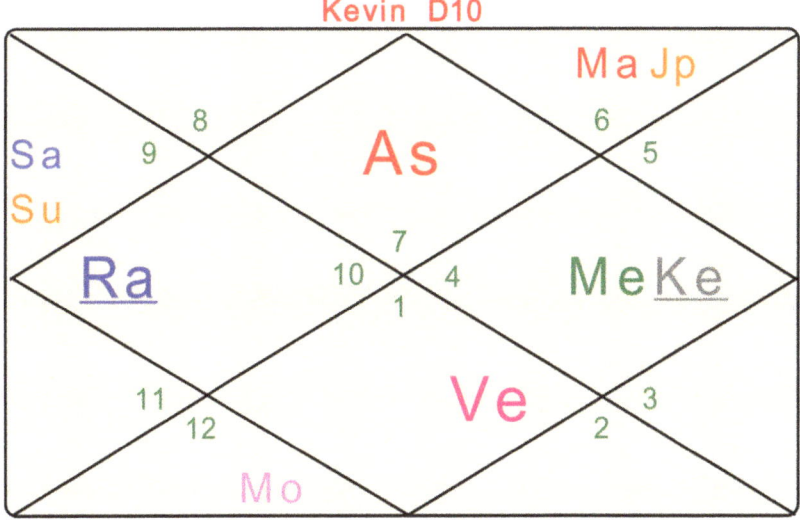

Mo	Ve		
	Kevin D10		Ke Me
Ra			
Su Sa		As	Ma Jp

Kevin: Vimshottari

Start Date			Age	Dashas	
12/	8/	1962	15.1	Ra	Su
11/	2/	1963	16.0	Ra	Mo
5/	3/	1965	17.5	Ra	Ma
5/	**22/**	**1966**	**18.6**	**Jp**	**Jp**
7/	9/	1968	20.7	Jp	Sa
1/	20/	1971	23.2	Jp	Me
4/	27/	1973	25.5	Jp	Ke
4/	3/	1974	26.4	Jp	Ve
12/	2/	1976	29.1	Jp	Su
9/	20/	1977	29.9	Jp	Mo
1/	20/	1979	31.2	Jp	Ma
12/	27/	1979	32.2	Jp	Ra
5/	**22/**	**1982**	**34.6**	**Sa**	**Sa**
5/	24/	1985	37.6	Sa	Me
2/	2/	1988	40.3	Sa	Ke
3/	12/	1989	41.4	Sa	Ve
5/	12/	1992	44.6	Sa	Su
4/	24/	1993	45.5	Sa	Mo
11/	23/	1994	47.1	Sa	Ma
1/	2/	1996	48.2	Sa	Ra
11/	8/	1998	51.0	Sa	Jp
5/	**22/**	**2001**	**53.6**	**Me**	**Me**
10/	18/	2003	56.0	Me	Ke
10/	14/	2004	57.0	Me	Ve
8/	15/	2007	59.8	Me	Su
6/	21/	2008	60.7	Me	Mo

Start Date	Age	Dashas	
	KK: Chara		
10/ 24/ 1966	19.0	Libr	Libr
10/ 24/ 1967	20.0	Virg	Libr
9/ 23/ 1968	20.9	Virg	Sco
8/ 24/ 1969	21.8	Virg	Sag
7/ 25/ 1970	22.8	Virg	Cap
6/ 24/ 1971	23.7	Virg	Aqu
5/ 24/ 1972	24.6	Virg	Pis
4/ 24/ 1973	25.5	Virg	Ari
3/ 25/ 1974	26.4	Virg	Tau
2/ 23/ 1975	27.3	Virg	Gem
1/ 23/ 1976	28.2	Virg	Can
12/ 23/ 1976	29.2	Virg	Leo
11/ 23/ 1977	30.1	Virg	Virg
10/ 24/ 1978	31.0	Leo	Virg
8/ 24/ 1979	31.8	Leo	Libr
6/ 24/ 1980	32.7	Leo	Sco
4/ 24/ 1981	33.5	Leo	Sag
2/ 22/ 1982	34.3	Leo	Cap
12/ 24/ 1982	35.2	Leo	Aqu
10/ 24/ 1983	36.0	Leo	Pis
8/ 24/ 1984	36.8	Leo	Ari
6/ 24/ 1985	37.7	Leo	Tau
4/ 24/ 1986	38.5	Leo	Gem
2/ 23/ 1987	39.3	Leo	Can
12/ 24/ 1987	40.2	Leo	Leo
10/ 23/ 1988	41.0	Can	Gem

According to his biography, 1972 was the year that Kevin Kline and several fellow Julliard graduates joined and began touring as the City Center Acting Company. Beginning in early 1971 and until late April of 1973, Kevin Kline ran his *Vimshottari* Jupiter – Mercury period. Both planets strongly manifest 12th house activation, as 11th lord Mercury joins 10th lord Sun and 12th lord Venus in the 12th house of the D-1. In Kline's D-9 and D-10, Mercury's sign of Virgo is on the 12th house and contains Jupiter, as 12th lord Mercury occupies the

10th house of the D-10. Concurrent with most of his Jupiter major period, Kevin Kline ran his 11-year Virgo *Chara dasha* starting at age twenty. In the birth chart the 2nd house (oratory) from Virgo holds the chart's AK, BK, and PK, as that combination of *grahas* also aspects the 12th house from Virgo. The 9th house (higher education, travel) has *Rahu* and is favorably aspected by five *grahas* – BK Venus, PK Sun, AK Mercury, AmK Saturn and Mars. From the sign of Virgo, the 11th house of gains, awards and entertainment holds Saturn and Mars and is activated by the Moon and Jupiter. It was during his Virgo -- Virgo period, in 1978, that Kevin Kline earned a Tony award for his performance as Bruce Granit in the successful revival of the Broadway musical *On the Twentieth Century*. His *Vimshottari dasha* at the time was Jupiter – Moon, activating the *Kesari* yogas of the birth chart and the D-10.

Kevin Kline's chart provides a solid example of the value and significance of divisional charts, as key to the determination of the degree to which the potential of a birth chart becomes fully realized in the life of the native. Kevin Kline would not have attained an equally high level of career success during his Virgo period without the strength of his D-9 and D-10. In both charts, it is seen that five *grahas* occupy angular houses during major or sub-periods of *dwishwabhava* signs. In Kline's D-9, Jupiter in Virgo is disposited by *swakshetra* AK Mercury in the 10th house in Gemini, as the *kendras* are also activated by PK Sun and Mars in Sagittarius and AmK Saturn in Pisces. Notice that the *dwishwabhava* signs benefit from occupation and/or aspect of their lords Mercury and Jupiter. In his D-10, the *Kesari* yoga is re-activated from the D-1 across the 1 – 7 axis from Virgo and occupants Jupiter and Mars, as DK Moon resides in the sign of Pisces while PK Sun joins AmK Saturn in the sign of Sagittarius.

The following chart is that of the prolific and influential film director Luis Bunuel (February 22nd, 1900, Calanda, Spain, 12:00 p.m., AA).

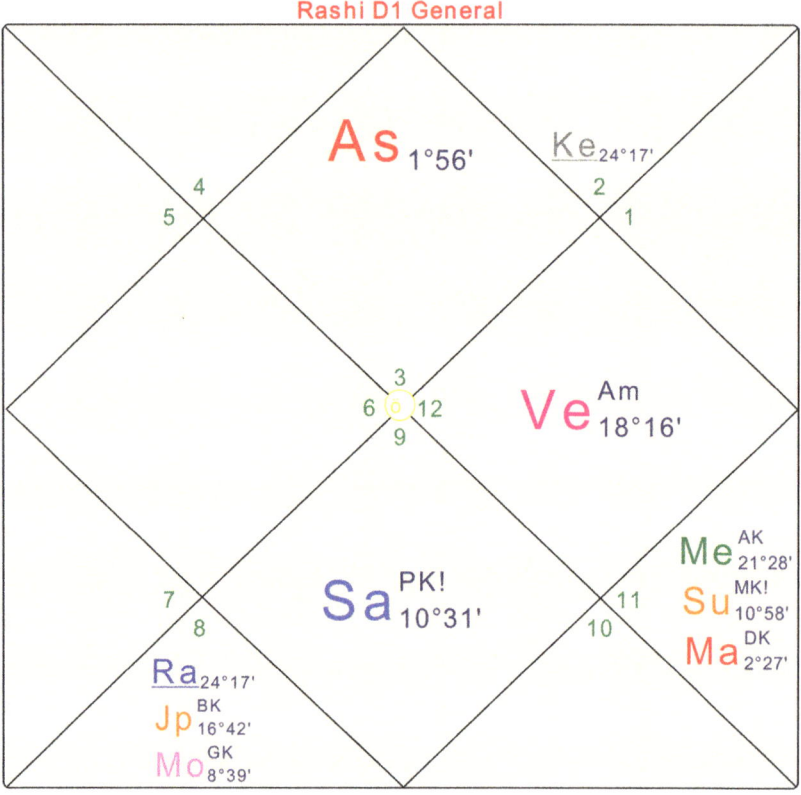

Rashi D1 General

	Ve Am 18°16'	Ke 24°17'	As 1°56'
Me AK 21°28' Su MK! 10°58' Ma DK 2°27'		ö **Luis Bunuel** Thu. 2/22/1900 12:00:00 Calanda, SPAIN	
Sa PK! 10°31'	Ra 24°17' Jp BK 16°42' Mo GK 8°39'		

At the age of twenty-five, Luis Bunuel moved from his native Spain to Paris, where he enrolled in the Academie du Cinema and studied film under the guidance of the French film director Jean Epstein. In 1929, in the context of a collaboration with Salvador Dali, Bunuel shot and directed his first film, *Un Chien Andalou* ("An Andalusian Dog"). Inspired by the dreams of the two men, *Un Chien Andalou* is still frequently shown in film schools and Bunuel retrospectives and is regarded as a ground-breaking surrealistic masterpiece. Over the course of his 50-year career, many of Bunuel's films served to reflect his iconoclastic social and religious views in the context of his unique artistic vision. His films included *L'Age d'Or* ("The Golden Age," 1930), *Los Olvidados* ("The Forgotten," 1950), *The Exterminating Angel* (1962), *Diary of a Chambermaid* (1964), *Simon of the*

Desert (1965), *Belle de Jour* ("Beauty of the Day," 1967), *The Milky Way* (1969), and *Tristana* (1970). Bunuel's 1961 film *Viridiana* was awarded the *Palme d'Or* for best film at that year's Cannes Film Festival. Luis Bunuel is perhaps best known for *The Discreet Charm of the Bourgeoisie* (1972), which won that year's Academy Award for Best Foreign Language Film, as well as Best Film and Best Director as chosen by the National Society of Film Critics. Luis Bunuel's last film, *That Obscure Object of Desire* (1977), was honored as Best Foreign Language Film and Best Director by the critics' National Board of Review, while Bunuel was also cited as Best Director by the National Society of Film Critics. In its 2012 list of the 250 best films in the history of cinema, the British Film Institute included seven films directed by Luis Bunuel.

Luis Bunuel's chart is that of Gemini rising, with ascendant lord Mercury in the 9th house with 3rd lord Sun and 6th and 11th lord Mars. Mercury's placement in *Purva Bhadrapada* and the Sun's location in *Shatabhisha* will confer skill and perception in the realm of visual expression. The chart is strongly defined by a prominent *Malavya* yoga, as 5th and 12th lord Venus occupies its sign of exaltation in highly imaginative *Revati nakshatra*. Venus in the 10th house receives a one-way aspect from 10th lord Jupiter. Venus therefore enjoys a powerfully benefic *sambandha* relationship with Jupiter, which aspects the 12th house as well as the lord; notice that the longitudes of the two planets configure them at less than 2 degrees of each other. In addition to its 12th house lordship from the ascendant, Venus rules the 12th house from the Moon.

As a creative artist Luis Bunuel was fascinated by the power of dreams and the capability of the media of film, beyond all others, to capture dreams. Bunuel's *New York Times* obituary quotes him as comparing a movie to "an involuntary imitation of a dream." (Peter B. Flint, *New York Times*, July 30, 1983). In a 2015 article entitled "25 Luis Bunuel Quotes on Art, Filmmaking and Dreams," writer Alison Nastasi quotes Bunuel: "*Un Chien Andalou* was born of the encounter between my dreams and (those of) Salvador Dali. Later, I brought the dreams directly into my films …" (Alison Nastasi, www.flavorwire.com, February 21st, 2015). Dreams and surrealistic dream imagery figure prominently in many of the films of Luis Bunuel; in his award-winning film *The Discreet Charm of the Bourgeoisie*, the dreams of four different characters are portrayed, as Bunuel employed three of his own recurring dreams in the film. (John Baxter, *Bunuel*, Carroll & Graf Publishers, 1994). The close connection between dreams and their visual depiction in his films is clearly indicated in the chart of Luis Bunuel. In addition to the placement of exalted 12th lord Venus in the 10th house, the 12th house is activated by the presence of *Ketu* and aspects from Jupiter, the Moon, and Mars. As owner of the 12th house from ascendant ruler Mercury, the planet Saturn aspects Mercury as well as the ascendant of the chart.

Mr. Bunuel's chart offers several of the *Jaimini Raj* yogas mentioned in BPHS chapter 40. These include: (40:4), the AmK (Venus in this chart) in exaltation, (40:6), the placement of AK and/or AmK in trine or angular houses (AK Mercury in the 9th and AmK Venus in the 10th), finally (40:11), the placement of the AK (Mercury) in the 9th house. The mutual glance between AmK Venus and PK Saturn is a *Raj* yoga in the *Jaimini* system, elevated in the chart by Venus' exaltation and 5th house rulership.

The Moon and Jupiter form a *Kesari* yoga in the 6th house from the ascendant. The Moon's debilitation is cancelled by the placement of Moon's dispositor Mars in the 4th house from the Moon, and that of Venus (owner of the sign where the Moon is exalted) in the 10th house from the ascendant. Taking the Moon as ascendant, Jupiter rules the 5th and aspects 5th house occupant (and 12th lord) Venus. The 10th house from the Moon is activated by aspects from three *grahas*, including 10th lord (from Moon) Sun in *Shatabhisha nakshatra*. The birth chart's *Kesari* yoga rises to *Gaja Kesari* status in Luis Bunuel's D-9, as *swakshetra* 3rd lord Jupiter is joined by ascendant ruler Venus, while the chart's 10th lord Moon goes to the 12th house. The likelihood of a 12th house-themed career is enhanced by way of 5th lord Saturn's placement in the 10th and aspect to 10th lord Moon in the 12th house; notice also Saturn's aspect to 12th lord Mercury in the 7th. Mercury is also enlivened by aspects from its dispositor Mars and 3rd lord Jupiter. In Bunuel's D-10, the 12th house holds 3rd lord Sun and *swakshetra* 5th and 12th lord Venus. Saturn again inhabits the 10th house of the chart and activates the 12th house and lord as does 11th lord Mars from its location in the 9th. Ascendant lord Mercury is exalted in the 4th house of the chart while 7th and 10th lord Jupiter achieves *Hamsa* yoga in the 7th house. Although the Moon – Jupiter arrangement in the D-10 does not strictly meet *Gaja Kesari* criteria, it does form a strong *Kesari* yoga as the Moon gains directional strength in the 4th house while both *grahas* occupy angular houses. In this context, it is worth noting that Luis Bunuel enjoyed his most successful period as a filmmaker after the age of sixty, concurrent with his *Vimshottari* Moon period. Certainly, the consistent presence of *Kesari* yogas (*Gaja Kesari* in D-9) across his D-1, D-9 and D-10 will contribute to Bunuel's success at this later time in his life. The Moon's 10th house rulership and location in the 12th of the D-9 is influential as well as the placement of six *grahas* (including *Rahu* and *Ketu*) in *kendra* houses from the Moon in Luis Bunuel's birth chart.

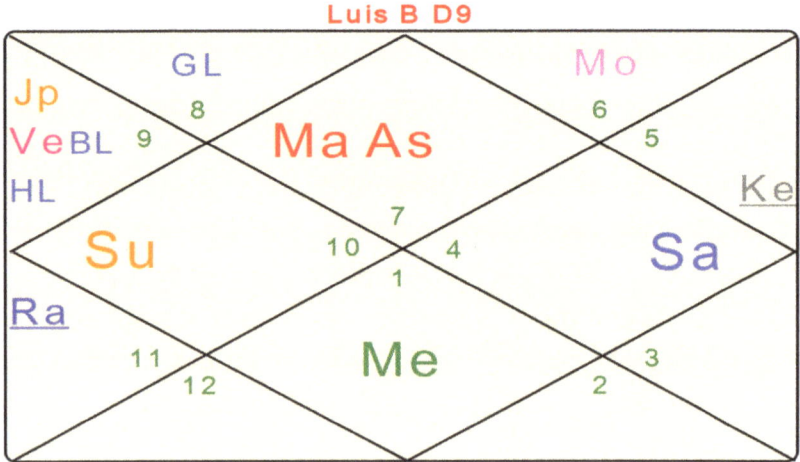

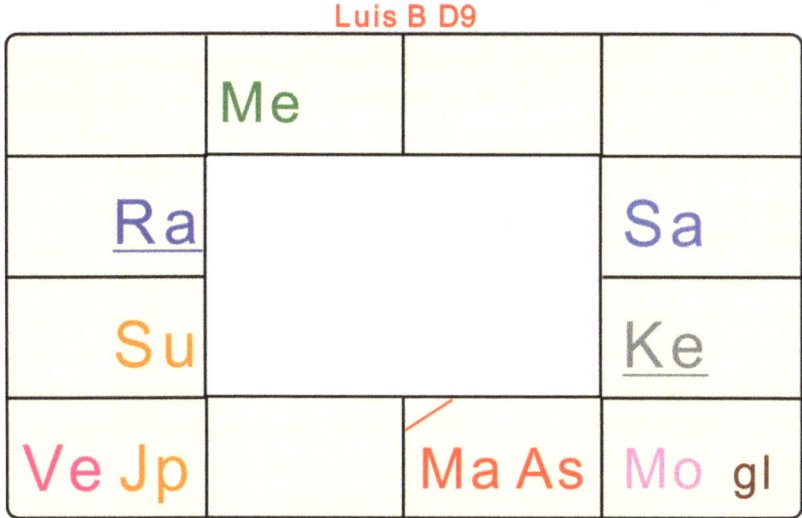

Luis B D9

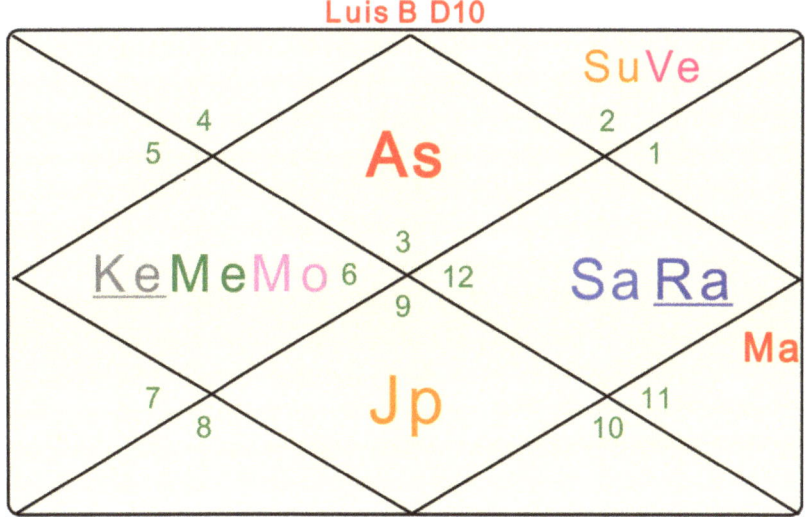

Luis B D10

Luis B D10

Ra Sa		Ve Su	As
Ma			
	Jp		Me Mo Ke

Luis: Chara

Start Date	Age	Dashas
2/ 23/ 1918	18.0	Ari
2/ 23/ 1928	28.0	Pis
2/ 23/ 1932	32.0	Aqu
2/ 23/ 1935	35.0	Cap
2/ 23/ 1936	36.0	Sag
2/ 23/ 1947	47.0	Sco
2/ 23/ 1950	50.0	Libr
2/ 23/ 1955	55.0	Virg
2/ 23/ 1962	62.0	Leo
2/ 23/ 1968	68.0	Can
2/ 23/ 1976 e	76.0	Gem
2/ 24/ 1984	84.0	Tau

Luis : Chara

Start Date	Age	Dashas	
5/ 25/ 1960	60.2	Virg	Can
12/ 24/ 1960	60.8	Virg	Leo
7/ 25/ 1961	61.4	Virg	Virg
2/ 23/ 1962	**62.0**	**Leo**	**Virg**
8/ 25/ 1962	62.5	Leo	Libr
2/ 23/ 1963	63.0	Leo	Sco
8/ 25/ 1963	63.5	Leo	Sag
2/ 23/ 1964	64.0	Leo	Cap
8/ 24/ 1964	64.5	Leo	Aqu
2/ 23/ 1965	65.0	Leo	Pis
8/ 24/ 1965	65.5	Leo	Ari
2/ 23/ 1966	66.0	Leo	Tau
8/ 25/ 1966	66.5	Leo	Gem
2/ 23/ 1967	67.0	Leo	Can
8/ 25/ 1967	67.5	Leo	Leo
2/ 23/ 1968	**68.0**	**Can**	**Gem**
10/ 24/ 1968	68.7	Can	Tau
6/ 24/ 1969	69.3	Can	Ari
2/ 23/ 1970	70.0	Can	Pis
10/ 24/ 1970	70.7	Can	Aqu
6/ 25/ 1971	71.3	Can	Cap
2/ 23/ 1972	72.0	Can	Sag
10/ 24/ 1972	72.7	Can	Sco
6/ 24/ 1973	73.3	Can	Libr
2/ 23/ 1974	74.0	Can	Virg
10/ 24/ 1974	74.7	Can	Leo

Luis : Vimshottari

Start Date			Age	Dashas	
7/	24/	1928	28.4	Ke	Ke
12/	20/	1928	28.8	Ke	Ve
2/	19/	1930	30.0	Ke	Su
6/	27/	1930	30.3	Ke	Mo
1/	26/	1931	30.9	Ke	Ma
6/	24/	1931	31.3	Ke	Ra
7/	12/	1932	32.4	Ke	Jp
6/	18/	1933	33.3	Ke	Sa
7/	27/	1934	34.4	Ke	Me
7/	25/	1935	35.4	Ve	Ve
11/	23/	1938	38.7	Ve	Su
11/	23/	1939	39.7	Ve	Mo
7/	24/	1941	41.4	Ve	Ma
9/	23/	1942	42.6	Ve	Ra
9/	23/	1945	45.6	Ve	Jp
5/	24/	1948	48.2	Ve	Sa
7/	25/	1951	51.4	Ve	Me
5/	25/	1954	54.2	Ve	Ke
7/	25/	1955	55.4	Su	Su
11/	11/	1955	55.7	Su	Mo
5/	12/	1956	56.2	Su	Ma
9/	17/	1956	56.6	Su	Ra
8/	12/	1957	57.5	Su	Jp
5/	31/	1958	58.3	Su	Sa
5/	13/	1959	59.2	Su	Me
3/	18/	1960	60.1	Su	Ke
7/	24/	1960	60.4	Su	Ve
7/	24/	1961	61.4	Mo	Mo
5/	25/	1962	62.2	Mo	Ma
12/	24/	1962	62.8	Mo	Ra
6/	24/	1964	64.3	Mo	Jp
10/	24/	1965	65.7	Mo	Sa
5/	25/	1967	67.2	Mo	Me
10/	23/	1968	68.7	Mo	Ke
5/	25/	1969	69.2	Mo	Ve
1/	23/	1971	70.9	Mo	Su
7/	25/	1971	71.4	Ma	Ma
12/	21/	1971	71.8	Ma	Ra
1/	8/	1973	72.9	Ma	Jp
12/	14/	1973	73.8	Ma	Sa
1/	23/	1975	74.9	Ma	Me

Although Luis Bunuel continued to work in the film industry in Spain, the U.S., and Mexico during the 1940s and 1950s, it was not until the 1960s that he was given the opportunities to produce and direct the set of films for which he earned acclaim as a visionary film maker. With the onset of his *Vimshottari* Moon period in July of 1961, Bunuel simultaneously began his *Jaimini* Virgo – Virgo period, as *Viridiana* was released and he began production of his next film, *The Exterminating Angel*. The sign of Virgo holds exalted AK Mercury and the Moon in Bunuel's D-10 chart, as *swakshetra* BK Jupiter and PK Saturn occupy the 4th and 7th houses, respectively. In his D-9, Virgo is the sign on the 12th house and holds the Moon while Jupiter and AmK Venus are located in Sagittarius. In the birth chart, the *kendra* houses are activated by exalted 5th lord/AmK Venus and PK Saturn.

Bunuel's film successes continued during his subsequent 6-year Leo *Chara dasha*; the Sun resides in the 10th house (from Leo) with *swakshetra* Venus in Bunuel's D-10. In the D-9, the sign of Leo is aspected by sign owner Sun, AK Mercury, and DK Mars as the 10th house from Leo is activated by the Sun, Mars, and PK Saturn. In his D-1, the placement of seven *grahas* in *kendras* from the sign of Leo, including AK Mercury, Sun, and DK Mars in the 7th, is favorable for career strength and self-determination, as was the case during this phase of Luis Bunuel's career. The specific theme of creative expression during the Leo period is enhanced in the D-1 by the presence of PK Saturn in the 5th house, where it is aspected by exalted natal 5th lord/AmK Venus. In both his D-9 and D-10, BK Jupiter inhabits its own sign of Sagittarius in the 5th house from Leo. Jupiter is joined by Venus and both are aspected by the Moon in the D-9 while the 5 --11 axis in the D-10 is favorably influenced by Mercury, Jupiter, the Moon, and Saturn, along with *Rahu* and *Ketu*. The *dwishwabhava* signs in Luis Bunuel's D-10 are occupied and/or aspected by their ruling planets, exalted Mercury and *swakshetra* Jupiter.

The following chart in this section will be that of pioneering photographer Edward Steichen (March 27th, 1879, Bivange, Luxembourg, 6:00 a.m., AA).

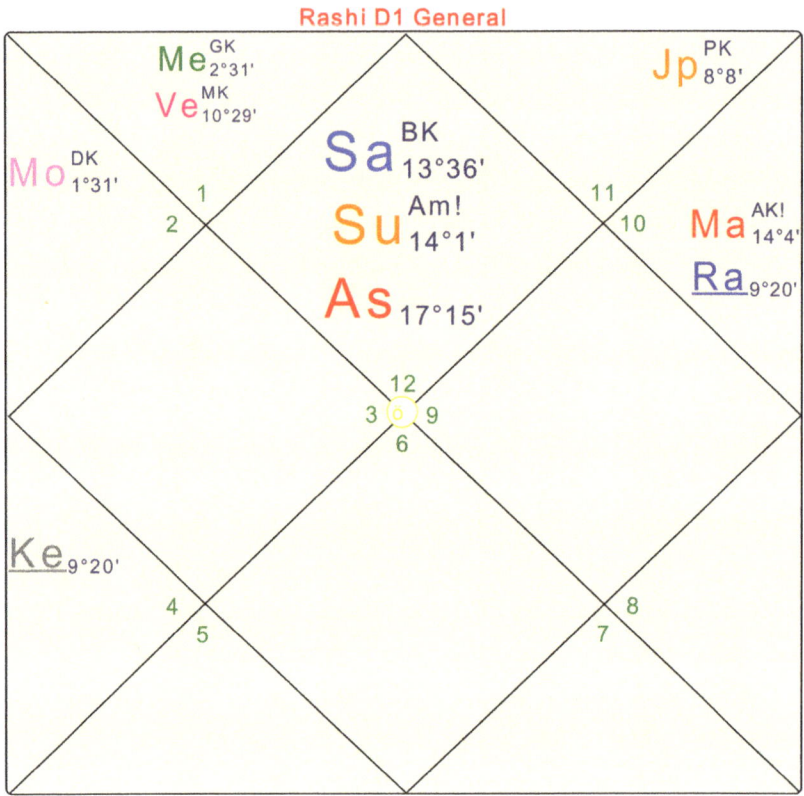

Creativity in the Vedic Astrology Chart

```
Rashi D1 General
┌─────────────────┬─────────────────┬─────────────────┬─────────────────┐
│ Sa  BK          │ Me  GK          │ Mo  DK          │                 │
│     13°36'      │     2°31'       │     1°31'       │                 │
│ Su  Am!         │                 │                 │                 │
│     14°1'       │ Ve  MK          │                 │                 │
│ As  17°15'      │     10°29'      │                 │                 │
├─────────────────┼─────────────────┴─────────────────┼─────────────────┤
│                 │                                   │      Ke 9°20'   │
│ Jp  PK          │                                   │                 │
│     8°8'        │              ö                    │                 │
│                 │                                   │                 │
│ Ma  AK!         │       Edward Steichen             │                 │
│     14°4'       │       Thu. 3/27/1879 6:00:00      │                 │
│                 │       49°32'39"N 6° 8'16"E        │                 │
│ Ra  9°20'       │                                   │                 │
├─────────────────┼───────────────────────────────────┼─────────────────┤
│                 │                                   │                 │
└─────────────────┴───────────────────────────────────┴─────────────────┘
```

Edward Steichen's family immigrated to the U.S. when Steichen was eighteen months old, settling first in Michigan, then finally in the state of Wisconsin. As a teenager, Steichen pursued interests in drawing and painting, and left high school to serve a four-year apprenticeship in lithography in Milwaukee. Edward Steichen purchased his first camera in 1895 and took thousands of photographs, several of which were featured at a photographic exhibition in Philadelphia in 1899. The following year Steichen was introduced to Alfred Stieglitz, who purchased three of Steichen's photographic prints and later enlisted Steichen's expertise in designing the cover logo for Stieglitz's new photographic journal, *Camera Work*. Over the 15 years of *Camera Work*'s quarterly publication, Edward Steichen's photographs were featured more frequently than those of any other contributor. During

World War I, Steichen served in France as an aerial cameraman with the U.S. Army Signal Corps and was awarded a Distinguished Service Citation. Steichen gained prominence in the realm of fashion and portrait photography in the time between the two world wars. In 1923, Edward Steichen signed a contract with Conde Nast publications to photograph for *Vanity Fair* and *Vogue* magazines; his subjects included Charlie Chaplin, Greta Garbo, Isadora Duncan, Martha Graham, Mary Pickford, Paul Robeson, Lillian Gish, J.P. Morgan, and John and Lionel Barrymore. During World War II, Steichen served as Director of the Naval Aviation Photographic Unit and directed the 1944 documentary film *The Fighting Lady*, which won best documentary feature at the 17th Academy Awards in 1945. For his service, Steichen earned the rank of Captain, and was awarded the World War II Victory Medal as well as several Asiatic and Pacific Campaign Medals.

In 1947, Edward Steichen was named Director of Photography at the Museum of Modern Art in New York. Steichen held this appointment for 15 years, during which time he curated the notable 1955 exhibit *The Family of Man*. In 1963, Edward Steichen was conferred the Presidential Medal of Freedom by President Lyndon B. Johnson. Edward Steichen's *New York Times* obituary characterized him as the country's "most celebrated" photographer, and "a craftsman of genius who transformed his medium into an art." (Alden Whitman, *New York Times*, March 26th, 1973). The website of Edward Steichen, www.edwardsteichen.com, includes this quote from Steichen: "The mission of photography is to explain man to man and each man to himself. And that is no mean function."

The Pisces rising chart of Edward Steichen features a *Parivartana* yoga between houses 1 and 12, with ascendant ruler Jupiter in the 12th house and 12th lord Saturn placed in the ascendant. At 17 degrees, the chart's ascendant lies in the innovative *nakshatra* of *Revati*. Both Jupiter and Saturn will exert strong influence on the career, as Jupiter in a Pisces chart also rules the 10th house, and Saturn as 12th lord aspects the 10th house from the ascendant. Jupiter and exalted 5th lord Moon form a *Kesari* yoga with Jupiter in the 10th house from the Moon in *Shatabhisha nakshatra*. Exalted *Krittika* Moon's potential for creative expression will manifest through photography due to 12th lord Saturn's aspect to the Moon. The ascendant and occupants Sun and 12th lord Saturn are flanked by all the natural benefics, with Jupiter in the 12th and the combination of Venus and Mercury in the 2nd house. From the Moon, dispositor Venus joins 5th lord (from Moon) Mercury in the 12th house as both are aspected by their exalted dispositor, Mars.

The sign of Taurus becomes the chart's KL, as Edward Steichen's AK Mars at 14 degrees is in the 5th *navamsha* from Capricorn. Exalted natal 5th lord/DK Moon occupies the KL and is *Jaimini* aspected by exalted 12th lord (from KL) AK Mars. 12th house emphasis persists from the *Jaimini* perspective; while the 12th house from the KL benefits from its ruler's exaltation status, the house itself is occupied by two natural benefics, Venus and Mercury, and is aspected by a 3rd, PK Jupiter. Referring once more to BPHS Chapter 40, we find several configurations which meet criteria for *Raj* yoga status. These include: (40:3), the association of the AmK (the Sun in Edward Steichen's chart) and AK dispositor (Saturn), (40:5), placement of the AmK in the ascendant, (40:8), the chart's 9th lord/AK (Mars) in exaltation, and (40:11), the *arudha* of the 9th house identical with the ascendant. As described in BPHS chapter 33 verses 57 – 60, the placement of a benefic (Jupiter in this chart) in the 10th house from the KL, with aspects from Venus and Mercury, is said to grant sagacity, wealth, strength, and the capacity for "great deeds."

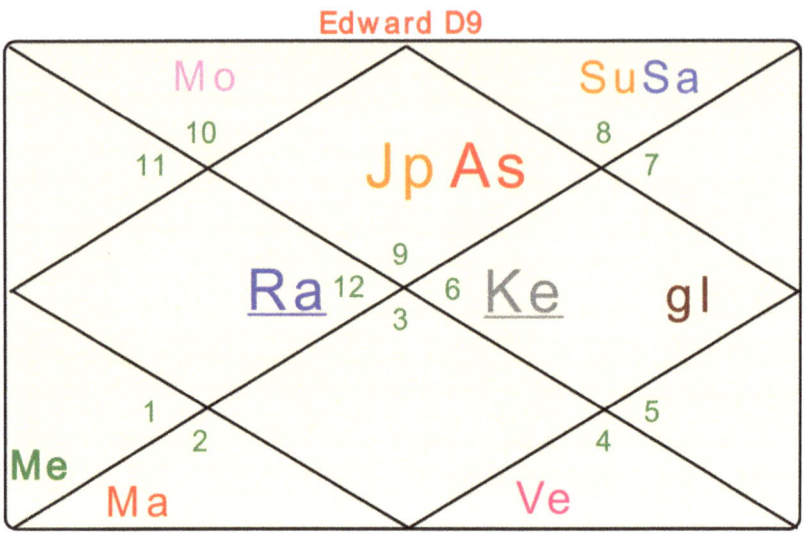

Creativity in the Vedic Astrology Chart

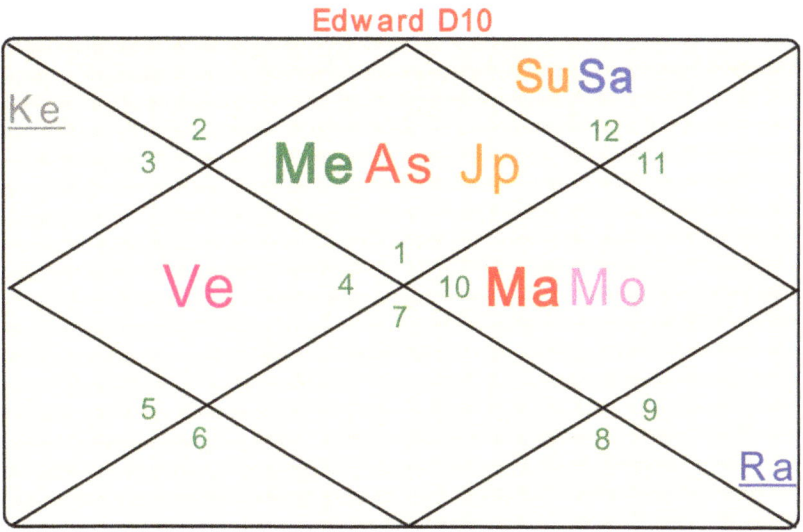

Edward D10

ES: Vimshottari

Start Date	Age	Dashas	
11/ 18/ 1890	11.6	Mo	Ve
7/ 19/ 1892	13.3	Mo	Su
1/ 17/ 1893	**13.8**	**Ma**	**Ma**
6/ 16/ 1893	14.2	Ma	Ra
7/ 4/ 1894	15.3	Ma	Jp
6/ 10/ 1895	16.2	Ma	Sa
7/ 19/ 1896	17.3	Ma	Me
7/ 16/ 1897	18.3	Ma	Ke
12/ 12/ 1897	18.7	Ma	Ve
2/ 11/ 1899	19.9	Ma	Su
6/ 19/ 1899	20.2	Ma	Mo
1/ 18/ 1900	**20.8**	**Ra**	**Ra**
10/ 1/ 1902	23.5	Ra	Jp
2/ 24/ 1905	25.9	Ra	Sa
1/ 1/ 1908	28.8	Ra	Me
7/ 20/ 1910	31.3	Ra	Ke
8/ 8/ 1911	32.4	Ra	Ve
8/ 8/ 1914	35.4	Ra	Su
7/ 2/ 1915	36.3	Ra	Mo
12/ 31/ 1916	37.8	Ra	Ma
1/ 19/ 1918	**38.8**	**Jp**	**Jp**
3/ 8/ 1920	40.9	Jp	Sa
9/ 19/ 1922	43.5	Jp	Me
12/ 25/ 1924	45.7	Jp	Ke
12/ 1/ 1925	46.7	Jp	Ve
8/ 1/ 1928	49.3	Jp	Su
5/ 20/ 1929	50.1	Jp	Mo
9/ 19/ 1930	51.5	Jp	Ma
8/ 26/ 1931	52.4	Jp	Ra
1/ 19/ 1934	**54.8**	**Sa**	**Sa**
1/ 22/ 1937	57.8	Sa	Me
10/ 2/ 1939	60.5	Sa	Ke
11/ 10/ 1940	61.6	Sa	Ve
1/ 10/ 1944	64.8	Sa	Su
12/ 22/ 1944	65.7	Sa	Mo
7/ 24/ 1946	67.3	Sa	Ma
9/ 2/ 1947	68.4	Sa	Ra
7/ 8/ 1950	71.3	Sa	Jp
1/ 19/ 1953	**73.8**	**Me**	**Me**
6/ 17/ 1955	76.2	Me	Ke
6/ 14/ 1956	77.2	Me	Ve

ES: Chara

Start Date	Age	Dashas
3/ 26/ 1889	10.0	Tau
3/ 27/ 1900	21.0	Gem
3/ 28/ 1910	31.0	Can
3/ 27/ 1912	33.0	Leo
3/ 27/ 1917	38.0	Virg
3/ 28/ 1922	43.0	Libr
3/ 27/ 1928	49.0	Sco
3/ 28/ 1930	51.0	Sag
3/ 27/ 1932	53.0	Cap
3/ 28/ 1942	63.0	Aqu
3/ 28/ 1953	74.0	Pis
3/ 28/ 1954	75.0	Ari

At age twenty, Edward Steichen began his 18-year *Vimshottari Rahu* period. This was the time during which Steichen met Alfred Stieglitz, had his photographs regularly published, and saw his reputation as a photographer begin to flourish. In the birth chart, *Rahu* joins exalted 2nd and 9th lord Mars in the 11th. *Rahu*'s sign dispositor Saturn and *nakshatra* dispositor Sun both occupy the ascendant, while the 10th house from *Rahu* is aspected by all three natural benefics including its own lord. In Edward Steichen's D-9, *Rahu*'s 4th house placement in the sign of Pisces benefits from dispositor Jupiter's double strength in the D-9 *lagna*. *Rahu* is again disposited by directionally strong 9th and 12th lord Jupiter in the D-10, as Jupiter aspects *Rahu* with its 9th glance. In its 9th house placement, *Rahu* also receives 10th and 11th lord Saturn's one-way aspect from the 12th house. Notice the D-10 repetition of the pattern seen in the birth chart, as the 10th house ruler is placed in the 12th while the 12th lord is in the chart's ascendant. The birth chart's *Kesari* yoga is replicated in the D-10, and becomes *Gaja Kesari* as Jupiter is joined by Mercury in the ascendant.

Steichen's subsequent Jupiter period brought him continued success; we have noted Jupiter's status as 1st and 10th lord in the 12th house of his birth chart and Jupiter's directional strength in the ascendant in both the D-9 and D-10 charts. In the D-9, *Hamsa* yoga Jupiter receives 12th lord Mars' one-way aspect from the 6th. In

Edward Steichen's D-10, Jupiter as the 12th lord is accompanied in the ascendant by 3rd lord Mercury; Mercury also achieves directional strength as both *grahas* are disposited and aspected by *vargottama* (in D-10) exalted chart lord Mars, which forms *Ruchaka* yoga and enjoys directional strength in the 10th house. Steichen's 1923 opportunity with Conde Nast publications occurred in his *Vimshottari* Jupiter – Mercury period. Along with its D-10 strength, Mercury rules the 10th house of the D-9, where it is found in the 5th house, is aspected by ascendant ruler Jupiter, and is disposited by 12th house ruler Mars.

Several weeks after the onset of his *Vimshottari Rahu* major period, Edward Steichen began a 10-year *Jaimini Chara dasha* of the sign of Gemini. In his D-1 and D-10, AmK Sun and BK Saturn occupy the 10th house from Gemini. The Sun gains directional strength in this placement as both planets achieve *vargottama* status in the D-10. In the birth chart, the 12th house from Gemini holds exalted natal 5th lord/DK Moon who is aspected by exalted AK Mars while the 3rd house of skills, the sign of Leo, is activated by Mars, Mercury, and Venus. Mercury and Venus in the 11th house from Gemini are in *Jaimini sambandha* with PK Jupiter. As the 12th from Gemini, the sign of Taurus in both D-9 and D-10 is favorably aspected by the combination of sign ruler Venus and the Moon. AK Mars occupies Taurus in the D-9 and aspects Taurus from its sign of exaltation in the D-10. Finally, and no less significant, is the exchange between Saturn and Jupiter which from the sign of Gemini becomes a *Maha Parivartana* yoga occurring between houses 9 and 10 in Edward Steichen's D-1. (Further appreciation of the life and work of Edward Steichen can be found at the website of the National Gallery, www.nga.gov/collection.)

The penultimate chart for this section will be that of the contemporary actress Kristen Stewart (April 9th, 1990, Los Angeles, CA, 9:21 a.m., AA).

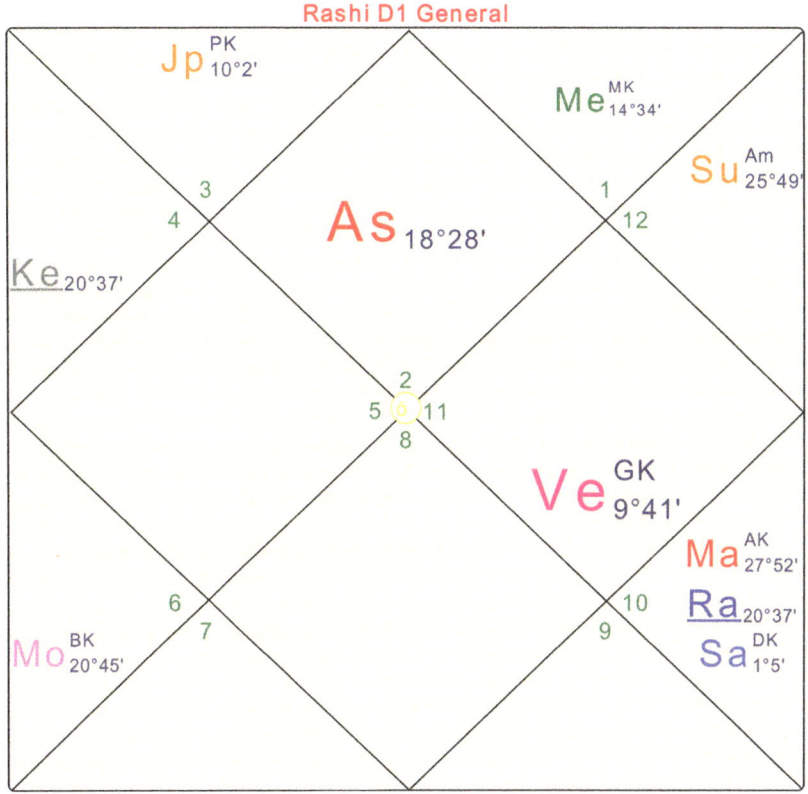

```
                    Rashi D1 General
┌─────────────┬──────────────┬──────────────┐
│             │      MK      │      PK      │
│    Su Am    │   Me 14°34'  │   Jp 10°2'   │
│      25°49' │              │              │
│             │   As 18°28'  │              │
├─────────────┼──────────────┼──────────────┤
│             │              │              │
│   Ve GK     │              │   Ke 20°37'  │
│     9°41'   │      Ö       │              │
│             │              │              │
│   Ma AK     │ Kristen Stewart             │
│     27°52'  │ Mon. 4/9/1990 9:21:00       │
│   Ra 20°37' │    Los Angeles, CA          │
│   Sa DK     │                             │
│      1°5'   │                             │
├─────────────┼──────────────┼──────────────┤
│             │              │     BK       │
│             │              │   Mo 20°45'  │
└─────────────┴──────────────┴──────────────┘
```

Kristen Stewart's film career began at the age of nine with several small roles. At age eleven she appeared in *The Safety of Objects* (2001), and in 2002 Ms. Stewart co-starred with Jodie Foster in *The Panic Room*. Kristen Stewart played her first starring role in *Catch That Kid* (2004), and since then has worked almost continuously, with leading performances in more than forty films. In 2008, Kristen Stewart made her first appearance in the *Twilight* saga, a series of five films produced over the following four years, in all of which she played the leading role of Bella Swan. At its 63rd annual awards ceremony in 2010, the British Academy of Film and Television Arts (BAFTA) honored Kristen Stewart with its Rising Star award. For her performance in the 2014 film *Clouds of Sils Maria*, Kristen Stewart was conferred the French Cesar Award for Best Supporting Actress;

she was similarly honored by the New York Society of Film Critics. Kristen Stewart's portrayal of Princess Diana in the 2021 biographical drama *Spencer* earned Stewart an Academy Award nomination for best actress. Kristen Stewart has directed two short films, *Come Swim* (2017), and *Crickets* (2020). Ms. Stewart was named Forbes magazine's highest earning actress in 2012.

The Taurus rising chart of Kristen Stewart has *Rohini nakshatra* on the ascendant at 18 degrees while chart lord Venus occupies the 10th house in visionary *Shatabhisha*. Venus in the 10th is stabilized by 11th lord Jupiter's 9th aspect and forms the yoga known as *Amala* (stainless). The *trikona* placement and *swakshetra* status of Venus' dispositor Saturn gives *Phaladeepika Parvata* yoga. The chart's potential for a career related to 12th house themes becomes evident as exalted 12th house ruler Mars combines with *Rahu* and *swakshetra* and *vargottama* 9th and 10th lord Saturn in the 9th house; notice that at 27 degrees 52 minutes, Mars is within 8 minutes of, and approaching, its precise degree of highest exaltation. The 12th house itself holds 5th lord Mercury and is enlivened by the 4th aspect of its ruler Mars from the 9th. Jupiter and a benefic full Moon form *Kesari* yoga as the Moon rules the 3rd house of artistic expression and resides in the 5th; the same pattern occurs from the Moon as 3rd lord Mars is exalted in the 5th house with *swakshetra* 5th lord Saturn. The 12th house from the Moon is activated by aspects from Mars and Venus. The chart benefits from two *Shubha Kartari* yogas, as the ascendant is flanked by natural benefics Jupiter and Mercury (*Shubha* yoga), while the Sun achieves *Shubha Ubhayachari* yoga through its flanking by Mercury and Venus. Kristen Stewart's D-9 has 12th lord Venus aspecting the ascendant from the 7th house while 10th lord Jupiter activates the 12th house from its location in the 8th. Jupiter's debilitation is cancelled by its association with Saturn as well as the position of both planets opposite *swakshetra* Moon. In her D-10, 5th and 10th house ruler Mars in the 12th in Gemini has mutual aspect with 7th and 8th lord Saturn.

Kristen Stewart's 12th lord Mars happens to be her AK. The AK in exaltation, in the 9th house and in aspect with the 9th lord qualifies for *Raj* yoga status as delineated in BPHS 40:6 and 40:8. The sign of Virgo is Ms. Stewart's KL and is occupied by the full Moon, as BK Moon enjoys mutual *Jaimini* aspect with AmK Sun and PK Jupiter. BPHS Chapter 33, verses 57 – 60 informs us that (placement of) the luminaries in aspect to Jupiter in the 10th house from the KL affords the native "acquisition of a kingdom."

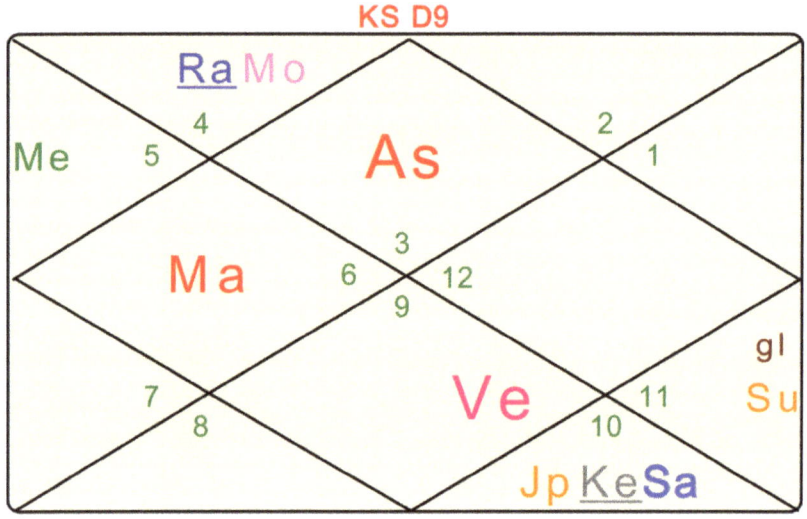

Creativity in the Vedic Astrology Chart

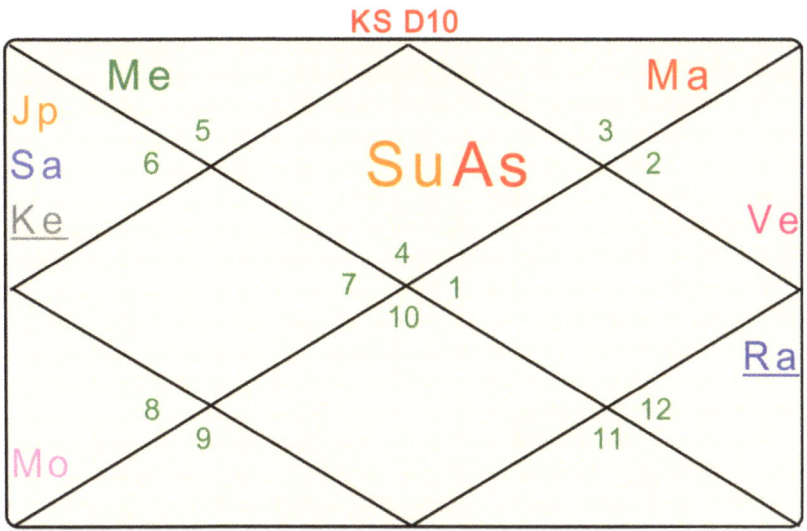

KS: Vimshottari

Start Date	Age	Dashas	
9/ 8/ 1996	6.4	Ma	Ke
2/ 4/ 1997	6.8	Ma	Ve
4/ 6/ 1998	8.0	Ma	Su
8/ 12/ 1998	8.3	Ma	Mo
3/ 13/ 1999	**8.9**	**Ra**	**Ra**
11/ 23/ 2001	11.6	Ra	Jp
4/ 18/ 2004	14.0	Ra	Sa
2/ 23/ 2007	16.9	Ra	Me
9/ 11/ 2009	19.4	Ra	Ke
9/ 30/ 2010	20.5	Ra	Ve
9/ 29/ 2013	23.5	Ra	Su
8/ 24/ 2014	24.4	Ra	Mo
2/ 23/ 2016	25.9	Ra	Ma
3/ 12/ 2017	**26.9**	**Jp**	**Jp**
5/ 1/ 2019	29.1	Jp	Sa
11/ 11/ 2021 n	31.6	Jp	Me
2/ 17/ 2024	33.9	Jp	Ke
1/ 23/ 2025	34.8	Jp	Ve
9/ 24/ 2027	37.5	Jp	Su
7/ 12/ 2028	38.3	Jp	Mo
11/ 11/ 2029	39.6	Jp	Ma
10/ 18/ 2030	40.5	Jp	Ra
3/ 12/ 2033	**42.9**	**Sa**	**Sa**
3/ 15/ 2036	45.9	Sa	Me
11/ 23/ 2038	48.6	Sa	Ke
1/ 2/ 2040	49.7	Sa	Ve

KS: Chara

Start Date			Age	Dashas
4/	9/	1990	-0.0	Tau
4/	9/	1999	9.0	Ari
4/	9/	2008	18.0	Pis
4/	9/	2017	27.0	Aqu
4/	9/	2018 n	28.0	Cap
4/	9/	2030	40.0	Sag
4/	9/	2036	46.0	Sco
4/	9/	2038	48.0	Libr
4/	9/	2042	52.0	Virg
4/	9/	2047	57.0	Leo
4/	9/	2052	62.0	Can
4/	9/	2062	72.0	Gem

Concurrent with the onset of her 9-year Aries *Chara dasha*, Kristen Stewart's film career began at the age of nine. Aries is the sign on the 12th house of the chart and holds natal 5th lord Mercury in mutual aspect with Venus. Aries sign ruler exalted AK Mars achieves directional strength in the 10th house of career in the company of 10th lord Saturn and *Rahu*. As the chart's AmK and owner of the 5th house from Aries, the Sun in the 12th house is aspected by PK Jupiter and bright BK Moon, reinforcing the potential for creative expression in the realm of film. In Ms. Stewart's D-9, we find *swakshetra* and *vargottama* DK Saturn and PK Jupiter with *Ketu* in the 10th house from Aries in mutual *Jaimini* aspect with natal 5th lord Mercury. AmK Sun and natal 5th lord Mercury aspect the sign of Aries while the 3rd and 12th houses from Aries are activated by aspects from Mars and Venus. Mercury again resides in Leo in the 5th house from Aries in Kristen Stewart's D-10, as Mercury and the Moon aspect Aries; the 10th house gains the aspects of Mercury and Moon as well as that of *swakshetra* Venus. Note that in Ms. Stewart's D-9 the 5th and 10th houses from Aries benefit from the combined activation of Jupiter and Mercury, while Venus and the Moon similarly aspect the 10th house from Aries in her D-10. Kristen Stewart's D-10 displays overall strength as AmK

Sun in the ascendant is aspected by BK Moon and *swakshetra* Venus. The 3rd and 12th houses from Aries in the D-10 are activated by AK Mars' location in the 3rd along with aspects from DK Saturn, PK Jupiter, and *Rahu* and *Ketu*.

Kristen Stewart began her 18-year *Vimshottari Rahu* period less than a month before the start of her *Jaimini* Aries *Chara dasha*. The placement of *Rahu* in the 9th house with 10th lord Saturn comprises a *Chaya Graha Raj* yoga and enables *Rahu* to grant the high degree of artistic and commercial success enjoyed by Ms. Stewart during her *Rahu* major period. *Rahu*'s other influences include exalted 12th lord Mars and *nakshatra* dispositor 3rd lord Moon. In Ms. Stewart's D-9, *Rahu* is found in the 2nd house with *swakshetra* Moon where it is aspected by 9th lord Saturn and 10th house ruler Jupiter. *Rahu* in the 9th house of her D-10 is disposited and aspected by Jupiter while also receiving the aspect of 7th and 8th lord Saturn.

Creativity in the Vedic Astrology Chart

This section concludes with a private chart of a successful writer, producer, and director of documentary films who will be identified as Filmmaker 0312 (no birth data provided).

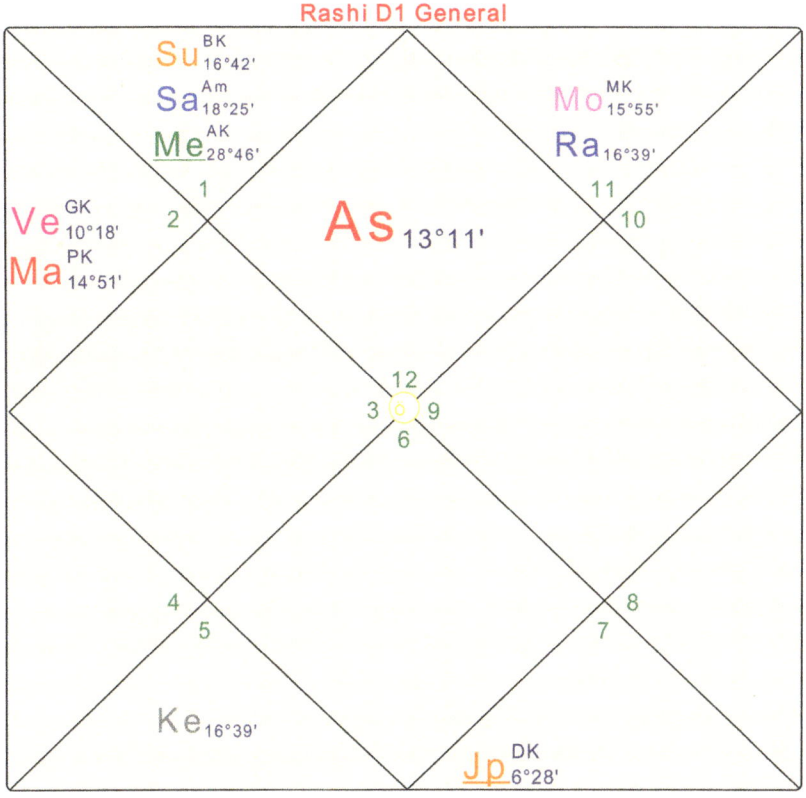

Rashi D1 General

As 13°11'	Su BK 16°42' Sa Am 18°25' Me AK 28°46'	Ve GK 10°18' Ma PK 14°51'	
Ra 16°39' Mo MK 15°55'			
			Ke 16°39'
		Jp DK 6°28'	

Here is a rather straightforward chart which encompasses a number of the principles set forward in this section. 5th house ruler Moon in the 5th from ascendant ruler Jupiter occupies the 12th house of visual expression with *Rahu* in the *nakshatra* of *Shatabhisha*. Ascendant and 10th house ruler Jupiter and 12th lord Saturn are in *sambandha* across the 2 – 8 axis. From the 8th house, Venus-disposited Jupiter aspects the 12th house and *vargottama* 5th lord Moon, accentuating the potential for a 12th house-related career. From the Moon, 10th lord Mars is joined in the 4th house by its *swakshetra* dispositor Venus as both Venus and Mars (in strength due to its *vargottama* status) occupy creatively abundant *Rohini nakshatra* and aspect the 10th house. The 12th house from the Moon is aspected by its owner Saturn. Saturn's debilitation is cancelled secondary to its association with exalted Sun, as well as by the location of Venus (ruler of Saturn's exaltation sign) and Mars (Saturn's dispositor) in a *kendra* house from the Moon, and in *kendra* (1st) from each other. The Libra rising D-9 of Filmmaker 0312 replicates the birth chart's placement of the 5th lord in the 12th house, while 10th lord Moon is joined by *vargottama swakshetra Rahu* forming *Chaya Graha Raj* yoga in the 5th house in the sign of Aquarius. 3rd lord Jupiter participates in *Kesari* yoga with the Moon and aspects the 10th house from its placement in the 2nd. The chart is also enabled by *lagna* lord Venus' aspect to the ascendant from the 7th house. As the ascendant and 10th house ruler of the D-10 of Filmmaker 0312, *swakshetra* Jupiter forms *Hamsa* yoga in the 10th. The D-10 is strongly drawn in the direction of a career in film, as exalted 12th lord Saturn aspects both 10th house and lord as well as the 5th house and its *swakshetra* lord Moon. Saturn's potential for artistic expression is emphasized by its *sambandha* with dispositor Venus.

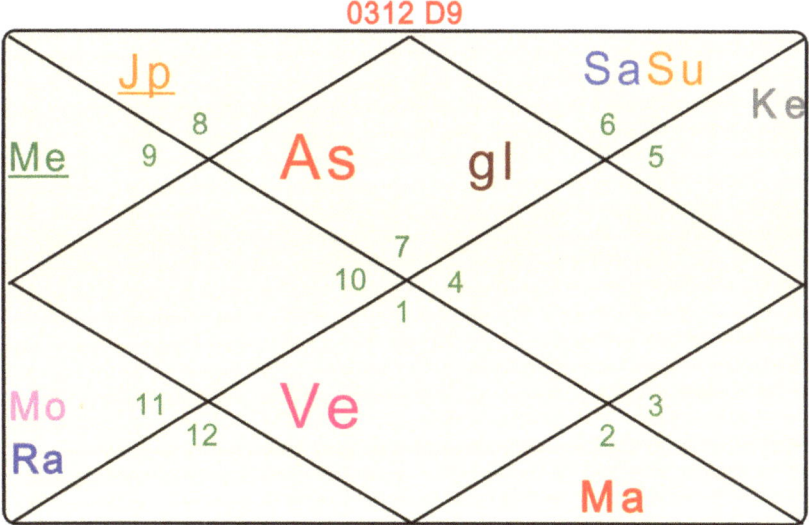

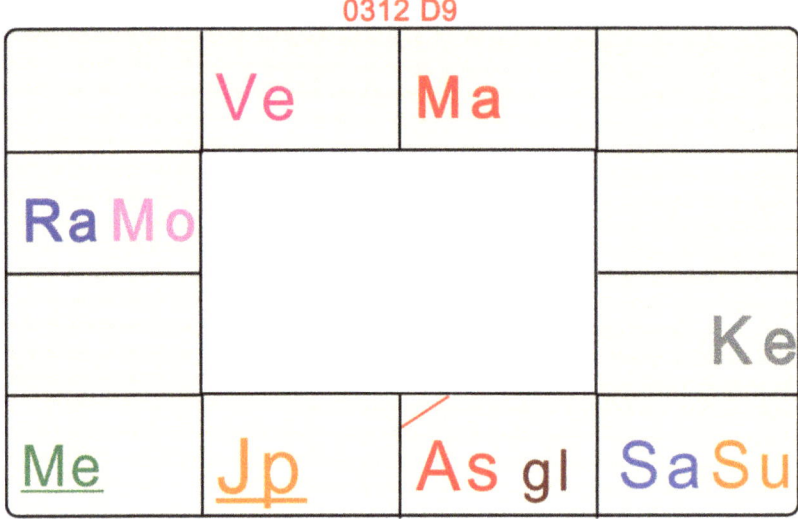

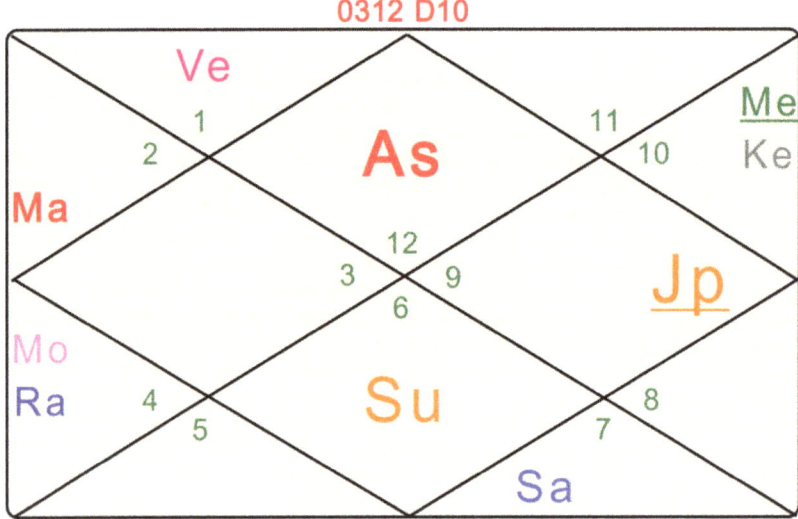

```
            0312 D10
┌─────┬─────┬─────┬─────┐
│ As  │ Ve  │ Ma  │     │
├─────┼─────┴─────┼─────┤
│     │           │Mo Ra│
├─────┤           ├─────┤
│Me Ke│           │     │
├─────┼─────┬─────┴─────┤
│     │ Jp  │  Sa │ Su  │
└─────┴─────┴─────┴─────┘
```

The 12th house of the birth chart and tenants 5th lord Moon and *Rahu* derive benefit from the *Jaimini* aspect of Aquarius owner AmK Saturn to its own house, as well as those of exalted BK Sun, AK Mercury and DK Jupiter. Additional *Jaimini Raj* yoga is obtained as the result of the Moon's activation by five *grahas*, including *Rahu*. The 5th house of the chart similarly benefits from the aspect of its lord Moon as well as those from *Rahu*, *swakshetra* Venus and *vargottama* PK Mars. 5th house confluence is found through the presence of a *Jaimini Raj* yoga formed by AK Mercury and AmK Saturn in the 5th house from the chart's Sagittarius KL, as Mercury, Saturn, and exalted Sun enjoy mutual aspect with 5th lord Moon. In the D-9 of Filmmaker 0312, the 3rd house has AK Mercury while AmK Saturn and BK Sun are placed in the 10th house from Mercury, the 12th house of the chart.

Although dates are not provided for this private chart, the 5-year *Jaimini Chara dasha* of Cancer proved to be seminal in the career of Filmmaker 0312. The AK/AmK/exalted BK *Raj* yoga combination is situated in the 10th house from Cancer. Cancer is the sign on the 10th house of the D-9 and is aspected by its lord as well as by Jupiter, Mars, and *Rahu*. The 10th house from Cancer holds Venus in mutual aspect with the Moon, Jupiter, *Rahu*, and *Ketu*. In the D-10, the sign of Cancer is occupied by its natal/local 5th lord Moon in mutual aspect with PK Mars. In both the D-9 and D-10 charts of this film maker, we find Venus and Mars involved in a 10 – 11 *Parivartana* yoga from Cancer.

This concludes our final section. In the charts of Ansel Adams, Greta Garbo, Ron Howard, Beverly D'Angelo, Herb Ritts, Luis Bunuel and Edward Steichen, the 12th lord either aspects or occupies the 10th house. There is *sambandha*, a direct relationship between the rulers of houses 10 and 12, in the charts of Ansel Adams, Robert Frank, Haskell Wexler, Kevin Kline, Kristen Stewart and Film-maker 0312. The 12th house of the chart is occupied or aspected by the 10th lord in the charts of Greta Garbo, Kevin Kline, Luis Bunuel, Edward Steichen, and Filmmaker 0312. The prevalence of *Shatabhisha nakshatra* in this set of twelve charts of photographers, actors and filmmakers is also notable; ten of the twelve charts presented here feature *grahas* prominently located in *Shatabhisha*. Another quote from director Luis Bunuel serves to remind us of the role of the 12th house in the lives and careers of visual artists: "'Don't worry if the movie's too short' I once told a Mexican producer. 'I'll just put in a dream.'"

Bibliography

Agarwal, G.S. *Practical Vedic Astrology* (New Delhi, India: Sagar Publications 2004)

Behari, Bepin. *Fundamentals of Vedic Astrology* (Twin Lakes, WI, USA: Lotus Press 2003)

Bhat, M. Ramakrishna. *Fundamentals of Astrology* (Delhi, India: Motilal Banarsidass 1967)

Boney, Marc. *Secrets of the Dashamsha* (Cardiff, California, USA: Saraswati Publications 2018)

Charak, Dr. K.S. *Essentials of Medical Astrology* (Delhi, India: UMA Publications 2005)

Charak, Dr. K.S. *Subtleties of Medical Astrology* (New Delhi, India: Systems Vision 1996)

Chugh, Sumeet. *Timing of Events* (New Delhi, India: Sagar Publications 1996)

Danielou, Alain. *The Gods of India; Hindu Polytheism* (New York, NY, USA: Inner Traditions 1985)

deFouw, Hart, and Robert Svoboda. *Light on Life* (Twin Lakes, WI, USA: Lotus Press 2003)

Greene, Liz. *Relating* (York Beach, ME, USA: Samuel Weiser, Inc. 1982)

Hand, Robert. *Planets in Transit* (Atglen, PA, USA: Whitford Press 1976)

Hickey, Isabel M. *Astrology, A Cosmic Science* (Sebastopol, CA, USA: CRCS Publications 1992)

Jain, M.C. *Rahu and Ketu in Predictive Astrology* (New Delhi, India: Sagar Publications 1994)

Kelleher, James. *Path of Light, Vols. I & II* (San Francisco, CA, USA: Ahimsa Press 2006)

Khot, Maj. S.G. *Astrology and Diagnosis* (New Delhi, India: Sagar Publications 1993)

Mantreswara. *Phaladeepika* G.K. Ojha (trans.) (Delhi, India: Motilal Banarsidass 2008)

Mathur, Dinesh S. *How to Time an Event* (New Delhi, India: Sagar Publications 2006)

Mathur, Dinesh S. *Predictive Astrology, an Insight* (Delhi, India: Motilal Banarsidass 1999)

Moore, Thomas. *The Planets Within* (Great Barrington, MA, USA: Lindisfarne Press 1990)

Parasara, Maharishi. *Brihat Parasara Hora Sastra, Vols. I & II* R. Santhanam (trans.) (New Delhi, India: Ranjan Publications 2009)

Pfau, Susan (Radhe). *Divine Forces of the Lunar Nakshatras* (Charleston, SC, USA: Shree Ganapati Productions 2014)

Rao, Dr. Jagannath. *Principles and Practice of Medical Astrology* (New Delhi, India: Sagar Publications 1972)

Rao, K.N. *Astrology, Destiny and the Wheel of Time* (Lucknow, India: Vani Graphics 1995)

Shil-Ponde. *Hindu Astrology* (New York, NY, USA: Willey Book Company 1944)

Sullivan, Erin. *Saturn in Transit* (Delhi, India: Motilal Banarsidass 2000)

Trivedi, Prashant. *The Key of Life* (New Delhi, India: Sagar Publications 2002)

Trivedi, Prashant. *The 27 Celestial Portals* (New Delhi, India: Sagar Publications 2004)

Varahamihira. *Brihat Jataka* B. Suryanarain Rao (trans.) (Delhi, India: Motilal Banarsidass 2005)

Varma, Kalyana. *Saravali, Vols. I & II* (New Delhi, India: Ranjan Publications 2014)

Wilkins, W.J. *Hindu Mythology* (New Delhi, India: DK Printworld 2009)

www.ingramcontent.com/pod-product-compliance
Lightning Source LLC
Chambersburg PA
CBHW050928240426
43671CB00019B/2951